# LATIN AMERICA
# IN THE NEW
# INTERNATIONAL SYSTEM

A project of the
Latin American Program
of the Woodrow Wilson International
Center for Scholars

# LATIN AMERICA
## IN THE NEW
## INTERNATIONAL SYSTEM

edited by
Joseph S. Tulchin
Ralph H. Espach

LYNNE
RIENNER
PUBLISHERS

BOULDER
LONDON

Published in the United States of America in 2001 by
Lynne Rienner Publishers, Inc.
1800 30th Street, Boulder, Colorado 80301
www.rienner.com

and in the United Kingdom by
Lynne Rienner Publishers, Inc.
3 Henrietta Street, Covent Garden, London WC2E 8LU

**Library of Congress Cataloging-in-Publication Data**
Latin America in the new international system /
    edited by Joseph S. Tulchin and Ralph H. Espach.
    Includes bibliographical references and index.
    ISBN 1-55587-940-3 (hc : alk. paper)
    ISBN 1-55587-917-9 (pb : alk. paper)
    1. Latin America—Foreign relations .I. Tulchin, Joseph S., 1939– . II. Espach, Ralph H.

JZ1519.L38  2000
327'.098—dc21                                                    00-034207

**British Cataloguing in Publication Data**
A Cataloguing in Publication record for this book
is available from the British Library.

Printed and bound in the United States of America

The paper used in this publication meets the requirements
(∞) of the American National Standard for Permanence of
Paper for Printed Library Materials Z39.48-1984.

5  4  3  2  1

# Contents

v

# 1

# Latin America in the New International System: A Call for Strategic Thinking

*Joseph S. Tulchin & Ralph H. Espach*

The international system has evolved rapidly since the end of the Cold War. The acceleration of international economic and political activity has deeply affected politics and society at the national and even local levels. The world is increasingly integrated by the spread of democracy, political freedom, and international markets, spurred on by advances in global communications. At the same time, however, the fault lines of ethnic differences and the North-South dichotomy between wealthy, economically developed nations or communities and those that remain marginalized or poor are more glaring.[1] The new international system is best described as multi-layered. International power is distributed differently in economic influence, where it is increasingly diffuse; military capacity, which is strongest in the United States; and political influence, which currently is dominated by the United States but is under constant challenge. Also, enhanced activity on the part of multilateral institutions and nonstate actors complicate what has traditionally been a structure based on sovereign nation-states. The United States, thus far uncertain in the role of global superpower, tends to make foreign policy in response to crises and within constraints imposed by domestic politics, and strives to act cooperatively by means of multilateral institutions such as the United Nations.[2]

Without the rigid ideological and geostrategic structure of the Cold War, Latin American nations receive less attention than before from the world powers. Regional affairs are low on the priority list of U.S. government interests, with the exception of its relationship with Mexico, its concern with drug trafficking, and its awkward policy toward Cuba, dominated by a peculiar mix of domestic special interests.[3] Despite some recent rhetoric, Europe also is too preoccupied with its own integration project and with security issues on its southeastern flank to give Latin America more than casual interest. Latin America is commonly hailed as a promising economic market, but issues of trade tariffs, subsidies, and competitive export markets come low on the strategic agendas of the greater powers. For their part, the nations of Latin America have been unassertive in projecting any importance in the global system beyond economics. In terms of international power, these nations—with the possible exception of Brazil—are still third- or fourth-tier players in international affairs, and continue to be "ruletakers" and not "rulemakers."

This volume responds to the question, "What type of policies can these nations enact to alter this pattern and enhance their role in the international system?" The region is neglected largely because it is perceived to pose no threat to the nation-states that dominate international affairs, but also in part because the nations of the region do not assert themselves. Exceptions prove the rule: it was only U.S. security concerns that in the 1980s turned Central America into a Cold War hot spot. Even today tiny, dilapidated Cuba—or, sadly, a single 6-year-old Cuban boy—can throw Washington into paroxysms while Brazil and Argentina go years without a U.S. ambassador. A realist perspective suggests that this will remain true until or unless a Latin American nation develops first-world economic weight or military capacity and achieves sufficient stability and political will to apply that power within the international system. From this perspective, probably only Brazil and Mexico have the potential to develop global influence.

However, a broader view—the one taken by this volume—argues that the nations of Latin America are increasingly important in economic and security terms to the global hegemon, even if its leaders are slow to recognize this fact, and to the world at large. Relations with Latin America are inextricably woven into many of the key issues facing the world and the United States in particular—drug trafficking, illegal migration, the need for export growth, and international crime. This fact does not guarantee increased power for Latin America in these historically asymmetrical relations. In many cases what it guarantees are greater tensions. If the tensions that come with rising economic and political interdependence are not met on both sides with openness and a willingness to cooperate, the United States is likely at some point to slip again into thinking in unilateral, interventionist terms. As the nations of Latin America seek to improve their positions in international affairs, their greatest opportunities and challenges are likely to come in the design and management of their tightening interrelations with the United States.

The pressures of the Cold War and U.S. regional involvement served as a straitjacket on the policy options of Latin American nations.

Nationalistic, authoritarian governments were encouraged to discriminate sharply, within the region and their own societies, among friends and foes of the state. Policies corresponded to an introspective and defensive vision of national interests and a preoccupation with sovereignty and control. Distrust among the nations of the region led to zero-sum competitive strategies, including Brazil's and Argentina's nuclear race and a region-wide buildup of arms.

The 1980s saw the spread of democracy and free market economic policies across the hemisphere. The end of the Cold War and the relaxation of U.S. security fears ushered in a period of remarkable regionwide agreement on basic principles and objectives. Free trade and integration projects emerged across the hemisphere with the blessing of the United States. The hawks in Washington or Europe turned their attention to the former Soviet Union, the Middle East, or terrorist threats, and Latin American nations found themselves with more maneuvering space than most had enjoyed since the nineteenth century.

Their response to this window of opportunity, however, has been less than ambitious. The legacy of hemispheric asymmetry and of U.S. unilateralism weighs heavily on the nations of Latin America. In most cases they continue to define their strategic options in terms of responding to the United States—friendly, hostile, cooperative, or resentful. During the 1990s, as the United States indicated a disposition to cooperate, such as in dealing with drug trafficking, with arms limitations, or with environmental issues, most Latin American nations held back, unsure about how to take advantage of the opening. With the exception of Argentina's atypical pro-U.S. position and Mexico's dramatic shift from traditional anti-U.S. posturing to joining NAFTA, the nations of Latin America have shown little confidence or innovation in exploring options for enhanced roles in world affairs. Until they learn to be more assertive, their strategic options will continue to be limited. Only this time they will to a large degree be self-limited, restricted as much by their own inabilities to move beyond traditional concepts of strategy and national sovereignty as limited by exogenous factors and forces.

An important theme of this book is that the nations of Latin America must engage themselves consciously and seriously in strategic planning. The reflections by Robert Keohane and Ernest May both indicate surprise at the shallowness of regional long-term thinking. The new international system requires a strategic vision different from that of the last century, which was fixed on government control over resources and people, military capacities, and a strict adherence to the principle of sovereignty. The nations of Latin America must learn to view such projects as economic liberalization, intellectual property rights legislation, science and technology programs, the promotion of high-technology or communications industries, improved education, and proactive participation in international institutions as potential elements of an integrated, multidimensional strategic policy. The strengthening of the region's democratic institutions, such as the judiciary, law enforcement agencies, and regulatory bodies, will be crucial to such policies. The new international system rewards political stability and economic agility and innovation. These qualities demand an active, responsive democratic system that provides its people and businesses the freedom and support to be competitive in the global market.

## Assessing the New International System

The international system is in a period of transition from the bipolar structure of the Cold War to one more multidimensional and dynamic. The nature of this emerging system, the direction of its evolution, and its implications for the power and behavior of nation-states and other important actors over the coming decades are a source of debate not only among policymakers but also in the academic community. To understand the emerging system, it is important to understand the sources of rules by which the system will be judged and governed. Who are the rulemakers and who the ruletakers? During the Cold War this distinction was clear, at times with brutal implications. Today, power is more diffuse and is wielded more flexibly, through a variety of instruments. Despite the continuation of U.S. regional hegemony, this new dynamism offers the nations of Latin America a broader range of options.

In the post–Cold War era, nations are growing more interdependent both economically, through the growth of international trade and investment, and in terms of security, due to the transnational nature of such threats as the international drug trade, the proliferation of nuclear or chemical arms, and economic instability. This intensification of international ties is the result of advances in communications and technology and the almost worldwide acceptance of the benefits of free markets and democratic rule. Even such critics of capitalism and liberal democracy as China, Iran, or Cuba have come to allow some free market practices within their economies in order to compete internationally. However, these liberal economic and political models have come under increasing criticism for their failure to reduce inequalities or to provide economic stability. In response to these shortcomings of the neoliberal model, a variety of proposals have arisen known as the Third Way. These new policy models represent an effort to bring the state back in and restore elements of social welfare to vulnerable populations, while preserving a free-market structure and a reduced government role in most other aspects of the economy. Far from the triumphant enthusiasm of the early 1990s, epitomized by Francis Fukuyama's suggestion of "the end of history," the existing capitalist and democratic models are increasingly questioned, especially in less developed regions of the world.[4]

## The Conceptual Debate over the Nature of the International System

Among theorists and scholars of international relations, a fierce debate has arisen about the nature and implications of the new international system. Before discussing the regionally focused themes and positions presented in this volume, it is useful to give a brief overview of the most prominent current conceptual approaches to assessing international relations. As in the past, the direction of this international debate will shape the perceptions and ideas of policymakers as they approach the challenges of the new international arena.

During most of the twentieth century, international relations were perceived almost exclusively through the lens of "realist" theory, which assumes an international arena without order in which rational, unitary nation-states compete for power and resources. Realists or neorealists argue that the international arena is characterized principally by interstate conflict and the self-interested pursuit of power by sovereign nation-states. Violent conflict is prevalent in many areas of the world, especially between ethnic groups in unconsolidated nations. Without the imposition of a framework for such conflict, such as that previously provided by the dominance of U.S.-Soviet tensions, the world is increasingly contentious. Nationalism—or the nationalist energies of ethnic or religious groups—is a persistent source of conflict.[5] According to realists or neorealists, international institutions and alliances have little significance beyond their temporary usefulness to the dominant parties. Realists point to the incoherence and lack of autonomy of institutions like NATO and the United Nations as evidence of these claims. It appears that without U.S. leadership or support for these bodies, they would be completely ineffective, and that the United States cooperates with them only when that suits its interests.

The most prominent competing conceptual approach to international relations emphasizes that the increasing importance of institutions is changing interstate relations, behaviors, and strategies. Institutionalist scholars emphasize deepening interdependence and the expansion of shared interests and principles, and argue that states increasingly pursue their interests through participation in international institutions. The proliferation of international ties and transactions requires recognized rules, standards, and norms of conduct, often formalized and enforced by international institutions such as the United Nations or the World Trade Organization (WTO), and often articulated by international networks of nonstate actors. Interdependence raises the costs of interstate violence and uncooperative behavior and provides incentives for peaceful means of conflict resolution that do not disturb economic flows or societal principles. Viewed in this light the current international system is as conflictive as ever, but institutional mechanisms exist so that those conflicts can be solved through negotiation, helping to make international relations more stable, predictable, and less prone to belligerence. Nations continue to pursue their own interests and the expansion of their power, but without the zero-sum mentality that previously dominated the international system.

According to prominent institutionalists, power is defined not only in terms of military might but also economic competitiveness, skills, and high-technology capacity, and the ability to assert political and cultural influence abroad.[6] For nations that wield little power in the realist sense, such as those of Latin America, participation in international institutions diffuses power and provides the nations an arena for negotiation in which they can enhance their influence over the design of those institutional values and rules. In this way, rulemaking now appears to occur through a wide variety of mechanisms and has become less hierarchical.[7]

Other recent descriptions of the international system highlight growing disparities among nations in terms of income, standards of living, and political and economic development. Many analysts predict that the gap between the industrialized world (the North) and nonindustrialized world (the South) will continue to widen and divide the world into roughly two regions with conflicting interests. The central challenge to addressing many of the most contentious issues in international affairs, including migration, drug trafficking, terrorism, and environmental conservation, is to bridge this divide. Samuel Huntington draws these fault lines between regions of differing ethnicities or religions. For example, he predicts increasing conflict between Muslim Africa and the Middle East and Christian Europe.[8] Other analysts sensitive to regional differences divide the globe based on degrees of democratic stability, international behavior, and state capacity. The industrialized democracies form a "zone of peace," where interstate military conflict carries such high economic and social costs that it has almost become obsolete, while most of the rest of the world constitutes a "zone of conflict," in which nations and communities fight among themselves over a diminishing portion of the world's economic pie.[9] In other words, peace and relative stability can be expected to continue in the institutionalized, modern world as further technologies and economic links deepen common interests and values, but political and economic conditions in underdeveloped regions—which inhabit a less lawful, more realist world—are far less certain.[10]

The United States supports this discrimination between an "us" of democratic, institutionally linked nations and a "them" in its labeling of certain nations—Iraq, North Korea, and Cuba, for instance—as "rogue states," and its unilateral certification of nations as either friends or foes in the fight against drug trafficking. The official identification of these nations as outsiders tends to make it true by creating measures that restrict their ties and trade with the international community. These measures are punishment for a nation's refusal to adhere to internationally accepted norms of conduct as interpreted by the prominent institutions of the global system, and can be reversed in response to a change in that nation's policies.[11] Institutionalism does not mean the end of global power politics, and organizations like the United Nations, the WTO, or the World Bank did not develop out of altruism. Institutions are increasingly relevant because they serve primarily the interests of their members, in particular those with the most power. This book argues that institutional participation offers the nations of Latin America a promising avenue for enhancing their international importance and protecting themselves from the type of unilateral interference they have suffered in the past from the United States. However, membership in institutions has its costs as well as its benefits.

## The Rise of Nontraditional Issues and Actors

The past two decades have seen a rise in international activity regarding issues such as human rights, anticorruption, and environmental protection. The political focus on these issues at the global level came principally from the civil society of the democratic powers. The international environmental movement and groups committed to protecting human rights developed successful campaigns of Western governments and multinational institutions, pressuring them to change their policies toward nations like Brazil, for the destruction of Amazon forests, or South Africa, for apartheid. International corporate associations and pro-free-market groups have advocated anticorruption reform and pushed the World Bank and the IMF to include such reform in the conditionalities of their loans. These developments illustrate two important trends: the worldwide diffusion of mainstream Western values and the enhanced power of nonstate actors.

At the beginning of 2000, two initiatives are under way at the supranational level that were unthinkable 20 years before. The human rights community and oppressed people around the world cheer the actions of the international war crimes tribunal at the Hague and the arrest in England of the former Chilean military dictator General Augusto Pinochet. However, these precedent-setting events challenge the traditional concept of national sovereignty, upon which the international system has been based since the Treaty of Westphalia in 1648. For the first time, supranational legal mechanisms are in place that make leaders and warriors accountable not only to their national communities, but to the world at large. More recently, the castigation of Austria by the rest of the European Union, Israel, and the United States following the election of the right-wing Freedom Party implies a wider, informal precedent for international response, even against a politically and legally legitimate domestic action. Although this latter event may prove over the long term to be extraordinary, the trend is clear. This increasing power of the international community to enforce its values upon national governments, individuals, and even democratic communities could herald a dramatically different international order.[12]

This trend is not without its critics. Many analysts are skeptical of the idealist claims behind these institutional actions, and argue that the United States rose to its current predominance by convincing other nations of the benefits of participation in an international economic and political system it dominates.[13] The United States will use its national resources to provide stability and—if pushed—security beyond the means of most other members, but the system will function only so long as it benefits U.S. strategic and commercial interests. A similar argument states that, in an era of heightened economic competition, the West pressures less developed nations to act under its rules and principles—including the creation of minimum wage levels, environmental protection measures, and workers' rights—in order to reduce those nations' competitive advantage as cheap and unregulated sites for production.

However, the forces behind this spread of Western values and the expansion of international institutional activities are too complex to be explained as a rational strategy of the industrialized democracies. The United States is far from consistent in its commitment to human rights or environmental protection, as demonstrated by its contradictory policies toward Cuba, China, and the Middle East. When ideological values conflict with economic or strategic interests, the latter generally prevail.

Today, however, the influence of these values is increasing worldwide through the spread of democracy, the free market, communications technologies, and global news and media industries. The growing connectedness and, some argue, homogenization that these phenomena bring, and especially their promotion of liberal Western values around the world, will continue to influence the development of the new international system.

Traditional notions of state sovereignty and the international system are also challenged by the increasing influence of nonstate actors. International nongovernmental organizations (NGOs) and other special-interest networks have demonstrated their capacity to pressure domestic policies around the world on issues such as environmental management and human rights, while the internationalization of investment and business has increased the political power of multinational corporations. These groups are active across political borders and increasingly influence the agendas of multinational institutions, including the World Bank.[14] The groups are both agents and beneficiaries of the spread of political freedom, and as such are bound to multiply as democracies around the world are increasingly consolidated and integrated. Their enhanced autonomy and power challenge the traditional sovereignty of states in making political and economic policies. Especially in less developed countries, decisions of multinational corporations or private investors can dramatically affect the lives of citizens: national governments and multinational institutions responsible to governments must monitor and negotiate with these entities daily. Today official foreign government visits to Washington must include, in addition to meetings at the White House and Congress, meetings at the International Monetary Fund (IMF) and development banks, research centers, and special interest groups, and with the heads of banks, investment groups, and business associations.

### Latin America Since the Cold War: From Isolation to Cooperation

Before examining the implications of this new international system for the nations of Latin America, it is important to review recent trends in regional security policies and international relations. These trends in policy and the conceptual approaches they represent continue to serve as the framework for strategic thinking across the region. This framework, we will argue, has been productive, but without enhancement is inadequate to support the multidimensional and internationally oriented strategic thinking required by the new international system.

During the Cold War, the preoccupation of the United States and the Western community of nations with the threat of communism encouraged the governments of the region to focus their energies on security, both external and internal. While the United States purported to support democracy in the region, in situations where democratic expression was perceived to be socialist in character, the United States either allowed or aided the rise of antidemocratic, often brutal authoritarian governments. Lacking a legitimate external threat, these governments applied their extensive security apparatuses inward against their own people. This persecution in the name of national security deepened social divisions and mistrust between the people and their national governments and security forces, a tragic legacy that continues to haunt these national communities.

The fixation of the United States on fighting communism exaggerated the asymmetry of power between it and its neighbors to the south. Its actions ranged from monitoring to the disbursement of aid as an incentive for U.S.-friendly policies, to covert involvement in domestic affairs, to military invasion. Such pressure made policies viewed as uncooperative in this fight extremely costly, and gave powerful incentives for Latin American countries to toe the line. Public policy, foreign and domestic, could not be formulated without considering the response it would receive from Washington. As a result, during the Cold War the nations of Latin America basically had three strategic options: they could ally themselves with the United States and cooperate with U.S. security operations, oppose the United States and risk the consequences, or hide. Their space for autonomous action in the international system was severely limited.

During the 1980s, crippling economic crises stifled the ability of Latin American governments to think in any but the most immediate terms, much less to consider innovative strategic policy. State-based economic models were widely discredited, along with the authoritarian governments that had overseen them. A wave of support for democratization and economic liberalization swept across the region. Sooner or later most nations decided they had little choice but to undertake an arduous process of price stabilization, fiscal cuts, trade liberalization, privatization, and other free-market reforms. These reforms suited the policy recommendations of the international lending agencies and the U.S. government, referred to collectively as the "Washington consensus." These reforms were generally effective in stabilizing the region's economies and brought growth from increased investment, much of it from abroad. As the public—and arguably the poor as much as anyone else—warmed to economic stability and more consumer choice, the critics of this neoliberal model on the traditional Left as well as the Right lost legitimacy and influence in regional politics. Policy alternatives, analogous to the Third Way in Europe, did not appear until the end of the 1990s when the persistence of poverty, income disparities, and unemployment revived calls for a rethinking of neoliberal orthodoxy.

With the end of the Cold War, and as democracy and free markets were consolidated across Latin America, the region's strategic importance as a battleground against the spread of socialism was diminished. From outside, the region was declared a promising "emerging" market for trade and investment. Across the Americas, the early 1990s witnessed an unprecedented convergence of political and economic ideology. The spirit of pan-Americanism was revived, and some policymakers proclaimed that the future of the Americas depended on further political and economic partnership and integration.

The renewal of hemispheric goodwill and cooperation peaked in late 1994 with two significant events: the Miami Summit that launched the Free Trade Area of the Americas (FTAA) project, and the inception of the North American Free Trade Agreement (NAFTA). Both occasions were hailed for building tighter inter-American relations. However, they represented contradictory versions of how these relations were to be consolidated. The summitry initiative, which led to a series of hemisphere-wide meetings at various levels throughout the 1990s, offered a new model of political relations between the United States and Latin America. Summitry was designed to capitalize on the climate of enthusiasm and shared interests to energize the FTAA project and to push through the bureaucratic obstacles and delay that often characterize international negotiations. Presidents, ministers, and other officials at the highest level, given a relatively flexible format for negotiations and political maneuvering, saw that they would gain from the international limelight increased political capital and motivation to push through reforms that met the objectives of increased hemispheric integration. According to the model, each country would progress individually toward a more open economy and a shared set of laws and standards based on democratic and free-market principles, such as protection for human rights, improved social development, and environmental responsibility. Summitry treated all of the region's democracies as equals (the only country not invited was nondemocratic Cuba), and the success of the project depended on the coordinated progress of all nations. From the perspective of U.S. policymakers, it was an efficient way to pay attention to Latin America. The defense ministerial and other ministerial "summits" were designed to forge the broadest possible consensus among a set of nations with diverse interests. Follow-up to the summit was assigned to a variety of state agencies and NGOs.[15]

NAFTA, on the other hand, was a painstakingly negotiated accord among three partners aimed at boosting economic growth by encouraging trade and investment among three already closely linked nations. Other nations of Latin America perceived the exclusive trade zone as a threat to their access to the enormous U.S. market, upon which depended many of their export industries. The advantage of membership provided a strong incentive to join. This was possible, however, only through individual negotiations with the NAFTA countries, a strategy that strengthened the hand of the United States (and of Mexico and Canada) in the process toward hemispheric integration. Brazil, in particular, questioned the commitment of the United States to open, multilateral integration and positioned itself and the Mercosur trade pact as an alternative to NAFTA-dominated regional integration. From the beginning, the project of pan-American integration was challenged by conflicting strategic agendas.

Within weeks of the Miami Summit, assassinations and political intrigue in Mexico, as well as the Zapatista revolt and the precipitous devaluation of the peso, shattered the euphoria. The resulting "tequila crisis" that spread across Latin America was to many investors and policymakers a shocking reminder of the region's potential for instability. The Clinton administration had spent enormous political capital pushing NAFTA through a reluctant Congress and had oversold the benefits of the pact in its arguments to the public. Mexico's economic crisis reduced the short-term gains to the United States of NAFTA implementation, and its critics howled. The administration was compelled to circumvent Congress in putting together a $40 billion loan package to support Mexico's stabilization. Political support for further integration faded in Washington. When the Clinton administration failed to obtain fast-track negotiating power, observers in Latin America (Chile in particular) saw it as a sign of the unreliability of U.S. leadership in the project of hemispheric integration. The deepening of U.S.–Latin American relations slowed as the United States entered a phase of domestic introspection. In the reshuffling of U.S. government priorities, Latin America fell even lower in the deck.

## The Late 1990s: Return to Instability

By the end of the 1990s, the model of open economies that had generated such excitement proved not without its dangers. Economic crises in Mexico in 1995, and Brazil and Ecuador in 1999, exposed the region's vulnerability to external economic factors. Latin America has joined developing nations around the world in reconsidering the risks of unregulated trade and investment flows. The chief instrument of the global financial safety net, the IMF, has come under fire for the lack of political and social sensitivity in its policy prescriptions and its inability to help countries avoid or reduce the costs of economic crises.

The costs of embracing global markets have hit home not only in Mexico and Brazil (and by extension to all members of Mercosur, which are increasingly dependent on the health of the Brazilian economy), but also in the smaller economies. Small, Eastern Caribbean island nations dependent on the banana industry have been distressed by a case brought to the WTO by the United States and Central American nations against European banana quotas. These micronations, dependent upon a handful of primary export goods, find the challenge of global competition especially daunting. Even larger countries, such as Argentina and Brazil, have criticized the commitment of the United States and Europe to open markets and a level playing field in international trade. Because of problems like these, policymakers across Latin America have begun to include economic security as a prominent, if ambiguous, item in their national security agendas. The most promising instrument available to them for promoting their economic interests seems to be subregional trade blocs. These blocs build economic legitimacy and promote collective bargaining and active participation in international institutions such as the WTO.

Recent turbulence in Latin America has led governments and analysts abroad to shift their focus back to issues of security. Political and social crises in Colombia, Ecuador, and Paraguay, as well as delicate political situations in Mexico, Guatemala, and Venezuela—to name a few—indicate that the stability of these democracies is less than secure. Traditional interstate threats such as border disputes have been stabilized, but they have not disappeared. A border dispute between Peru and Ecuador that in 1995 led to military clashes was solved only through the intervention of the guarantor countries of the Rio Treaty, Argentina, Brazil, Chile, and the United States. Other areas of contention, for instance between Colombia and Venezuela, Guyana and Venezuela, and Panama and Colombia, also remain sensitive.

In addition to these traditional security threats a number of nontraditional, transnational threats, such as drug trafficking, migratory flows, international crime, and environmental degradation, have grown more acute. Political and economic instability, which served historically to legitimize intervention by the United States and other nations, has reappeared as a potential threat to regional security. Colombia's war against guerrilla insurgents, who control nearly half of Colombian territory, threatened to spill over into Venezuela, Panama, Ecuador, and Brazil, leading to heightened tensions and additional troops at these borders. Moreover, U.S. policy toward Colombia promises to expand the dimensions of that conflict.

These transnational threats require cooperative responses. Although there are instances of ad hoc cooperative response to crises, with the United States often the primary actor, the region has been slow in creating institutional mechanisms of cooperative response. Currently no legitimate hemispheric framework exists to address serious international crises, and most of the region's security forces are too unorganized, unprepared, and unwilling to engage in a large-scale multinational effort. Therefore, if a regional crisis erupts, for instance if the cross-border activities of the FARC in Colombia expand to threaten stability in the border regions of Ecuador, Peru, or Brazil, there exists no mechanism for international response except one led—perhaps unilaterally—by the United States.

Without dramatic reform and increased resources, existing multilateral institutions like the Organization of American States (OAS), the Inter-American Defense Board, or the security component of the summitry process appear incapable of formulating an effective multilateral response to these security issues. Progress has been achieved in specific areas at the operational level, as in the growing fabric of collaboration against drug trafficking within the Inter-American Drug Abuse Control Commission (CICAD), an agency of the OAS.[16] However, in times of crisis these institutions have had difficulty working quickly or effectively and are perceived as weak or vacillating in their commitments. This is not solely the result of inaction or a lack of coordination by Latin American governments. The United States often withholds the support that would make these institutions effective.

The questions of what kind of institutional framework is most appropriate to address these different kinds of threat, and what instruments are in place to address nontraditional, transnational sources of instability, are increasingly pressing. Examples of successful multilateral interventions exist, such as the assistance of the Rio Treaty guarantor nations in resolving the Ecuador-Peru border conflict in 1995, and the Contadora Group's success in the late 1980s at legitimizing the transition of armed guerrilla groups into political parties in Central America.[17] These examples are scarce, however, and at any rate were short-term actions designed to address specific issues or crisis situations. Faced with the threat of a multinational security crisis, such as that of the ever expanding and increasingly sophisticated drug trafficking operations, at present the architecture of hemispheric security relations appears woefully inadequate. As a result, the United States remains the only legitimate actor capable of effecting fast, effective responses to security crises throughout the hemisphere.

Today, the models of democracy and free market economics so popular at the beginning of the decade are increasingly criticized across Latin America. Venezuela's President Hugo Chavez owes his popularity to his image as a revolutionary populist. Chavez's message, that the democratic system in its current state was hopelessly corrupt and unresponsive to the real concerns of the public, struck a chord across Latin America. In the eyes of many Latin Americans, democracy—or at least democratic politicians—have done little to address the poverty, social inequalities, and lack of development that plague their nations. Citizens of democracies that seem mired in corruption or political in-fighting wonder whether leaders like General Pinochet, or milder versions such as Fujimori or Chavez, are more likely to institute the dramatic changes they want. If this frustration with the results of economic liberalization and democratic reforms continues, more people may be tempted to gamble on radical reformers who have little regard for the institutions or processes of constitutional democracy.

As hindsight becomes distorted by current problems, many people tend to overlook or play down the tragic costs of the repression and civil division of those military regimes.[18] A return of the populism, nationalism, or, at worst, the authoritarianism of earlier decades could be disastrous for the current inter-American system of shared interests and values. This would put an end to Latin American aspirations for an enhanced political role in global affairs, and tarnish the nations' allure to foreign investors. These high costs imposed by the international community make such political insurrection as military coups almost unimaginable. A potential coup in Paraguay in 1998 was quelled largely by threats from its Mercosur partners to cut off all trade, and one in Ecuador in 2000 lasted only 3 hours before military leaders were convinced of its impossibility, allegedly through word from the U.S. embassy.

The governments of Latin America must chart a course between two dangers. On the one hand they must continue to show commitment to the democratic and free-market values of the international system, even as they experiment with those definitions; otherwise they risk severe marginalization. On the other hand, they must find the political energy to distribute more equally the gains from economic liberalization and to address the poverty and long-standing frustration that afflict so many of their people.

## Latin America Today: Foreign Policy Options in an Institutionalized International System

With the success of Mercosur and other regional cooperative and integrative projects, an institutionalist account of international behavior is most suitable for assessing the Latin American case. In an increasingly institutionalized international system, Latin American nations enjoy an advantage in their efforts to greater insertion into it due to their familiarity with the processes and trade-offs of greater cooperation and the diplomacy and flexibility required for the system to be effective. In this system, a nation's international influence is partly determined by the nature and extent of its involvement in the institutions available to it. Is the nation a responsible, active partner; a passive, nonparticipatory partner; or an obstructionist element in the institution? Canada and Sweden, for example, have formulated successful, very active roles for themselves despite their limited economic or military power. Their influence, disproportionate to a purely realist assessment of their hard (that is, military and economic) power, is a result of the legitimacy they have earned through active participation and even leadership in various international institutions and initiatives—their soft power.[19]

Institutionalist theory suggests that international institutions benefit ruletaker, or less powerful, nations in two ways. First, it offers them a more equal forum for the expression and pursuit of their interests, and, second, the powerful nations' commitment to these regimes restrains them from acting unilaterally and gives them incentives to pursue their interests through coordinated, multinational initiatives.[20] Institutionalism offers ruletaker nations a strategy by which they can position themselves to become rulemakers.

Effective insertion into—and openness toward—the international system is not a one-way street, as Austria most recently discovered. Because the structure and values of the system are still in formation, and may be so indefinitely, nations that are not at the cutting edge of democratic, liberal norms can find themselves pinched by the system's zealousness. Chile enjoyed considerable international influence in the early 1990s as the model for effective neoliberal economic reform. Whatever imperfections existed in Chile's democracy were overlooked by many in the North who praised Chile's bold liberalization program and its economic growth. This success enhanced Chile's image abroad, and Chilean economists were welcomed around the developing world to discuss the "Chilean model." Things changed quickly, however, in 1999, when the nation's governing elite was taken by surprise by the arrest of General Augusto Pinochet in Britain at the request of Spanish judge Baltazar Garzón on charges of violating the human rights of Spanish and Chilean citizens during his dictatorship. The Chileans' enthusiastic embrace of the economic rules of the global market did not exempt them from the emerging rules of the international community regarding human rights and universal justice, even though those rules are still in formation. As it turns out, Pinochet's arrest had the salutary effect of strengthening Chile's court system and advancing its legal processes for dealing with cases from its authoritarian period, thereby better protecting the nation from future shocks of this sort. The writing is on the wall. Nations that do not measure up to international standards in legal punishment of human rights violations, or in other sensitive areas, may face international condemnation, and should take steps to address those discrepancies. In the region, Argentina, Colombia, and Guatemala—and perhaps Brazil (if it is not perceived as committed to protecting its tropical forests)—could someday be vulnerable to such international action.[21]

Considering the historical legacy of outside intervention in regional affairs, the success of institutions that reduce the likelihood of similar actions in the future is crucial to the interests of Latin America. However, effective multilateral institutions require from their members a willingness to participate in and devote resources to cooperative activities at the regional and global level, including some that are sensitive areas of national policy. If Brazil, for example, is serious in its claim to a permanent seat on the UN Security Council, it must reverse international perceptions that it is unwilling or unable to address its fiscal problems, human rights record, severe poverty, and environmental destruction. International legitimacy requires more than rhetorical adherence to the values and objectives of the international community.

Becoming a rulemaker abroad demands that a national government is able to be a rulemaker at home. This issue is not restricted to developing nations. When President Clinton was unable to win from Congress fast-track authority for negotiating free-trade agreements, the United States lost significant ground in its influence over the integration process, a slippage from which Brazil, Chile, and Mercosur nations in particular have benefited.

An international system characterized by increasing globalization requires a multidimensional conceptualization of foreign policy. A decision by a state to commit itself to economic integration and greater political coordination tends to weaken the power and autonomy of its centralized government. What previously were domestic policy decisions—interest rates, currency exchange levels, wage rates, and environmental laws, for instance—now have international implications. This growing "intermestic-ity" of issues challenges policymakers across the globe. It is particularly difficult for many larger, less centralized nations, where federal governments responsible for international policies have to contend with state and local governments. Foreign policy projects can be vulnerable not only to external shocks, but also to shocks from within, as happened in 1999 when Itamar Franco, governor of Minas Gerais, a major Brazilian state, announced a moratorium on debt payments to Brasilia. What was basically a personal political attack on President Cardoso precipitated Brazil's currency devaluation and contributed to a regionwide economic recession. More than ever, successful foreign policy requires coordination with state and local governments and other domestic parties—particularly the private sector and prominent NGOs—and requires that local government institutions have the capacity to implement national-level decisions.

Dynamic, open democratic systems tend to complicate the formulation of coherent foreign policies. More actors are involved in international relations, not just multinational institutions or corporations but also state and local governments and citizens. What has long been the case in the United States is increasingly true in much of Latin America: formulation of international policy is characterized by linkages and interrelations among domestic and external forces. These new linkages are difficult to assimilate, especially for elite groups that are historically accustomed to making decisions of national strategic or security policy with a high degree of autonomy. In an international community that places high value on transparent democratic practices, breaches of constitutional conduct can bring into question a government's legitimacy. For example, Venezuela's idiosyncratic President Hugo Chavez found that although he and his supporters believed that closing down congress and the supreme court were necessary for national reform, the profound skepticism and worry this generated among international investors and regional partners forced him to moderate his actions.

What are the objectives and available instruments of national policy in this new international system? How do the features of modern democracy and open, internationally connected societies affect the perceptions and conduct of relations among states? Will institutions like the United Nations, NATO, or the OAS prove effective over the long term, or will powerful nations decide they can be more successful acting alone? In financial crises or disputes, will organizations like the IMF or the WTO play expanded roles? Add the fact that nonstate actors can apply tremendous pressure on governments, and it is understandable that many nations, including the United States, are having difficulty finding their footing in the new, still evolving international system.

## Themes of the Volume:
## A Call for Strategic Thinking

This book assesses Latin America's situation in the international system of the post–Cold War era and the strategic options available to the nations of the region to pursue their interests and enhance their roles internationally. These chapters are the result of a project of the Latin American Program of the Woodrow Wilson International Center, supported by the Ford Foundation. The Latin American Program has an ongoing interest in questions of hemispheric international relations, regional strategic thinking, and the foreign policies of Latin American nations.[22] Most of the chapters present the viewpoints of policymakers and scholars from Latin America. These regional perspectives are complemented by the reflections of two preeminent U.S. scholars of international relations, whose areas of expertise are institutions and foreign policy making at the global level. From this range of analyses emerge four principal themes: increasing heterogeneity of the strategic interests and options of subregions and nations; variations in the degree of U.S. regional influence; the need for multidimensional strategic planning; and the fundamental importance of strengthening democratic institutions.

### Widening Divergence Among the Subregions and Nations of Latin America

The unidimensional approach the United States took toward the region during the Cold War, based on which governments or groups were or were not potentially communistic, blurred the contrasts among nations. Whether it was Chile, Brazil, or Nicaragua, policies from Washington were fundamentally the same. Under the confining ideologies and security fixations of the times, nations in the region often perceived each other in similar reductionist terms. Since the end of the Cold War, this mentality has given way before expanding social, economic, and political ties between the countries of the hemisphere and their global partners. Increased knowledge of and interaction with the region have put Latin America's complexities into high relief.

The international interests and preoccupations of the various subregions of the hemisphere (e.g., the Andean nations, the Southern Cone, Central America) sometimes overlap, but are clearly distinct. Often the economic, political, or social-historical characteristics even of neighboring countries yield strikingly different international profiles. For example, even though they share one island, the political and economic systems of

Haiti and the Dominican Republic differ significantly. Although students of the region and Latin Americans themselves have known for years that the national characteristics and interests of Bolivia, Peru, and Chile diverge widely, this fact is rather novel to many policymakers in Washington. To lump Brazil with the numerous small states of the hemisphere into one category is not a useful assumption, as Brazilians often point out to their colleagues from the North who speak of Latin America as a coherent geographical entity. Even comparing the strategic interests of Brazil or Argentina with those of Mexico is complicated by subregional, historical, and institutional differences, as is evident in the chapters by Guadalupe González and Thomaz Guedes da Costa. While this book frames issues in a similar, regionwide approach, the range of perspectives and approaches discussed indicate increasing regional heterogeneity.

The dynamics and effects of globalization are not evenly distributed among countries or subregions.[23] Key variables in the determination of a nation's international role—the size and development of its economy, the strength of its military, the nature and degree of U.S. influence in its regional affairs, the competitiveness of its industries in the global marketplace, and its degree of economic integration and partnership—vary dramatically. Moreover, the forces of globalization and regional integration seem to be increasing these differences instead of reducing them, which complicates Latin American solidarity in the face of negotiations with the larger powers.

Efforts at subregional integration exist across the region. However, some have been more effective than others. These disparities mostly reflect differences among the degrees of compatibility between regional domestic markets, and differences among the flexibility and efficiency of the private sectors of various nations, as well as the effectiveness of their government institutions in providing support and structure for these relations. The success of Mercosur has benefited each of its member nations and associate members in terms of their economic growth and political stability in a way that membership in the Andean Pact has not. Alberto Van Klaveren, in particular, indicates that the future growth of these trade blocs and their potential for deeper integration are key questions in the minds of many Latin American policymakers. Will Mercosur lead to a South American free trade zone, and if so by what rules will Brazil play as its dominant member?[24] Will membership in Mercosur or another trade bloc complicate future efforts to join NAFTA—which remains the grand prize due to the sheer size and voraciousness of the U.S. domestic market—or to establish free trade with the United States by another means? How compatible are South American markets with each other? If you are the Ecuadoran minister of trade, will your exports bring greater and more stable profits in Brazil, Mexico, Japan, Korea, or the United States? Does subregional integration force you to choose?

The answers to these questions vary from country to country, as Peter Smith emphasizes in his discussion of differing strategic options. Options made available to Chile by its bustling niche export economy and the development of its fishing and agricultural industries are not equally available to Nicaragua or even to Mexico, the industrial and trade portfolios of which are quite different. Each nation of the region will have to determine its preferred path to greater insertion in the international system according to the tools and advantages it has, and those it has not, which indicates that Latin America's heterogeneity will only increase in the coming decades.

This trend is painfully clear in the recent WTO dispute over European quotas for banana imports. Ecuador, Costa Rica, and other Central American nations, in cooperation with the massive U.S. banana industry, brought a suit to the WTO that attacked the foundation of the economies of many Eastern Caribbean islands. If not managed through forward-thinking, cooperative international initiatives, the pressures of increased global and regional competition can undermine partnership among the nations of the Americas and lead them into a trap of zero-sum competition, by which the region as a whole would suffer. Again, this requires more legitimate and active multinational institutions for cooperation and dialogue at the subregional and hemispheric levels, and this depends on greater national commitment to regional cooperation.

### Variations in the Degree of U.S. Influence in Regional Affairs

The different viewpoints represented in this book make clear that the degree and nature of the United States' influence in regional affairs vary along subregional and national lines. Chile, for instance, is relatively distant from the United States, is less affected by the drug trade, and historically has had a more balanced trade portfolio than do its neighbors to the north. As Heraldo Muñoz points out, Chileans today are as interested in the political and economic news from Brasília, Buenos Aires, and São Paulo as they are in those from New York or Washington. Authors from the Southern Cone countries—Guedes da Costa, Muñoz, and Van Klaveren—emphasize a balancing strategy as a central facet of their nations' strategic relations. Increased economic and political ties within the region, institutionalized in Mercosur, and also with Asia or Europe, are viewed as a means of protection from undue dependence on the United

States, and as a source of increased leverage vis-à-vis the United States within the broader global system.

The idea of engaging in a policy of strategic balancing against the United States is hardly novel. Indeed, recent cooperative initiatives also have a long history.[25] The diversification of trade and investment is beneficial in economic theory, but has proven throughout the history of the region to have limited effectiveness in providing protection from price volatility. Politically, to a student of inter-American history these efforts are redolent of other strategic efforts, likewise unsuccessful, in which options were constrained conceptually by the ideological fixation on the need to resist the dominant position of the United States. In most cases trade should follow natural market flows and seek out higher returns, regardless of whether those returns are achieved from selling to the U.S., European, or Asian markets. The appeal of the idea of diversified trade as a strategic policy is more ideological than economic, and implies government intervention in the private sector using subsidies or other supportive actions, which would likely lead to price distortions and inhibit competitiveness.

The long-term political significance of these more diverse economic and political ties, especially regional integration, is one of the most contentious issues of the volume. Although Muñoz and Van Klaveren present broader trade relations as a key element of Latin American long-term policy, Peter Smith doubts the political will and economic benefit behind tighter relations with Europe or Asia. Regardless of the rhetoric, actual trade policy in both regions is in large part controlled by domestic interests. For example, at present the European Community defense of the Common Agricultural Policy makes commodity exports from Latin America all but impossible. The U.S. domestic market is far from perfectly open, with clear protections in place for important regional industries. However, of the major markets it is far and away the most accessible, even to nations without NAFTA membership.

In his analysis, Smith bases the strategic options of these nations on the structures of their interhemispheric and regional trade relations. Robert Keohane doubts the political significance and durability of regional integration and cautions against optimistic comparisons with the project of the European Community. Keohane argues that Europe's modern economic structure, its strategic rationale for political congruence and a unified security system, and historical experience provide it with powerful political motives for integration that Latin America lacks. Without long-term political motivation, Keohane suggests, integration projects in the region are likely to remain shallow and vulnerable to political shocks. Yet, without economic integration and the wider international political cooperation that it fosters, Latin America risks becoming marginalized within the global system. Keohane states that ultimately the international position and influence of each country will depend upon its responses to pressures of globalization, and they will depend on the strength and flexibility of its domestic democratic and free-market systems.

In the cases of Mexico, Central America, and the nations of the Caribbean, the pressures of globalization will continue to strengthen and deepen their interrelations with the United States. As González describes it, economic liberalization is leading to trade substitution and greater dependence on the U.S. market, and the security threats that these countries share with the United States as well as the heavy migratory flows make cooperation imperative. For the Andean nations, as long as supply-side interdiction and crop reduction remain the principal elements of the U.S. strategy against illegal drugs, these nations will have to negotiate the specialized attention this industry brings.

Closer ties to the United States and the sharing of that nation's regional interests can be detrimental, beneficial, or in most cases both. Especially in the cases of smaller countries, negotiating with the United States to gain medium- or long-term benefits from increasing cooperation may be an optimal solution, given those countries' range of options. The key is in the nature of the nations' behavior in these asymmetrical relations. Because of the uncertainty in its global foreign policy and its satisfaction with free-market democracies in Latin America, the United States today is open to recommendations and models for cooperation from its neighbors to the south. The official rhetoric of "partnership" heard from the Clinton administration, from the drug czar Barry McCaffrey, and from the U.S. Southern Command is an important shift of diction from the accusatory language of the preceding decades.[26] The nations of Latin America should work aggressively, not with caution, suspicion, or sheepishness, in the formulation of their relationship with the United States. Simply complaining about U.S. policies, such as its unilateral certification process, which they know to be tied up with complicated domestic bipartisan issues, is not constructive. They must bring to the bargaining table viable multilateral options that are responsive to U.S. interests, which are by and large the same as theirs, as well as sensitive to their valid concerns with sovereignty and reciprocity.

As an example, important officials of U.S. government agencies, as well as members of Congress, have expressed either officially or unofficially their interest in finding alternatives to the country's awkward, anachronistic policies of unilateral certification and the embargo against

Cuba. Creative ideas for the replacement of these unilateral instruments with legitimate multilateral ones that serve the region's collective interests—that help reduce drug trafficking and support the democratization of Cuba—would be a welcome sign to Latin America's friends in Washington and a significant step forward for inter-American relations. There is an opportunity for Latin America to take the initiative and work with the United States to create a new architecture for hemispheric relations. Working with it is here understood to be different from reacting to or subordinating to the United States. It is a foreign policy posture that begins with the defense of each nation's interests, but looks openly to shared interests and values and energetically explores potential areas for cooperation.

As long as the convergence of political and economic values across the Americas holds up and the primary interests of the region coincide with those of the United States (i.e., increased economic trade, political freedom, reduced drug trafficking, regional stability), Latin American nations enjoy far more autonomy of international action than they did during the Cold War. They must take advantage of this window of opportunity, for it is impossible to predict what crises or changes might cause it to close. A growing U.S. focus on fighting drugs above other regional policy objectives threatens to reduce this opportunity. In the first decade of 2000, the nations of Latin America must be more assertive and innovative than they were in the 1990s. Latin American nations, working together, have an unprecedented chance to reshape the hemispheric community more to their liking, if they would assume responsibility and leadership in doing so.

## The Need for Multidimensional Strategic Planning

For the most part, the chapters by Latin Americans and scholars of Latin America present options for trade and economic integration as the core of these countries' strategic policies. Ernest May finds this troubling in that it seems to assume the perpetuation of the international economic system in its current form and stability. In light of the global economic turmoil of 1998–1999, and the precarious and inexplicable nature of the current buoyancy of the U.S. economy, any policy based on this assumption is of limited use over the long term. According to May, such a focus on short- and medium-term economic policies hardly qualifies as strategic. Keohane notes the lack of traditional foreign policy behavior, such as strategic alliances, nationalist projections, or balancing strategies. In other regions of the world, such as South Asia or Africa, the end of the Cold War brought a resurgence of traditional political competitiveness and maneuvering. Although the regionwide convergence of values, widespread respect for international sovereignty, and the decline of many traditional rivalries, such as those between Brazil and Argentina or Chile and Argentina, are to be welcomed, policymakers should not see economic partnership and liberalization as the only remaining instruments for building regional power. To May and Keohane this is an unnecessarily narrow approach.

Regional integration projects are as important for their political and security implications as they are for their economic benefits. As Guedes da Costa notes, the deepening of Mercosur and the expansion of trade ties with its other neighbors is the centerpiece of Brazil's strategic policy. Politically, these multilateral ties are central to the consolidation of Brazil's position as the leader of South America. By fomenting interdependence, Mercosur has contributed to the subregion's stability and security as well as to its economic growth. As it was when constructed in the mid-1980s, Mercosur continues to be an important tool for the fortifying of democracy among its members. This is evidenced by the pivotal role its member nations played in their firm response to an attempted military coup in Paraguay in 1998.

Closer economic and political ties among Chile, Argentina, and Brazil have paved the way for improved security in the Southern Cone. Before the 1980s the traditional hypotheses of conflict for all these nations were intraregional: they each perceived one another as principal rivals and potential military aggressors. However, in the 1990s joint military exercises between former antagonists became routine. In early 1999 the governments of Chile and Argentina resolved their last remaining territorial dispute. Brazil and Argentina have agreed to joint production and repair of naval vessels, and Argentina and Chile have planned to hold their first bi-oceanic joint naval operations in the year 2002.

Across the hemisphere, enhanced regional economic and political relations have improved security. The Latin American Guarantor Nations of the Rio Group—Argentina, Brazil, and Chile—worked assertively to mediate a solution to the border conflict between Peru and Ecuador in 1995. For years, many nations of the Caribbean have coordinated their military or coast guard maneuvers, frequently including the United States. The Eastern Caribbean Regional Security System, which consists of the naval forces of the English-speaking Eastern Caribbean nations, provides a successful model for cooperation, though its expansion toward more diversity has proven problematic.

In strategic terms, it is not always clear how foreign policy can support a nation's drive toward sustainable development and economic competitiveness. Under Carlos Menem, Argentina made an explicit decision to throw itself into UN peacekeeping efforts as a way to demonstrate its reliability. The Menem government also sent boats to the Persian Gulf to show its new solidarity with the United States, offered to send personnel to Brazil to fight forest fires, and—in a gesture of community support that was embarassing to all—offered in August 1999 to send troops to Colombia. By contrast, Brazil, Chile, and Mexico have been slower and more reluctant to participate in collective peacekeeping. Brazil, which has declared openly its ambition to be a permanent member of the UN Security Council, continues to be diffident in the assertion of its international influence. Like other nations of the region, Brazil's rhetoric of support for regional collective action in response to security crises is weakened by its long-standing insistence on the preservation of national sovereignty and nonintervention as foreign policy principles. Foreign Minister Luiz Felipe Lampreia has indicated that Brazil would be an unassertive hegemon, although his hardline positions in Mercosur negotiations since its currency devaluation in 1999 indicate limits to Brazilian diffidence.

Keohane cautions against overestimating the durability and long-term significance of subregional integration projects, suggesting that until they are much more formalized they remain vulnerable to an international economic meltdown or a rise in interstate tensions in the region. The sharp bickering between Brazil and Argentina since the devaluation seems to bear out this point. Even if successful over the long term, regional integration does little to enhance these nations' political importance beyond the hemisphere. Nevertheless, considering the conceptual chains of mistrust and assumed antagonism that had constricted the foreign policies of Latin American nations for over a century, the importance of these cooperative initiatives should not be underestimated.[27] In varying degrees, they have virtually eliminated long-standing conflictive and mutually suspicious strategic and security conceptions and laid the groundwork for further partnership in a range of areas.

A principal argument of the book is that the nations of the region should look beyond economic liberalization and regional integration toward a broader, more innovative set of instruments for strategic policy. Policies that have traditionally been thought of as domestic now assume international dimensions. Improving economic competitiveness, the development of high-technology industries, the growth of social capital, and the enhancement of the national image abroad are all aspects of modern strategic policy. Cultivating domestic expertise and skill in high-technology areas and supporting scientific research are important steps toward improving international competitiveness. In Costa Rica, for example, attracting an

Intel production facility brought jobs and economic development and raised the country's credibility as a market for foreign investment. Other nations, including Brazil and Chile, have thriving software- and computer-manufacturing industries, vital segments to any competitive modern economy. State support of and promotion of public-private partnerships for research and training regarding satellites, computer software, Internet communications, and other such high-technology, cutting-edge industries are valuable elements of a long-term plan for economic development.

Public-private cooperation on research and development has played an important role in the development of high-technology industries in the United States and other industrialized nations, yet it hardly exists in much of Latin America. The establishment of intellectual property laws and viable mechanisms for their effective enforcement are crucial to this effort. Public education systems are often the victim of budget cuts and are poorly managed and inefficient across the region, although the education level of a population is crucial to its productiveness and to improving national competitiveness. When faced with deep public debt and economic turmoil, governments find it difficult to think beyond daily constraints and crises. However, economic and political investments made today in these areas should be viewed as elements of long-term strategic planning and as necessary steps toward expanding a country's strategic capabilities in the future.

Narrowly focused foreign policy formulations are anachronistic in the new international system. Without the Cold War, Latin American governments can no longer manipulate the interests of the United States or, in Cuba's case, the Soviet Union to secure favors. Policies of aggressive third-world solidarity, as were popular in the 1960s and 1970s, can be damaging in an era marked by the benefits of global openness and interdependence. Also disastrous would be the revival of traditional concepts of regional power based on military threat or territorial expansion. There is a growing divide between the nations that act within the institutional norms of international behavior and those that choose instead to defy the system. Even though the system has its flaws and is asymmetrically weighted toward the interests of the great powers, the nations of Latin America benefit from its stability and enjoy more freedom to pursue their interests within its parameters than without.

The recent expansion of the powers of the international community to enforce its values—demonstrated by the arrest of General Pinochet, the international court at the Hague, and the response of the European Union to Austria's new government—has many critics. For developing nations in particular, the imposition of social and cultural values perceived to come from the outside can appear threatening, especially to groups whose power, impunity, or freedom of action may be targeted. However, the emergence of these values offers nations that esteem democratic principles and that cooperate internationally opportunities to influence the formation of institutional mechanisms for their expression. Informal and formal measures that limit such phenomena as corruption, human rights violations, child labor, political coups, or unduly destructive environmental practices appear assured to become significant elements in future international relations. To fight such measures merely on principle would be a dangerous and outdated policy. Instead, the nations of Latin America should take advantage of the inchoate state of the international institutional mechanisms relevant to these values and be active and outspoken in their ongoing formulation: they can become rulemakers.

## The Fundamental Role of Democratic Institutions

Keohane emphasizes that a nation's success under the forces of globalization will depend on the flexibility and strength of its democratic system. Policies like the promotion of high-technology industries, defense against fluctuations in short-term capital flows, regulation of the banking industry, unequivocal protection for intellectual property, the setting of socially responsible but economically competitive wage levels, and increasing involvement in multinational initiatives require effective public institutions. Deepening international ties can affect the structure and function of these institutions, as has happened to Mexican national and state police and the judicial system since they have been forced to cooperate with their U.S. counterparts in fighting drug trafficking. After the recent economic crises, international investors are more wary of suspect business, banking, and legal environments. Greater economic openness often reveals problems of corruption, ties to illegal activities, or general mismanagement, the removal of which requires stronger, more autonomous judicial and regulatory systems.

Virtually every nation of the region has implemented important reforms over the last decade.[28] Economic liberalization and the privatization of state-held companies have improved efficiency and competitiveness, and governments are working now to bring state institutions up to the task of monitoring and regulating these dynamic economic arenas. This progress must continue if Latin American economies are going to open up further and continue to grow and become more competitive in the globalized market. In the broad sense, the strengthening of democracy and democratic institutions at home is fundamental to a state's capacity to engage in strategic policymaking.

## Policies for National Promotion Abroad

Many nations are rightly concerned about the effects that the influx of foreign media and culture—particularly those of the United States—could have on their national values and cultures. Government protection for local media industries, as exists in France and Canada, is growing popular. Uruguay, for instance, has instituted a cultural promotion program called "Defensa de la Identidad Uruguaya" to respond to the inundation of products and media from its Mercosur partners. But what is a threat can also be an opportunity. This spread of culture and image can serve as a promotional piece for national interests.

Analogous to Joseph Nye's concept of "soft power," international dissemination of Latin American culture and news increases the attention the region receives and, over time, builds greater awareness, interest in investment and tourism, and political legitimacy. This spread of information occurs naturally through the internationalization of the communications industry. Today Latin American news, films, and television are broadcast via the Internet or on television around the world. Governments should support this export of information, culture, and national imagery through creative promotion campaigns abroad, including support for academic research, art and music exhibitions, modern studies programs, and the offering of Spanish- or Portuguese-language classes.[29]

The growth and increasing political organization of Latino communities, primarily in the United States, contributes to this greater awareness of regional interests. Such communities are gaining influence over policymaking at all levels of the U.S. political system. The nations of Latin America can benefit by maintaining ties with their expatriate communities and encouraging their interest in the issues that affect their nation of origin and the state of relations between their nation of origin and the nation in which they reside. Another indication of increased globalization is the fact that political and economic events in New York City, New Jersey, and Miami are now deeply linked with the national politics of the Dominican Republic, Puerto Rico, and Cuba, and vice versa. This form of potential influence could be particularly advantageous to the nations of the Caribbean and Central America, producing an indirect benefit of their intense social and economic ties to the United States.

## New Concepts and Broader Cooperation
## with New Actors

In his reflections, May points out that during the 1950s and 1960s Latin America was a hotbed of intellectual enterprise. Latin American scholarship generated seminal models and theories that contributed to a major shift in the predominant thinking on issues of international development and economic relations. Chile in particular earned a reputation as a locus of important intellectual activity—especially the prestigious UN Economic Commission for Latin America, headed up by the influential Argentine economist Raul Prebisch—and Brazil proclaimed itself a champion of third-world political unity against the North. These initiatives were largely in response to and were conditioned by the structure of the Cold War, but they represent a political energy and spirit of innovation lacking in the region today.

In light of the indifference they receive from the governments of the United States and other powers, Latin American nations could gain from strengthening their relations with partners that are showing more interest.[30] While Washington continues to be shortsighted and to suffer from attention deficit disorder regarding Latin America, the U.S. business community is increasingly aware of and active in the region. Contrary to some of the uglier instances in the history of U.S.–Latin American relations, today private-sector groups in the United States can be an important regional ally in pressuring their government on a variety of issues, from support for fast-track negotiations to assistance in research and institutional capacity building. Public-private partnerships and cooperative work with international NGOs can bring cutting-edge technology and skills to regional product research and development, environmental resource studies, energy production, education, and many other pressing issues. The same can be said about the nongovernmental sector of the European Union. Transnational linkages between regional and extraregional business groups, NGOs, universities, cultural or social organizations, and other entities are multiplying under the region's democratic freedom. The nations of Latin America should encourage and fortify these informal ties to insert their communities as well as their political objectives into those of the wider democratized world.

Because these ties, and much of today's growing international activity, are in areas in which international regulation and structure are still undefined, farsighted policymakers in Latin America can make a special effort to position their nations' specialists at the forefront of the shaping of relevant international norms. Many new issues require addressing in the international system, such as Internet regulation and design, environmental valuation and sustainable development laws, and standards and processes for human rights protection. The nations of Latin America—if they are innovative and assertive in their participation in the international debate over these issues—can assume significant roles in these negotiations. That is, they can progress to being rulemakers instead of ruletakers.

The purpose of these nontraditional instruments of foreign policy is to gain legitimacy in the international system. A nation increases its legitimacy by improving its own democratic practices and institutions, participating actively and responsibly in international initiatives, expressing a clear and consistent agenda, and building stronger economic, political, and social ties between itself and the rest of the world. In a world shaped more by the rules, standards, and actions of institutions than by interstate militarized oppression, enhanced legitimacy translates into power. The nations of Latin America must understand that it is through this power, the power that comes from a sound democratic legitimacy and responsible international participation, that their interests will best be pursued in the new international system.

## Notes

1. See James Rosenau, *Along the Domestic-Foreign Frontier: Exploring Governance in a Turbulent World* (Cambridge Studies in International Relations, 53).

2. Such has been the U.S. strategy under President Clinton. At the same time, many U.S. strategists and policymakers openly criticize the United Nations and urge either a return to isolationism (political pundit Patrick Buchanan, for instance) or the use of alternative multilateral instruments that will more effectively respond to U.S. interests.

3. See Jorge Dominguez, "The Americas: Found, Then Lost Again," *Foreign Policy* 112 (Fall 1998): 125–137.

4. Francis Fukuyama, "The End of History?" *National Interest* 25: 3–18.

5. Carlos Floria, "Nationalism as a Transnational Question. Political Analysis of Nationalism in Contemporary Argentina," Woodrow Wilson International Center for Scholars, Latin American Program, Working Paper Series, 220. There are Spanish and French versions of this monograph.

6. For an explanation of Joseph Nye's concept of "soft power," see Joseph S. Nye, *Bound to Lead: The Changing Nature of American Power* (New York: Basic Books, 1991).

7. See Robert O. Keohane and Joseph S. Nye, *Power and Interdependence* (Boston: Little, Brown, 1977); Robert O. Keohane and Joseph S. Nye, *After Hegemony: Cooperation and Discord in the World Political Economy* (Princeton University Press, 1984); and Lisa Martin, and Beth Simmons, "Theories

and Empirical Studies of International Institutions," *International Organization* 52: 4.

8. Samuel Huntington, *The Clash of Civilizations and the Remaking of World Order* (New York: Touchstone Books, 1998).

9. Hans-Henrik Holm and Georg Sorensen, *Whose World Order? Uneven Globalization and the End of the Cold War* (Boulder, Colo.: Westview Press, 1995).

10. For a discussion of the relevance of Western international relations theory to the reality of politics and statehood in less developed regions, see Stephanie G. Neuman, ed., *International Relations Theory and the Third World* (New York: St. Martin's Press, 1998).

11. See Robert S. Litwak, *Rogue States and U.S. Foreign Policy* (Washington, D.C.: Wilson Center Press/Johns Hopkins University Press, 2000).

12. On the power of the rule of law argument in creating a new code of good behavior in international affairs, see Thomas Carothers, "The Rule-of-Law Revival," *Foreign Affairs* 77, 2 (March/April 1998). The halting, cacophanous response of the hemispheric community to the electoral farce in Peru in June 2000 suggests the limits to this approach.

13. The classic, unblushing statement of U.S. strategic interest and the use of power is Alfred Thayer Mahan, *The Influence of Sea Power upon History, 1660–1783* (New York: Hill and Wang, 1957). For analysis of U.S. strategic thinking and its participation in institutions, see John Ikenberry, "Distant Gains: Hegemony, Institutions, and the Long-Term Returns on Power," in Daniel Deudney and Michael Mastanduno, eds., *Power and Power: Essays in Honor of Robert Gilpin* (forthcoming); Richard N. Haas, "What to Do with American Primacy?" *Foreign Affairs* 78, 5 (September/October 1999): 37–50; Robert Kagan, "The Benevolent Empire," *Foreign Policy* (Summer 1998); and Josef Joffe, "How America Does It," *Foreign Affairs* 76, 5 (September/October 1997): 13–27.

14. See P. J. Simmons, "NGOs in Global Affairs: Resistance Is Futile," *Foreign Policy* (Fall 1998).

15. See Richard E. Feinberg, *Summitry in the Americas: A Progress Report* (Washington, D.C.: Institute for International Economics, 1997). See also Richard Feinberg and Robin Rosenberg, eds., *Civil Society and the Summit of the Americas: The 1998 Santiago Summit* (Miami: The North-South Center Press, 1999).

16. For official documents and information on CICAD, see the Web site at *www.cicad.oas.org*.

17. For analysis of the successes and failures of such transitions in six countries, see Cynthia J. Arnson, ed., *Comparative Peace Processes in Latin America* (Washington, D.C.: Woodrow Wilson Center Press and the Stanford University Press, 1999).

18. Not so Spanish Judge Balthasar Garzon, who changed global legal principles by indicting General Augusto Pinochet in 1999 for violations of human rights during his rule. Since then, Garzon has also indicted former military officials in Argentina and has caused panic among former dictators and their officials throughout Latin America.

19. Andrew Hurrell, Andrew Cooper, Ricardo Sennes, Srini Sitaraman, and Guadalupe González, "Paths to Power: Institutional Foreign Policies of Middle-Power Nations," Woodrow Wilson International Center for Scholars, Latin American Program, Working Paper Series, 244.

20. See Robert O. Keohane, "Lilliputians' Dilemmas: Small States in International Politics," *International Organization* 23, 2 (1969). Also see John Ikenberry, "Distant Gains: Hegemony, Institutions and the Long-Term Returns to Power," paper presented at the Woodrow Wilson Center, Washington, D.C.

21. During his official visit to the United States in June 2000, Argentine president Fernando de la Rua paid a visit to the Holocaust Museum and apologized for his country's willingness to provide a haven for Nazi war criminals after World War II. In this way he hoped to mitigate Argentina's image in the United States as anti-U.S. and anti-semitic, both long-standing stains on Argentina's international reputation.

22. Heraldo Muñoz and Joseph S. Tulchin, eds., *Latin American Nations in World Politics* (Boulder, Colo.: Westview Press, 1996).

23. See Holm and Sorensen, 1995.

24. For instance, the crisis between Brazil and Argentina in July and August of 1999 nearly broke Mercosur apart, and continuing disputes regarding tariffs on car parts, shoe manufacturing, and other industries important to national markets worry regional analysts.

25. In the 1950s, Argentina's President Juan D. Perón attempted to form the ABC Alliance based on a coincidence of political style and ideology. His partners were in Brazil (Getúlio Vargas) and Chile (Bernardo Ibáñez). This effort, after a number of diplomatic exchanges, came to nothing.

26. See Richard Quirk, "The Cooperative Agenda of the U.S. Armed Forces in the Caribbean," in Joseph S. Tulchin and Ralph H. Espach, eds., *Security in the Caribbean Basin* (Boulder, Colo.: Lynne Rienner Publishers, 2000).

27. See Andrew Hurrell, "Security in Latin America," *International Affairs* 74, 3 (1998): 529–546.

28. For a discussion of the role of effective markets and competition policy, see Moisés Naím and Joseph S. Tulchin, *Competition Policy, Deregulation, and Modernization in Latin America* (Boulder, Colo.: Lynne Rienner Publishers, 1999).

29. Brazil is currently engaged in such a project, led chiefly by Ambassador Rubens Barbosa, first in England, where Oxford University established a Centre for the Brazilian Studies, and now in the United States, where Ambassador Barbosa proposes to help a variety of institutions develop permanent divisions or study centers on Brazil.

30. See Jorge I. Dominguez, *Foreign Policy* 112 (1998).

# 2

# Strategic Options for Latin America

## *Peter H. Smith*

*Look, it's simple. There is an Americanization of the world. We cannot go in the opposite direction. At last we are going to make America here.*
—Carlos Alfonso Ferraro, Peronist Governor
of Jujuy, Argentina (1998)

Latin America faces a perplexing world. The end of East-West conflict means that the region no longer serves as a battleground for superpower rivalry. Within Latin America, passage of the Cold War has relaxed the terms of ideological contention, strengthened centrist elements, reinforced processes of liberalization under way throughout the 1980s, and enhanced the prospects for democratic consolidation. These changes have prompted the hope that Washington could come to evaluate and appreciate Latin America on its own terms, respecting regional aspirations and supporting national efforts for social and political development.

It has also been anticipated that the conclusion of the Cold War would expand the range and quality of policy options for Latin America. This may or may not be so. Leaders in the region currently confront two pressing imperatives. One is to find a viable position in the newly emerging global economy, a niche that could provide a foundation for long-term development and growth. The other is to forge a response to changing patterns in the distribution of international power, and, in particular, the intensification of U.S. hegemony in the Western Hemisphere. How might Latin America address these concerns? What is the range of plausible choice? For which countries of the region?

The goal of this chapter is to assess strategic options for Latin America at the outset of the new millennium. I begin with a brief survey of the post–Cold War international context. I then analyze contemporary strategies: unilateral liberalization, integration with the United States, subregional integration, and quests for extrahemispheric alliances. A principal part of this analysis argues that different strategies are available to different countries in differing degrees. A conclusion evaluates these policy alternatives and offers speculation about potential changes in the future.

A central pillar of this argument is the concept of "strategic options." As used here, the term applies to opportunities for (and variations of) relatively long-term, consistent policies—"grand strategies," in the argot of international relations theory—to protect and promote the interests of nation-states. They entail realistic appraisals of changing configurations of international power. While using the nation-state as the unit of analysis, I am not claiming that the state is the only relevant actor in the international arena or that it is unitary and rational.[1] Nor do I assume that leaders pursue strategic goals with maximum effectiveness or utmost rationality. Indeed, the intent of this chapter is merely to outline the range and content of options currently available to the nations of Latin America. Whether they make constructive use of these choices is quite another matter.

## The International Context

Sweeping transformations during the late 1980s ushered in an era of optimism, hope—and uncertainty. The crumbling of the Berlin Wall, the reunification of Germany, the liberation of Eastern Europe, and the consolidation of superpower detente marked the end of the 40-year Cold War and left substantial confusion in its wake. What kind of world order appears to be emerging?

One pervasive reality is economic multipolarity. After decades of transformation, the global economy has three distinct poles. One is the United States. Second is the European Community, whose combined gross domestic product (GDP) of 1990 was just about equivalent to that of the United States. Third is Japan or, more broadly, the Pacific Rim. As of 1960 the combined GDP of Asian-Pacific countries (excluding the United States) was merely 7.8 percent of world GDP; by 1982 it had more than doubled, to 16.4 percent, and by 1990 it had risen to 23.0 percent. A strong economic recovery in the United States and market uncertainties in Europe and Asia somewhat modified this pattern in the late 1990s, but the overall structure remained multipolar.

A second development has been the consolidation of U.S. military preeminence. The implosion of the Soviet Union meant that the United States would have no serious military rival anywhere in the world: it could enjoy a "unipolar moment" of unchallenged superiority. Yet there are complications. One is the threat of nuclear proliferation, as epitomized by the emergence of rogue "weapons states" (Iraq and North Korea among them) and by midlevel countries seeking to join the nuclear club (such as India and Pakistan). Moreover, military capability has limited political utility. For the most part, challenges and conflicts of the 1990s do not lend themselves to military solutions. The Gulf War of 1991 was a glaring exception; the protracted, contradictory, and painful struggles of Somalia and Bosnia seem more likely to represent the rule.

A third feature is the increasing role and importance of nonstate actors and transnational forces. Private corporations allocate massive investments in line with global strategies. Communications networks spread information and ideas with lightning speed around the world. Grassroots movements, social groups, and NGOs make contact with each other, distribute resources, build agendas, and help shape the terms of transnational discourse: civil society has begun to play a major role in world affairs. Organized crime, drug cartels, smuggling rings, and other unsavory groups also take advantage of illicit opportunities.

It remains far from clear whether and how the post–Cold War world will manage to achieve a workable code for international behavior. As Joseph Nye has written, "No single hierarchy describes adequately a world politics with multiple structures. The distribution of power in world politics has become like a layer cake. The top military layer is largely unipolar, for there is no other military power comparable to the United States. The economic middle layer is tripolar and has been for two decades. The bottom layer of transnational interdependence shows a diffusion of power."[2] This configuration seems unlikely to produce stability—and, under current conditions, one could imagine that the international power structure might evolve in any one of several directions (as contemplated in the conclusion of this chapter). One of the defining features of the international arena is the absence of any firm set of rules of the game. As of the century's turn, uncertainty prevails.

## The United States and Latin America: Hegemony Regained

As the global arena moves toward complexity, the Western Hemisphere reveals simplicity: a reassertion of U.S. hegemony. The distribution of power resources remains extremely unequal. In 1950 the populations of all Latin America and the United States were nearly the same, just over

150 million; by 1990 the population of Latin America was almost 75 percent larger, 436 million compared with 250 million. Even so, the economic productivity of the United States has consistently overwhelmed Latin America's regional output: U.S. GDP was seven times as large as Latin American GDP in 1950, seven times as large in 1970, and well over five times as large by 1990. In 1950 the GDP of the United States was 30 times that of Argentina, 33 times that of Brazil, 37 times that of Mexico; by 1990 the GDP of the United States was 58 times that of Argentina, 13 times that of Brazil, 23 times that of Mexico. In relation to population size, the spread in per capita output grew steadily throughout this period: in 1950 GDP per capita in the United States was just over seven times as large as in Latin America, and by 1990 it was nearly ten times as large.[3] By this standard, economic disparity has been increasing over time.

Ultimately, the end of the Cold War signified that the United States would no longer have an archenemy in the hemisphere. To be sure, Washington policymakers and media pundits had for decades drastically exaggerated the extent of Soviet influence within the Americas; Moscow's influence had never been very great. Yet it was also conceivable that, without the East-West conflict, the United States would not concern itself with Latin America. As Jorge Castañeda noted, this possibility created a serious dilemma for the region:

> Paradoxically, after so many years of worrying about excessive U.S. involvement, Latin America may soon suffer from U.S. indifference, compounded by the rest of the world's traditional, relative lack of interest. As the geopolitical motivation for U.S. policy toward Latin America fades, its economic component could also shrink. The hemisphere could well face the prospect of "Africanization"—condemnation to the margins of world financial and trade flows but also, inevitably, to neglect and irrelevance. It may well find itself caught in the bind of a perverse, contradictory tension: between new forms of U.S. intervention in domestic Latin American policies and new expressions of U.S. and world indifference to its needs.[4]

Without the Cold War, Latin America could face the prospect of marginalization.

As major powers wrestle with reconfiguration of the world community and struggle to devise new rules of the game, Latin America finds itself at a distinct disadvantage. The continent is not a global power center. It will have only a modest role in determining the shape of the post–Cold War world. From this position of relative weakness, it will have to make creative and constructive use of policy choices. The question is this: What can Latin America do?

Ideological zeal and political solidarity no longer offer feasible alternatives.[5] Aptly interpreting the tone of the post–Cold War era, Latin American leaders have fastened on economic relations. Resulting strategies emphasize economics over politics, opportunity over principle, pragmatism over ideology. They also conceal the danger identified by Castañeda: that some countries (and many people) might face isolation and abandonment.[6]

## Option One: Trading Around

One conceivable option is to undertake unilateral programs of economic liberalization, more or less according to the Washington consensus, and to strengthen commercial and financial ties with major power centers. A "plurilateral" approach toward economic intercourse seems to comply with multipolar realities of the new global economy, especially the rise of Europe and Japan. Systematic reduction of commercial barriers promises to achieve the anticipated benefits of free trade. Moreover, unilateral action has the advantage of maintaining flexibility. Within a general strategy of export-led development, the corresponding policy prescriptions are relatively straightforward: diversify products and partners, seek foreign investment from multiple sources, and avoid restrictive entanglements; in other words, embark on a unilateral project in the name of free trade.

Among all countries of Latin America, Chile pursued this option with the greatest alacrity. Like other nations of the region, Chile adopted an increasingly protectionist trade policy from the 1930s to the early 1970s—by 1973 the modal tariff was 90 percent, with a maximum of 750 percent, accompanied by an extensive network of nontariff barriers (NTBs) as well. From 1974 on the Pinochet regime imposed a radical change in policy. Most NTBs were eliminated at the outset, and tariffs were steadily lowered to a flat rate of 10 percent on nearly all items by 1979. In reaction to the debt crisis the government temporarily hiked tariffs back up to 35 percent in 1984, while avoiding NTBs, and subsequent steps brought tariffs back down to 11 percent by the early 1990s. The democratic governments of Patricio Aylwin and Eduardo Frei, Jr., continued the Pinochet emphasis on commercial liberalization. "Free trade has been widely accepted as an integral part of Chile's development model," according to one well-informed analysis, "and there is consensus that a return to protectionism is not a reasonable option."[7] In demonstration of this point, there was no meaningful opposition to reduction of the tariff rate from 15 to 11 percent in mid-1991.

Results of this outward-looking strategy have been dramatic. Exports as a share of Chile's GDP grew from 31 percent in 1974 to 71 percent in 1990. After sharp contractions in the early 1980s, the economy achieved strong and steady rates of economic growth, reaching a maximum of 10 percent in 1989, and far outperforming the region as a whole from 1986 through 1992. Chile further achieved unusual success in the diversification of its commercial partnerships. By 1991 Japan had replaced the United States as the country's largest customer. Chile also had extensive trade connections with the European Community, especially with Germany, and imported about as many goods from the community as a whole as from the United States. In time, as we shall see, Chile would supplement (or supplant) its go-it-alone strategy with alternative policies, but by the early 1990s unilateral liberalization could be scored as a success.

By developing commercial ties with Europe and Japan as well as the United States, Chile is not beholden to any single trade partner. By publicly advocating the virtues of free trade, Chile has claimed a leadership role throughout the region. Having restored its traditions of democracy, Chile has become a political model as well.

Other nations of the region would probably like to pursue the Chilean path, and several have attempted to do so. The fact, however, is that Chile has managed to capitalize upon unique advantages. Some are economic: the lack of a larger and dominant commercial partner; a relatively isolated location; natural resources in widespread demand; and, paradoxically, smallness of size—with a population of less than 14 million and a GDP of only $41.2 billion as of 1992, Chile threatens no one. The other main advantage is political. Since the transition to democracy, a strong consensus has emerged in favor of unilateral opening. This has occurred because adjustment costs were borne largely under the Pinochet dictatorship, because economic benefits have become clearly apparent, and because of the urgent need to maintain national harmony in the post-Pinochet environment. This unanimity—or, at minimum, this de facto truce among opinion leaders and policymakers—has been essential for continuation of this strategy.[8] As things have turned out, only Chile could reap full-fledged benefits from the Chilean model.

## Option Two: Joining with the North

A second general strategy is to find a way to join with the North, or, more specifically, with the United States. In the early 1990s Washington encouraged this prospect, perhaps more as a means of confronting economic rivals elsewhere in the world (especially Europe and Japan) rather than of proclaiming fundamental solidarity with neighbors in the hemisphere, but the resulting opportunity was nonetheless apparent. It has become conceivable, under these new conditions, for countries of Latin America to align themselves with the United States on economic grounds.[9] This alternative looks attractive because it ensures some form of integration with the world economy.

For this strategy Mexico has by far the most advantages: geographical proximity, petroleum deposits, a relatively skilled workforce, a large and growing consumer market. The complexity of the bilateral agenda, ranging from drugs to migration to foreign policy questions, creates further incentives for Washington.

Yet this was not Mexico's first choice. Early in his term President Carlos Salinas de Gortari attempted to pursue the kind of "plurilateral" strategy pioneered by Chile, reaching out through commerce and investment to multiple centers of world economic power (and, at the same time, carefully tailoring economic relations with the United States through a series of limited sectoral agreements). But this option proved not to be viable. Financiers in Europe were directing their resources toward the rehabilitation and reincorporation of Eastern Europe, and Japanese investors were proving reluctant to meddle in what they saw as a U.S. sphere of interest. Anxious to attract investment capital, Salinas then turned to the United States. An FTA with the United States would ensure access to the U.S. market, guarantee the continuation of his economic policies, and, most important, send a crucial signal to the business community. In one analyst's summation, an accord with the United States would provide "an excellent chance to advertise to the world the business opportunities available in Mexico."[10]

### North American Free Trade

As a result, Mexico undertook negotiations with the United States and Canada to create the North American Free Trade Agreement (NAFTA) in 1992. After ratification by legislatures of the three governments, it took effect in January 1994. Building on a bilateral free-trade accord between Canada and the United States (approved in 1988, initiated January 1989), NAFTA established the largest trading bloc in the world, with a population of 370 million as of 1992 and combined economic production of approximately $6 trillion.

In its final form, NAFTA displayed three outstanding characteristics. One is an implicit commitment to regional economic integration. Despite its title, NAFTA is not merely concerned with "free trade." With extensive chapters about investment, competition, telecommunications, and financial services, it envisions a more profound form of integration than its label implies. Second, NAFTA is essentially an intergovernmental accord. Unlike the European Community (later European Union), which created an elaborate structure for governance with supranational authority, NAFTA relies on negotiations and presumed consensus between national governments.

Third, like other enduring integration schemes, NAFTA possesses an underlying political rationale. The United States was seeking several goals: stability along its southern border; secure access to petroleum from Mexico; a useful bargaining chip in its trade negotiations with Europe, Japan, and the GATT; and diplomatic support from Mexico on foreign policy in general. For its part Mexico was seeking, first and foremost, preservation of its social peace; second, an opportunity for President Salinas to institutionalize his economic reforms, insulating them from the historic vagaries of presidential succession; third, international benediction for its not-quite-democratic political regime; and, finally, diplomatic leverage vis-à-vis the rest of Latin America and, by extension, the third world as a whole. Association with Canada and the United States linked Mexico with advanced industrial democracies, so Mexico could claim to serve as a "bridge" between the developing world and the developed world, as a representative and interlocutor for aspiring peoples of the South. NAFTA has prompted some analysts to charge that Mexico was turning its back on Latin America. The assumption in Mexico City, however, has been that NAFTA would in the long run strengthen Mexico's diplomatic and political prestige.

### From NAFTA to WHFTA?

From the beginning, NAFTA was envisioned not only as a three-way partnership but also as the stepping stone toward a hemispheric accord (soon nicknamed WHFTA, for Western Hemisphere Free Trade Area). As President George Bush proclaimed when launching the Enterprise Institute of America (EAI) in 1990, the ultimate goal was to create a free-trade zone "stretching from the port of Anchorage to the Tierra del Fuego." Expectations were soon running high. Chile, Argentina, Costa Rica, and, for a time, Colombia expressed immediate interest in the possibility of joining NAFTA. The question is whether this kind of institutionalized alignment with the United States offers the most constructive alternative for Latin America.

One concern focuses on potential trade diversion. This risk is substantial for countries with major commercial partners outside the hemisphere. Chile has thus insisted that any FTA involving the United States should have no adverse effects on its trade relations with Europe and Japan. The lower the unilateral barriers to imports, of course, the more plausible this approach; and the greater the prior concentration of trade with the United States, the less the room for trade diversion. For a country like Brazil, however, with extensive European connections and substantial import barriers, the prospects of diversion are genuinely worrisome. Partly for this reason, policymakers in Brasília have displayed considerable reticence toward the idea of special trade agreements with the United States.

A second issue deals with NAFTA itself. This is a highly specialized treaty, adorned with special provisions and festooned with supplementary agreements on environmental and labor issues. While it meets the particular concerns of its three members, it offers a cumbersome instrument for other countries. What Chile and Costa Rica and Argentina really wanted in the early 1990s were bilateral FTAs with the United States, straightforward and simple accords that would certify the signatories as secure and desirable sites for foreign investment and guarantee access to the U.S. market. NAFTA, with complex provisions ranging from rules of origin to environmental protection, was both more and less than they wanted.

Third is uncertainty about accession. NAFTA does not establish criteria for admission. In a deliberately uninformative clause, the treaty simply holds that new countries may join NAFTA "subject to such terms and conditions as may be agreed" by the member countries and "following approval in accordance with the applicable approval procedures in each country." This vague language means that member countries retain the right to establish arbitrary or impossible accession criteria if they so choose. It is similarly unclear whether NAFTA member states truly support expansion. Canada resisted negotiations with Mexico in the first place, and seems unlikely to welcome more Latin American countries. The United States might regard expansion of NAFTA as a means of consolidating economic and political influence—and of gaining access to new markets—but would have to balance these advantages against potentially negative impacts on relations with Europe and Japan. Mexico presumably wants to be the only NAFTA-approved site in Latin America for foreign investment, and would therefore oppose new accessions (admission of new members from the region would also dilute Mexico's political status as a unique interlocutor between Latin America and the United States). Decisions on accession would have to be unanimous at any rate, which means that each of the three member countries possesses the right of veto.

Finally, and perhaps most fundamentally, WHFTA lacks clear political motivation. For reasons explained above, NAFTA had the makings of a credible political bargain. WHFTA does not.[11] Geopolitical motivation could come about in response to major events, realignments, or developments in the international arena—which had not occurred as of the late 1990s.

Even so, NAFTA could lead to WHFTA in a variety of ways. One possibility is for countries of the Americas to enter NAFTA directly through accession: if NAFTA eventually was to include all countries of the hemisphere, it would automatically become a WHFTA. A second would be for the United States (or Mexico) to form a series of "hub-and-spoke" arrangements with Latin American countries that could ultimately lead to integration of the region by "filling in the rims." A third possibility would be for Latin American countries to accelerate their own processes of sub-regional integration (such as Mercosur, about which more below) so these groupings could then negotiate free-trade agreements with NAFTA. There is more than one route to a WHFTA.

### Hemispheric Summitry

Seeking to capitalize upon its hemispheric hegemony, the Clinton administration promoted and hosted a grandiose "Summit of the Americas" in the Latinized city of Miami in December 1994. Attended by thirty-four heads of state, with the conspicuous exception of Cuba's Fidel Castro, this was the first such gathering in nearly 30 years. The ostensible goal of the Miami summit was to develop a blueprint for collaboration into the twenty-first century. An implicit purpose, from Washington's perspective, was to provide assurances that the United States would neither neglect nor abandon Latin American countries outside of Mexico.

The meeting's principal achievement was to agree upon the creation of a Free Trade Area of the Americas (FTAA). Confidently predicting that FTAA "will stretch from Alaska to Argentina," Clinton boasted that the accord marked "a watershed in the history of the hemisphere." With a combination of amnesia and hyperbole, the U.S. president went on to proclaim that "the so-called lost decade of Latin America is a fading memory." With the exception of Cuba, he exulted, the region had "freed itself from dictatorship and debt, and embraced democracy and development."

What happened in fact is that the signatories in Miami designated the year 2005 as a deadline for the completion of negotiations for a free-trade area, with implementation to follow in subsequent years. This was an ambiguous result. Advocates hailed the agreement for its high-minded principles and ambitious goals. Skeptics lamented its vagueness and its drawn-out timetable, which meant that official talks could drag on for a decade or more.

Equally important, the Miami declaration shifted the most feasible route toward WHFTA. Instead of using NAFTA as the principal mechanism for expansion, the summit initiated a series of broad, hemispheric negotiations for creating FTAA (as a form of WHFTA). To complicate the picture, NAFTA members also invited Chile to commence negotiations on accession. As time has passed, however, hemisphere-wide discussions for FTAA appear to have supplanted the idea of accession of NAFTA. It further seems likely that the resulting accord will be relatively shallow—a lowest-common-denominator agreement or "FTA lite," one might guess, an FTA that will call for progressive reduction of tariffs without entailing the profound level of integration represented by NAFTA.

Even this prospect was cast into doubt in late 1997 by the refusal of the U.S. Congress to grant fast-track authorization to the Clinton administration. An alliance of organized labor, environmental groups, disgruntled Democrats, and intransigent Republicans effectively dismantled the administration's approach to the region. As one Peruvian columnist acidly noted:

> The repercussions of this legislative humiliation are potentially devastating. The immediate and practical effect will be that it will be impossible for U.S. officials to broach complex initiatives of major importance. In the absence of a continued U.S. drive, the Free Trade Area of the Americas (FTAA) has been condemned to what it has been so far: a bombastic rhetorical exercise rich in expressions of good will, but lacking concrete results. Chile's dream of joining NAFTA has likewise been cut short, and the same can be said about APEC trade opening talks.[12]

Without the fast track, most observers agree, there would be no FTAA or any other formal integration scheme involving the United States.[13]

A follow-up Summit of the Americas in Santiago de Chile in April 1998 exuded much uncertainty. Although President Clinton assured his fellow heads of state that "our commitment to the Free Trade Area of the Americas will be in the fast lane of our concerns," the U.S. delegates were unable to press these issues with force and credibility. Despite much public bonhomie, one Latin American finance minister confided that, "the reality is that we are growing frustrated and more and more skeptical that the United States is really committed to free trade."[14] To be sure, the Santiago summit resulted in a unanimous pledge to make "concrete progress" toward creation of an FTAA by the end of the century and to adopt an intensive schedule for negotiating sessions. Leaders of the hemisphere agreed to set up a multilateral process for evaluating progress against illicit drug trafficking, and to hold inter-American summits "periodically," with the next gathering to be hosted by Canada. Perhaps most important, they also adopted an ambitious plan (with anticipated loans of $6 billion from the World Bank and the Inter-American Development Bank) to provide universal access to elementary school education and high school education to 75 percent of the region's youth by the year 2010. Conspicuous, however, was Washington's low-key demeanor on the question of free trade. According to José Miguel Vivanco of Human Rights Watch, the educational plan represented "the silver lining to Clinton's failure to get fast track—a shift away from trade to human issues."[15]

## Option Three: Affirming Self-Reliance

A third alternative for Latin America entails regional (or subregional) economic integration. The region has a long history of efforts in this area. In the aftermath of debt crisis and the Cold War, Latin American leaders have sought new forms of regional integration.[16] The idea is not to foster growth through market protection, however, but integration with the global economy. As Sylvia Saborio described this integrationist revival:

> As part of the broader agenda of economic reforms, it is outward-oriented rather than inward-looking. It seeks rather than shuns foreign investment as a source of capital, technology, and distribution outlets. It relies primarily on market signals and competitive forces rather than on policy interventions to allocate resources. And, last but not least, it favors across-the-board, automatic measures over selective, piecemeal approaches to minimize backsliding and special interest pressure.[17]

A principal goal of this movement, as Monica Hirst has observed, is to "reduce [the possibility of] marginalization in the face of global economic processes."[18]

Given the diversity of interests and economic structures, Latin American leaders have focused not on continental unification but on subregional integration—projects for economic cooperation among groups of Latin American countries, rather than for the continent as a whole. During the 1990s this has led to three distinct strategies: (1) subregional integration as a path toward broader integration, (2) subregional integration as a means of consolidating markets and economies of scale, and (3) subregional schemes as a means of advancing geopolitical interests. As we shall see, these variations are not always mutually exclusive.

## Paths Toward Integration

As of the late 1990s, Latin America has created more than thirty collective or "minilateral" schemes for economic cooperation. Many are bilateral arrangements; some involve three or four countries. As such, they reflect legitimate fears of confronting the post–Cold War world all alone. There seems to be safety in numbers.

The Central American Common Market has been resuscitated, the Caribbean Community and Common Market (CARICOM) reinvigorated, and the Andean Pact reshaped and revitalized. The general goal of these schemes is to avoid exclusion from the global economy. The more specific goal is to utilize these schemes as means of gaining access to larger and more important groupings, particularly NAFTA or FTAA. Successful forms of subregional integration can assist this process in two ways: by demonstrating the capacity of member countries for submitting to the disciplines of international accords, and by consolidating markets and (perhaps) production processes. In tandem, it is thought, these features enhance the attractiveness of the group (and its members) in the eyes of larger nations and/or blocs.

This is particularly clear in the case of the Andean Group. On its own, the arrangement does not dramatically serve the economic interests of its members. But it strengthens the ability of members to negotiate with other subregional blocs and to contemplate possible prospects for the FTAA. As Miguel Rodríguez-Mendoza has written, such subregional groupings "are seen as 'paths' toward larger integration efforts at both the Latin American and hemispheric level."[19]

It is not always an easy process. There often exists a temptation for the more advanced or liberalized economies within a group to negotiate on their own, rather than together with other members of the group. One conspicuous case in point is Costa Rica. Its leaders have decided—for the moment— to negotiate with outside powers through the Central American Common Market, but critics argue that the country might well be able to advance its own interests more effectively by operating on its own. This is especially apparent with regard to NAFTA: Costa Rica might well gain admission by itself, while the isthmus as a whole has almost no chance at all.

*Mercosur*

A second form of subregional scheme involves the creation of markets for their own sake. The most conspicuous case of this model is the "Common Market of the South," known from its Spanish acronym as Mercosur. This effort began with a bilateral agreement between Argentina and Brazil, and soon included Uruguay and Paraguay. Under the Treaty of Asunción, reached in March 1991, the four member countries committed themselves to construct by December 1994 a customs union, with a common external tariff (CET), and to move toward a full-fledged common market in subsequent years. There have been some setbacks: the CET is not yet a reality, and both Argentina and Brazil have raised some tariffs in response to the Mexican "tequila effect" and the 1997 Asian crisis. In view of long-standing rivalries among its members, however, Mercosur has been a truly remarkable development. Its partner countries comprise nearly one-half of Latin America's GDP, more than 40 percent of its total population, and about one-third its foreign trade.[20]

Mercosur's internal trade has expanded at impressive rates, climbing from $4.1 billion in 1990 to $17.0 billion in 1996. During the same period, intra-Mercosur trade as a share of total exports increased from 11.1 percent in 1991 to 22.7 percent in 1996 (and a projected 24.7 percent by 1997).[21] By 1995 Mercosur had a combined GDP of $714 billion, making it the world's fourth largest integrated market, after NAFTA, the European Union, and Japan.

Beyond its economic agenda, Mercosur has clear political goals: the consolidation of democracy and the maintenance of peace throughout the Southern Cone. At the same time that Mercosur was taking shape, agreements were reached in the nuclear field between Argentina and Brazil, countries that shared significant nuclear capacity as well as historic rivalry. And, at a summit gathering in 1992, the presidents agreed to stipulate that "an indispensable assumption for the existence and development of Mercosur is that democratic institutions are in force."[22] In practical terms, Mercosur provides civilian democrats throughout the subregion with regular opportunities for consultation and mutual support, thus offsetting the long-established conclaves for chieftains of the armed forces.

From the start, Mercosur's designers have seen it as a dynamic institution, one that would evolve rapidly over time and also crystallize relations with economies of the North. Mercosur has become a powerful instrument for collective bargaining with the European Union and, potentially, with the United States. Contradictory tendencies also have emerged: Argentina for some time expressed eagerness to negotiate its own FTA with the United States (and/or seek membership within NAFTA), an act that would have led to the dismantling of Mercosur. Within all such sub-regional groupings, trade-offs between unilateral initiative and multilateral solidarity have presented individual countries with agonizing policy dilemmas.

## Hubs and Spokes

Inevitably, the plethora of integrationist agreements in the 1990s has led to "hub-and-spoke" formations. Under this system a central country, or hub, enjoys special preference in the market of each spoke country under a series of separate bilateral agreements. The spokes, however, do not have preferential access to each other's markets; even worse, they have to compete among themselves for preferences within the hub market. What is good for the hub is not always good for the spokes.

There were initial fears that the United States was intent on the formation of a hemispheric hub-and-spoke system with itself at the center. It was this concern, in fact, that prompted a reluctant Canadian government to join the U.S.-Mexican negotiations over what would eventually become NAFTA. Rather than become one of two competitive spokes in a North American market, it was preferable for Ottawa to take full part in the creation of a trilateral arrangement.

Efforts to avoid a U.S.-centric system have not, however, prevented Latin American countries from attempting to create their own hub-and-spoke arrangements. There are economic and, especially, political advantages in the hub position. By virtue of size and/or strategic location, only three nations have had realistic opportunities to pursue this strategy: Chile, Mexico, and Brazil.

Starting in the early 1990s, Chile supplanted its pattern of unilateral liberalization with a selective network of bilateral FTAs. In 1991, the Aylwin administration reached an agreement with Mexico for the purpose of establishing an FTA by January 1996. In 1993, the government forged compacts with Colombia for an operational FTA by 1994, and with Venezuela for the realization of free trade by 1999. Chile also concluded less ambitious agreements with Argentina, Bolivia, Costa Rica, Ecuador, and Uruguay. The goals of these negotiations were manifold: to open new markets, to ensure supplies of critical products (such as petroleum), and to establish Chile's position as a continental leader. As Patricio Meller has explained:

> Given the widespread proliferation of preferential trade agreements, the
> first best strategy for improving market exports for domestic exports is

to become a member of those agreements. It is usually said that the first best option for a small country is a multilateral free-trade world. However, a better option would be to enjoy preferential access, so that the small country can play the "hub and spokes game" in which Chile would be the center and its trading partners the spokes. By taking advantage of its good economic and political image, this is precisely what the recent Chilean trade strategy has intended.[23]

Moreover, membership in FTAs would provide Chile with a small measure of protection from the vagaries of an uncertain world.

This headlong pursuit of FTAs has led to problems. As Meller again has observed: "The Chilean government in the 1990s was willing to sign an FTA with all trading blocs; there existed the illusion that every trade agreement was keenly interested in incorporating Chile as a member. . . . Observers now say there was an overdose of wishful thinking about Chile's acceptance into FTAs, and the extreme optimism generated frustrations. . . ."[24] As in so many walks of life, moderation appears to be a virtue.

In contrast to Chile's approach, the Mexican strategy has been to establish itself as the central interlocutor between the United States and Latin America. This could be welcome to Washington, given its long and troubled history of relations with Latin America; it could also provide considerable leverage for Mexico, and compensate for Mexico's loss of independence in other areas of foreign policy. As a founding member of NAFTA, Mexico could exercise a veto over applications for admission. This alone represented a substantial source of hemispheric influence.

Mexico thus began pursuing a series of subregional negotiations: the bilateral pact with Chile (1991), a bilateral pact with Costa Rica (1991), pacts with other countries of Central America (1992),[25] and a trilateral arrangement with Venezuela and Colombia (1993) to create the Grupo de los Tres. The resulting pattern has created a good deal of confusion, but the political meaning is clear: so long as NAFTA expansion remains the preferred route toward WHFTA, any road to hemispheric integration (and the U.S. market) will have to go through Mexico. (By the same token, hemisphere-wide negotiations for FTAA tend to diminish the Mexican role.)[26]

Brazil has taken a still different tack, attempting to affirm its position as a subregional hegemon rather than as a conduit to the United States. Already the dominant country within Mercosur, Brazil officially launched in April 1994 its proposal for a South American Free Trade Area or SAFTA (Area de Libre Comercio Sudamericana, ALCSA). The goal of SAFTA is to create a free-trade zone for "substantially all trade" within the continent (in GATT-speak)—that is, on all products except those touching on "sensitive" national interests. This means about 80 percent of intraregional trade. SAFTA would accomplish this target largely through a linear, automatic, and progressive schedule of liberalization over the 10-year period from 1995 to 2005. It would remove nontariff as well as tariff barriers, though it would deal only with goods and not with labor or services.

Public intentions behind SAFTA are manifold: to capitalize on the experience of Mercosur, to reach out to neighboring countries (and groups), and to accumulate negotiating power for dealing with broader integration schemes in the Americas.

There is a political purpose as well. SAFTA would confirm Brazil's historic claim to be a continental hegemony, its long-standing sense of manifest destiny. By itself, without any formal link to North America or the United States, SAFTA would reflect and ratify regional domination by Brazil. Alternatively, during the course of any ensuing negotiations with the North, Brazil would become the principal intermediary between the continent and the United States. Either way, SAFTA would lead to the strengthening of Brazil's international position: Brazil would become the hub of South America.

SAFTA has had significant prospects for success. Apparently frustrated by the slowness of NAFTA negotiations, Chile became an "associate member" of Mercosur in mid-1996: this satisfied Brazilian aspirations for expansion as well as Chile's reluctance to take part in the CET. Bolivia followed suit shortly thereafter. As of late 1997/early 1998, Mercosur was holding active negotiations with the Andean Group (now Community). Piece by piece, SAFTA seemed to be falling into place.

This momentum came to a screeching halt in January 1999. Buffeted by international financial markets, Brazil had managed to negotiate a $41.5 billion package with the International Monetary Fund the previous November in order to sustain inflation, uphold exchange rates, and recapture the confidence of investors. Only two months later, newly reelected President Fernando Henrique Cardoso was forced to announce that the Brazilian *real* would float freely because the government could no longer afford to intervene in international currency markets (foreign reserves having dwindled from $75 billion to $30 billion in merely five months). The *real* promptly lost 40 percent of its value in relation to the dollar. This was a devastating turn of events, since exchange-rate stability had provided the key to an otherwise successful battle against inflation and to Cardoso's reelection. Behind this failure was the president's inability to maneuver IMF-required reforms past vested interests and thus reduce a budget deficit amounting to 8 percent of GDP. Support of the *real* became particularly implausible after Itamar Franco, a political rival and the governor of Minas Gerais, announced his refusal to continue payment on state debt due to the federal government. By the end of the month President Cardoso succeeded in getting some of his reforms thorugh a jittery Congress, but by that time much of the damage was done. With unemployment running at its highest level in fifteen years, Brazilians were holding Cardoso personally responsible for promising to defend the *real* and then failing to do so, and his approval rating dropped to merely 22 percent (compared with 56 percent two years before). Under these circumstances Brazil was forced to look inward, to put its economic house in order and to recover its sense of political purpose, rather than to concentrate on expanding its field of subregional influence. SAFTA would take a back seat for a while.

## Option Four: Seeking Extrahemispheric Partnerships

Early in the 1990s it appeared that Latin America would have no chance of striking major deals with extrahemispheric powers and thus offsetting the hegemonic position of the United States. Within the past few years, however, Latin American leaders have made remarkable efforts to develop economic (and political) ties to outside powers. In differing degrees, they have courted two possible allies: the European Union and the Asia-Pacific region, especially Japan.

### The European Campaign

Efforts to engage European powers in Latin America have a long historical tradition. In 1974, Europe made a modest reappearance in the Americas with the initiation of biennial meetings of parliamentarians. In 1984 Europe discreetly opposed the Reagan administration's policy in Central America through the San José dialogue. Since 1990 the European Community (now Union) has had steady interaction with the Rio Group.

There are significant economic ties as well.[27] The European Union takes in nearly 20 percent of Latin American exports. It is the region's second leading source of direct foreign investment (during the 1980s, in fact, Latin America received a larger share of net foreign direct investment from Europe than from the United States). Europe is also the largest source of overseas development assistance (ODA) for Latin America: in 1993 the combined total for the EU and member states accounted for 61.5 percent of total assistance to the region, far ahead of Japan and the United

States. By 1996 the European Union's aid commitment was nearly 50 percent greater than in 1991.

In view of these connections, some European analysts have expressed apprehension about U.S. designs on Latin America—as expressed in the Enterprise for the Americas Initiative, NAFTA, and FTAA proposal. One EU think tank has declaimed such developments as thinly disguised efforts to dress the Monroe Doctrine in new garb.[28] Off the record, EU officials are wont to denounce the prospect of "Anglo America." More recently, the Instituto de Relaciones Europeo-Latinoamericanas (IRELA) has affirmed that "Europe does not intend to assume a passive role in the face of western hemisphere trade integration. The EU has significant economic incentives to expand its presence in Latin America, which is a particularly dynamic market for European goods." And if the FTAA process were to continue, IRELA maintains, "EU-US economic rivalry in Latin America is likely to become increasingly explicit."[29]

On a rhetorical level, these economic ties are often reinforced by reference to common historic and cultural links. In the words of one EU document:

> Latin America's cultural identity is heavily imbued with the values that shaped Europe's character and history. Five centuries of uninterrupted relations between the two regions have caused European ideals to permeate to the core of Latin American societies, which have in turn exercised an irresistible pull on the old continent. Constitutions, legal principles and ideas of liberty and democracy found across Latin America are drawn from the body of philosophical and legal concepts that are Europe's heritage.[30]

This seems like a generous assessment, given complex legacies of conquest and imperialism, but it serves to make the point: Europe and Latin America have much in common, including rivalry with (or resentment of) the United States.

Within the European Union, Spain has taken the lead in promoting strong ties with Latin America. Since Spain joined the European Community in 1986, Spanish companies have poured billions of dollars into Latin America, purchasing telephone companies, banks, hotels, and airlines in such countries as Argentina, Chile, Peru, Venezuela, and Cuba. Spanish banks have invested at least $4 billion since 1992; Telefónica holds about $5 billion in assets in Latin America. About 60 percent of Spanish FDI now heads for Latin America. The government has organized state visits to key countries by King Juan Carlos I, intensified cultural exchanges, and, since 1991, sponsored an annual Ibero-American Summit. Televisión Española is carried on cable systems almost everywhere, and magazines like *Hola!* and *Interviú* are widely circulated. In Spanish circles, the overall policy is known as the creation of "an Ibero-American space."[31]

Spain's political clout in Latin America is greatly enhanced by its integration with Europe, of course, and expanding ties with Latin America can also bolster Spain's position within the European Union. "We will be much stronger in Europe as long as we grow in America, where we have a natural advantage," says Antonio de Oyarzábal, Spanish ambassador to the United States. The European Union's commissioner for Latin American affairs is currently a Spaniard, as are the secretary general of NATO and the chair of the European parliament. Largely at Spanish insistence, the European Union now has embassies in virtually every Latin American capital.[32]

Complications exist. Spain would like to maintain its position as the critical link between the European Union and Latin America—as the hub, in effect, between two large regional spokes. For their part, Latin American leaders would prefer to deal directly with the European Union as a whole.[33] They have little desire to leave their commercial links—and access to capital—in the hands of one of the European Union's junior members.

### Promoting Rapprochement

In October 1994 the European Council adopted a general policy proposal for a new partnership with Latin America. In December 1995 EU negotiators signed a framework agreement with Mercosur. Its immediate purpose is to promote close relations in political, economic, commercial, industrial, scientific, technological, institutional, and cultural fields. It seeks to strengthen democracy and respect for human rights and calls for regular political dialogue as well as economic cooperation. The eventual goal is "to pave the way for an Interregional Association in the medium term."[34]

The framework agreement has prompted extensive follow-up. In April 1997 foreign ministers of the European Union and Mercosur states met to review the December 1995 accord. An EU–Latin American summit took place in June 1999, a gala event amid fanfare that was designed, in Cardoso's words, to create "a diversity of centers of decision." But there was not much tangible achievement. While it had long been anticipated that the EU and Mercosur would use the occasion to announce plans for creation of an FTA, they were unable to agree on either a timetable or an agenda. There are practical obstacles—Europe's reluctance to open its market to agricultural goods from Latin America,[35] matched by Mercosur's reluctance to open service sectors and reduce barriers to automobiles and car parts. There are strategic issues as well. In particular, the lack of a deadline for concluding the negotiations raises serious questions about the relationship between EU-Mercosur discussions and the ongoing FTAA process. As Monica Hirst observed, "It is not at all clear where this will lead."[36]

EU negotiators have nonetheless started discussions with individual Latin American countries. In June 1996 the European Union reached a framework agreement with Chile, which was just about to become an associate member of Mercosur. Around that same time the European Union began talks with Mexico, which had managed to emerge from the 1994–1995 peso crisis as a plausible partner, partly because of its market, partly because of its access to the United States.[37] And from the Mexican standpoint, an EU accord offers a way to reduce dependency on the United States (apparently increasing under NAFTA). As Francisco Gil Villegas explained, the peso crisis intensified official interest in "the European option":

> Today the European Union provides the best alternative for Mexico to offset its excessive concentration of economic relations with the United States. When officials in the Foreign Ministry talk about a project of "diversification" for Mexican foreign policy, they are thinking fundamentally about Europe, and only then about Japan or Latin America.

At the same time, NAFTA provides Mexico with a valuable asset for negotiations:

> Mexico belongs to Latin America but is also part of North America, and is integrated into the grand regional pact that is NAFTA, something that is clearly different from any of Latin America's regional economic agreements. The special treatment that Mexico is receiving from the bosom of the EU is justified by the country's sui generis location. . . . To the suggestion that Mexico should align itself with other Latin American countries in order to negotiate jointly with the EU, the invariable reply should be that Mexico's own regional bloc is North America, not Mercosur or the Andean Pact. *Geopolitics is destiny,* and for once Mexico does not deserve to be pitied because of its proximity to the United States.[38]

In late 1997 Mexico and the European Union announced agreements for economic partnership, political cooperation, and cultural exchange, much along the lines of the Mercosur accords. Exulted Mexico's then–foreign minister José Angel Gurría: "With this agreement we initiate a new and ambitious relationship with the European Union. . . . Europe is today a high priority for our foreign policy." This offered the prospect for diversification of international ties and for an alliance, as well, with a "trustworthy partner" in confronting the United States. The allusion was quite clearly to the Helms-Burton law, which Mexico and the European Union both condemned. U.S. policy toward Cuba was thus encouraging Mexican ties with Europe.[39] But even as negotiations proceed, it is unclear where they will lead. The optimal result, in the Mexican view, would probably be a formal free-trade agreement.[40] For reasons explained below, the Europeans will probably settle for a good deal less.

### The Asia Card

In anticipation of the prospect of a "Pacific century," Latin American leaders have turned toward Asia as well. This was not only the world's most dynamic region through the early 1990s, with its development model it also appeared to hold the keys to economic success. The "Asia card" became a potential trump for Latin America.

One way to pursue this avenue is through bilateral ties—principally with Japan, thought to provide a useful counterweight to the United States, and to a lesser extent with China. Conspicuous here have been the efforts of Peru, which unleashed "Fujimori fever" throughout Japan with the 1990 election of a president of Japanese descent, and of Brazil, which hosts the world's largest Japanese émigré community. Mexico has also sought close links with Japan. President Ernesto Zedillo and Prime Minister Ryutaro Hashimoto exchanged state visits in 1996–1997, and in May 1997, after a hiatus of three and a half years (due to political and economic instability in Mexico), the two countries resumed bilateral private-sector talks.

The other mechanism for courting the Asia-Pacific has been APEC, the Asia-Pacific Economic Cooperation forum, which represents 40 percent of the world's population, 55 percent of its wealth, and 46 percent of all world trade. APEC is an unusual institution, preferring to work through consensus rather than traditional diplomatic agreements. Under pressure from the United States, to be sure, the organization has agreed to establish an FTA by the year 2020, but in general it evinces a loose form of association that relies on unilateral cooperation rather than political coercion.

In principle, APEC adheres to the high-minded (if oxymoronic) idea of "open regionalism"—a pattern of regional integration that would be outward oriented, not inward looking, designed to achieve integration with the world economy rather than protection from it. As construed in Latin America, open regionalism has implied two understandings: average external tariffs (and NTBs) by any member must not be elevated against non-FTA countries, and opportunities for accession by nonmembers should be clearly available. As practiced by APEC, however, open regionalism refers mainly to voluntary agreements by member countries to liberalize trade in concert according to a common timetable.

Three Latin American countries have gained accession to APEC. First was Mexico in 1993, largely under the shelter of NAFTA. Second was Chile, which had for some time aspired to establish connections with the Pacific Rim. During the 1980s, in fact, the Pinochet regime began to resuscitate nineteenth-century notions about the country's "manifest destiny" in the Pacific, while also searching for economic partners who would not condemn the regime for human rights abuse. And soon after its democratic transition, Chile launched a concerted diplomatic initiative toward APEC membership. Ebullient over the country's full and formal incorporation in November 1994, analysts predicted that this triumph would "open great opportunities for the continued expansion of Chile's international economic relations in the Asia-Pacific area." Accession to APEC thus crowned "the most advanced effort by any Latin American country" to forge meaningful links with the Pacific Rim.[41]

The most recent case is Peru, which, like Chile, mounted a persistent diplomatic campaign. At an early stage Malaysia, the largest importer of Peruvian tin, expressed support on the grounds that APEC "should not become an exclusive club restricted to certain countries only. Pacific countries are also entitled to become members, regardless of their economic status. For this reason, Malaysia supports and nominates Peru as a new member." And as the Malaysian foreign minister added, "Malaysia and Peru share the view that nontrade issues, such as labor relations, human rights, and the environment, must not become an obstacle to trade relations among countries grouped in the WTO. These nontrade issues can be discussed at other forums." Probably more crucial was the role of Japan—which was eager to express gratitude for Peru's support of Tokyo's bid to gain permanent membership in the UN Security Council (and, it is said, for Fujimori's decisive resolution of the Japanese hostage crisis of 1996–1997). So Peru received an invitation to join along with Vietnam and Russia in November 1997, just as APEC announced a 10-year moratorium on new memberships.

Although these APEC accessions represent genuine diplomatic triumphs, it is not entirely clear what benefits they bring. Precisely because APEC is such a loose organization, Latin Americans have not obtained

binding commitments from other members. Nor does it offer an unam-
biguous means of counteracting U.S. hegemony, since the United States is
APEC's most powerful member. Finally, the Asian crisis of 1997–1998
has reduced the practical and symbolic value of association with APEC.
Asia no longer looks like the answer to Latin America's development
problems; indeed, the crisis itself could have negative fallout for countries
of Latin America.[42]

### Prospects for Success? The Problem
### of Asymmetrical Significance

There is every reason for nations of Latin America, such as Mexico, Chile,
and Mercosur members, to seek close ties with extrahemispheric powers in
Europe and the Asia-Pacific. Since the mid-1990s Mexico has been stress-
ing the importance of "diversification" in economic and diplomatic relations.[43] Seeing itself as a "global trader," with commerce all over the world,
Brazil also aspires to consolidate links with Europe and the Asia-Pacific
region.[44] In particular, President Cardoso has recently insisted that Europe
is "central" to Brazil and, by implication, to the rest of South America.[45]

The question is whether Latin America's would-be partners share this
same conviction. How important is Latin America for Europe and Asia?

The sad truth is: not very. This condition of "asymmetrical significance" has serious consequences. It means that Latin America will give
high priority to extrahemispheric negotiations, but the European Union
and Japan will give them much less time, attention, and energy. Latin
America is likely to seek binding and long-term agreements; the European
Union and Japan will be inclined to settle for vague declarations of principle. Above all, the European Union and Japan will not want to undertake
any Latin American agreements that might jeopardize larger interests in
other parts of the world; in particular, they will not want to antagonize the
United States. Under such circumstances, the potential for miscommuni-
cation and disenchantment in discussions between Latin America and the
European Union or Japan becomes extremely high.

Trade indicators offer one insight into the extent of this asymmetry.
Table 2.1 shows the overall distribution of exports and imports as of 1996
for major trading partners—the United States, the European Union, and
Japan. The statistics tell a sobering story. First, all three countries trade
more with advanced industrial countries than with any developing area.
Second, only the developing countries of Asia have established significant
trade relations with major partners, principally Japan. Third, the United
States conducts 15 to 18 percent of its trade with Latin America, but more

**Table 2.1   World Trade Flows, 1996 (in percentages)**

|  | Exports | | | Imports | | |
|---|---|---|---|---|---|---|
|  | U.S. | EU | Japan | U.S. | EU | Japan |
| Industrial Countries[a] | 56.4 | 76.4 | 47.1 | 54.2 | 78.0 | 46.1 |
| Developing Countries: | 43.5 | 22.0 | 52.8 | 45.8 | 21.0 | 53.8 |
| Africa | 1.2 | 2.3 | 1.2 | 2.3 | 2.7 | 1.4 |
| Asia | 19.2 | 6.9 | 44.1 | 24.4 | 8.0 | 37.7 |
| Europe | 1.8 | 7.2 | 0.9 | 1.2 | 5.9 | 1.5 |
| Middle East | 3.7 | 3.0 | 2.6 | 2.4 | 2.2 | 10.1 |
| Latin America | 17.6 | 2.4 | 4.1 | 15.4 | 2.1 | 3.2 |
| Other | 1.0 | 0.1 | 0.1 | — | — | 0.1 |

*Source:* International Monetary Fund, *Direction of Trade Statistics Yearbook 1997* (Washington, D.C.: IMF, 1997).

*Note:* a. United States, Japan, Canada, Australia, New Zealand, Western Europe.

than half of that is with Mexico alone. The European Union carries on barely 2 percent of its total trade with Latin America—less than 5 percent as a proportion of external trade (discounting internal trade within the European Union).[46] Japan does only 3 to 4 percent of its trade with Latin America. The European Union and Asia might be important to Latin America, in other words, but Latin America is not very important to Asia or the European Union.

Two-way trade flows emphasize this point. In 1996 Brazil had $26.3 billion in trade with the European Union—which represented 25 percent of Brazil's total trade, but less than 1 percent of all EU trade (and less than 2 percent of the European Union's external trade). Mercosur shows a similar profile: 22.4 percent of its trade was with Europe, which represented only 2.4 percent of the European Union's external trade. Similarly, Chile conducted more than 10 percent of its trade with Japan, which amounted to less than 0.5 percent of all Japanese trade. Throughout the Americas, the United States continues to overshadow all extrahemispheric traders: it was somewhat less present in Mercosur than the European Union as a whole, but far more significant than any single country.[47]

Investment data confirm this general picture. Table 2.2 shows FDI flows to Latin America and the Caribbean during the 1990–1994 period. The cumulative figure for the United States ($6.7 billion) is nearly three times the combined figure for the European Union and Japan ($2.3 billion). Including investment in offshore money centers (such as the Cayman Islands), U.S. FDI ($9.6 billion) is still nearly twice as much as combined investment from the European Union and Japan. In virtually

**Table 2.2    FDI Flows to Latin America and the Caribbean, by Source, 1990–1994 (net flows, annual averages in millions $U.S.)**

| Country/Region | U.S. | EU | Japan |
|---|---|---|---|
| Mexico | 2,232 | 290 | 176 |
| Central America | 87 | 17 | 2 |
| Andean Group | 771 | 408 | 46 |
| Brazil | 2,243 | 567 | 132 |
| Mercosur | 2,918 | 962 | 154 |
| Latin America + Caribbean | 6,732 | 1,952 | 386 |
| Offshore Centers | 2,866 | 2,000 | 299 |
| Other | 19 | 498 | 3 |
| Total | 9,618 | 4,450 | 688 |

*Source: Foreign Direct Investment in Latin America in the 1990s* (Madrid: IRELA, 1996), Tables 23, 25, 26.

every country or subgroup in the region—Mexico, Central America, Andean Group, Brazil, and Mercosur—U.S. investment is dominant.

The same condition applies to accumulated stocks of FDI, as shown in Table 2.3. By the 1990s the United States held more investment than the European Union and Japan not only in Mexico, which might be expected, but also in Argentina and Chile, which comes as something of a surprise. It is only in Brazil where the accumulated stock of EU investment exceeds that of the United States, and that by a very small margin ($19.7 billion to $18.4 billion). Even then, the United States remained the largest single investor in Brazil, with 32.5 percent of the total; the runner-up was Germany, with only 11.2 percent of the stock.

**Table 2.3    FDI Stock in Selected Latin American Countries, 1990s, by Source**

| Country/Year | U.S. Amount[a] | % | EU Amount[a] | % | Japan Amount[a] | % |
|---|---|---|---|---|---|---|
| Mexico (1995) | 33,346 | 59.5 | 11,227 | 20.0 | 2,500 | 4.5 |
| Argentina (1992) | 6,063 | 39.5 | 5,190 | 33.8 | 227 | 1.5 |
| Chile (1995) | 6,122 | 41.5 | 2,801 | 19.0 | 463 | 3.1 |
| Brazil (1994) | 18,388 | 32.5 | 19,679 | 34.8 | 4,161 | 7.4 |

*Source: Foreign Direct Investment in Latin America in the 1990s* (Madrid: IRELA, 1996), Tables 40, 42, 43, 46.
*Note:* a. Millions $U.S.

**Table 2.4    Accumulated Stock of U.S., European, and Japanese Investment, by Destination (in percentages)**

|  | U.S. | | EU | | Japan | |
|---|---|---|---|---|---|---|
|  | 1980 | 1995 | 1987/88 | 1992/93 | 1980 | 1995 |
| United States | — | — | 57.6 | 44.3 | 23.8 | 40.5 |
| European Union | 44.8 | 50.3 | — | — | 12.1 | 18.5 |
| Japan | 2.9 | 5.4 | 0.0 | —[a] | — | — |
| Latin America | 15.2 | 15.6 | 6.4 | 11.7 | 14.8 | 11.9 |
| Asia (excluding Japan) | 3.8 | 12.1 | 2.8 | 10.9 | 27.3 | 17.6 |
| Other | 33.3 | 16.6 | 32.3 | 33.1 | 22.0 | 11.5 |

*Source:* Adapted from Table 7 in Keiichi Tsunekawa, "Assessing NAFTA's Effects for Mexico: A Japanese View," paper presented at symposium on "Japón y México hacia el nuevo siglo: situación actual y perspectivas del NAFTA," Tokyo, March 1998; and *Foreign Direct Investment in Latin America in the 1990s* (Madrid: IRELA, 1996), p. 91.
    *Note:* a. Negative value.

Finally, Latin American holdings represent modest proportions of total FDI for the investor countries. As revealed in Table 2.4, the major economic centers tend to circulate funds among themselves: to put it more precisely, the United States and Europe invest in each other, while Japan invests in both (but twice as much in the United States as in Europe). Latin America's share of accumulated Japanese FDI declined from 17 percent in 1980 to 12.6 percent in 1995, as Japanese investors became increasingly attracted to Europe and the United States.[48] Latin America increased its share of European FDI from 6.4 percent in 1987–1988 to 11.7 percent in 1992–1993, nearly a doubling of the proportion—but still not to very high levels, barely more than the percentage of European investments in Asia. Meanwhile Latin America held its ground as a site for U.S. investment, with 18 percent of the U.S. total as of 1980 and 17.8 percent in 1995. The region has thus been retaining its position relative to the United States, losing its (already modest) importance to Japan, and advancing as an investment site for Europe, but within strict limits. Despite its efforts and its aspirations, Latin America is not a major economic partner for Japan or the European Union.

    The problem of asymmetrical significance is thus pervasive and profound. The outside world might well be important to Latin America, but Latin America is not so important to the outside world (i.e., to the European Union, Japan, or China as of this moment). The *Economist* pithily observed about European Union–Mercosur relations: "The trouble is that Europe is not, in fact, central to Latin Americans, and still less so—far less so—are they to it. Uncle Sam has not for years been the only, all-powerful outside figure that counted to them, as myth had it. But he is still number one."[49]

The prognostication therefore has to be that Latin America will not get very far in its attempts to cultivate close and meaningful ties to extra-hemispheric powers. The effort makes consummate sense from the stand-point of Latin America, but Europe and Asia are not likely to respond in kind. There will be a good deal of talk, invocations of cultural heritage, and symbolic gesticulation. Unfortunately, however, the conditions for serious commitment do not appear to exist.

## Conclusion

It might appear that optimistic predictions about the post–Cold War environment have come true: Latin America has a broad menu of strategic options, and regional leaders can select from a variety of means to connect their countries with the global economy. Choices include unilateral liberalization for an open, plurilateral trade policy; formal alignment with the United States; subregional integration, a general approach with various subtypes; and partnerships with major powers outside the hemisphere. There is much that Latin America can do about its position in the world, one might conclude, and much is being done.

To emphasize the point, Table 2.5 sets out these different strategies, their application by specific countries, and (on a highly impressionistic basis) their apparent results as of mid-1998. The table shows, for instance, that Chile has employed a number of approaches, moving from unilateral liberalization in the 1970s and 1980s to the pursuit of accession to NAFTA, associate membership in Mercosur, formation of subregional hub-and-spoke arrangements, and full membership in APEC (plus negotiations with the European Union). Mexico has opted for alignment with the United States, through NAFTA, and has since attempted to diversify its economic and political relations through membership in APEC and discussions with the European Union. Brazil has focused its initial attention on the consolidation of Mercosur, now supplemented by the drive toward SAFTA (with Brazil as the hub) and negotiations with the European Union. Argentina and Colombia both entertained thoughts of accession to NAFTA until 1994 or so, then moved in differing directions: Argentina turned toward Mercosur and the European Union–Mercosur negotiations, while Colombia helped rejuvenate the Andean Community as a means for

**Table 2.5    Strategic Options and Preliminary Outcomes: Countries and Regions of Latin America**

|  | Unilateral Liberalization | Joining the North | Self-Reliance | | | External Partnership |
|---|---|---|---|---|---|---|
|  |  |  | Pathway | Market | Hub |  |
| Chile | s | a | — | s | a | m |
| Mexico | — | s | — | — | a | m |
| Brazil | — | — | — | s | m/s | a |
| Argentina | — | a | — | s | — | a |
| Paraguay/Uruguay | — | — | — | s | — | a |
| Colombia | m | a | m | — | — | — |
| Peru | a | — | m | — | — | m |
| Venezuela | — | — | m | — | — | — |
| Caribbean | — | a | a | — | — | — |
| Central America | — | — | a | — | — | — |
| Costa Rica | m | a | a | — | m | m |

*Notes:* s = relatively successful; m = moderate chance or degree of success; a = attempted with little chance or degree of success; — = not available, not attempted.

collective bargaining with other blocs. During the 1990s Colombia and Peru also made strides toward unilateral liberalization. Peru has in the meantime merged its reentry into the Andean group with trans-Pacific aspirations, as revealed by President Fujimori's special attachment to Japan and the successful campaign to join APEC. Venezuela has only one broad strategy, subregional integration as a means of gaining access to larger groups, although petroleum provides it with a potentially effective resource for negotiation on its own. Caribbean countries have clamored for special treatment under NAFTA and bolstered their collective capacity through both CARICOM and the Association of Caribbean States. Similarly, Central America has attempted to strengthen its hand through subregional integration, while Costa Rica—always a special case—has made progress on its own through unilateral liberalization and for a time had hopes of entering NAFTA.

So the menu looks fairly rich. Yet there are fundamental problems. One is that opportunities are not evenly distributed across Latin America. In theory, any country of the region (or the world) can apply any or all of these strategies. In practice, the range of feasible choice is restricted by key structural factors—geographic location, natural resources, demographic size, and level of development. The ability to capitalize on opportunities is further determined by political will. Only Chile and, to a lesser extent, Colombia, Peru, and Costa Rica have had the economic and political resources to make effective use of unilateral liberalization as the foundation for a long-term strategy. (Other countries have opened their economies, but mainly as a prelude to or part of some other option.)[50] Only Mexico, with the advantages of its size and location, has managed to join with the United States through NAFTA. Only Mercosur has established itself as an autonomous and more or less viable bloc; and only Brazil, with its size and strength, can entertain hopes of becoming a subregional hegemon. Only Mercosur, Chile, and Mexico have attracted enough interest from the European Union to initiate trade negotiations. Only Chile, Mexico, and Peru—with their special links to Asia—have gained membership in APEC. Options are not available in the same degree to everyone. While a few countries in the region have managed to pursue a variety of strategies, most have a slim range of choice.

As an extreme case in point, Cuba faces an extremely bleak horizon. The ideological thrust of the 1959 revolution has lost appeal in the Americas. The collapse of the Soviet Union has eliminated Cuba's principal source of international support and financial subsidies. Perpetuation of the U.S. embargo, recently intensified by Helms-Burton legislation, only tightens the economic stranglehold. Faced by these pressures, Fidel Castro has pursued two main options: cultivation of extrahemispheric support, especially from Europe, through expanding trade and investment opportunities; and subregional integration, most notably through the Association of Caribbean States (which is a political organization, not an economic integration scheme). Both strategies have helped to shore up the Castro regime, but neither can promise long-term solutions to the island's economic plight.[51]

## Missing: Option 5?

One additional option is most conspicuous by absence: concerted participation at the global level. Clearly, Latin American nations would benefit from a strong international regime for trade and finance. This would foster worldwide liberalization, guarantee access to markets and capital, and level the economic playing field: strong and weak countries would have to abide by uniform rules. To enhance such prospects, the most effective strategy for Latin America would be to vote as a uniform bloc in key international organizations (as it formerly did in the United Nations). This would require coordination, consultation, and commitment. It would hearken back to traditional notions of continental solidarity and, of course, the much invoked myth of the "Bolivarian dream."

Yet this strategy appears to have little support. It encounters classic problems of collective action.[52] There are too many incentives for too many countries to pursue their own alternatives, and this impedes coordination. From one perspective, the current menu of policy options offers Latin American countries a tempting array of possibilities; from another perspective, it leads to fragmentation and dispersion of effort. Option 5 remains merely a hypothesis, a missing item in the region's strategic inventory.

### Outcomes and Outlooks

Despite the range of policies in place, the prospects for success do not seem very good. Andean nations are using subregional integration as a means of connecting with larger blocs, perhaps starting with Mercosur, but the outcome is not yet clear; Caribbean countries and Central America have not so far made much headway in their attempts to deal with NAFTA. Mercosur is plainly a success, for its members and presumably for its associates, and Brazil seems to be forging this into an effective hub-and-spoke arrangement for South America. But as for extrahemispheric partnerships, it remains to be seen what Chile and Mexico and Peru will actually gain from APEC membership. It also remains to be seen what will emerge from negotiations between Europe and Chile, Mexico, and Mercosur—and the outcome remains much in doubt. In other words, *Latin American leaders have made creative and extensive use of options that are available, but most of these options have limited chances for success.*

Adding to this picture is uncertainty. The current array of grand strategies for Latin America might well undergo far-reaching change. Latin American leaders and officials have thus far forged rational responses to prevailing conditions in the post–Cold War world. If and as those conditions change, the plausible range of policy options will change as a result. Consider some alternatives.

*Scenario 1: Global hegemony for the United States.* Unequivocal assertion of U.S. supremacy might be accompanied by stagnation in Europe (and Russia), depression in Asia, retrenchment of Japan, and instability in China. The international system would no longer resemble a layer cake: the United States would reign supreme in economic, military, and political affairs. In a unipolar environment, Latin America's quest for extrahemispheric partnerships would no longer make sense; the most reasonable option would be alignment with the United States. This would precipitate intense competition among individual nations seeking to curry Washington's favor, weaken movements toward subregional integration, and probably accelerate negotiations for the eventual creation of a hemispheric FTAA—on terms dictated largely by the United States.

*Scenario 2: Intensification of multipolarity.* The international system of the twenty-first century could come to contain a half-dozen major powers: as Henry Kissinger has predicted, "the United States, Europe, China, Japan, Russia, and probably India—as well as a multiplicity of medium-sized and smaller countries."[53] The United States would be important but not dominant. Under these circumstances, it would make sense for Latin American nations to expand the pursuit of extrahemispheric partnerships to major power centers beyond the European Union and Japan to Russia, China, and India. This would diversify the region's economic and diplomatic relationships and lessen dependence on the United States. From Washington's standpoint, in fact, intensified multipolarity might increase the importance of FTAA; but in the Latin American view it would reduce the significance of FTAA. This could lead to fundamental disagreement. It might also help equalize the bargaining positions of Latin America and the United States during the course of FTAA negotiation and implementation.

*Scenario 3: Clash of civilizations.* A variation on this theme, propounded by Samuel P. Huntington, foresees the consolidation of eight or nine "civilizations" (Western, Latin American, African, Islamic, Sinic, Hindu, Orthodox, Buddhist, Japanese). These broad cultural groupings would transcend nation-states and shape the outlooks, associations, and interests of key actors in the world. Conflicts between them would be frequent (sometimes violent), compromise scarce, and tension permanent. Current realities would be likely to create antagonism between "the West and the rest," as rising cultures of the world seek to acquire and assert commensurate shares of power. Such predictions have engendered enormous controversy and debate.[54] If true, however, they offer clear guidelines for Latin America: to associate itself with the West, meaning Europe and the United States; to surrender aspirations in the Asia-Pacific region; and to accept a role as junior partner in a global contest of civilizations.

*Scenario 4: Formation of rival blocs.* This idea envisions a small number of powerful economic and political blocs headed by a major power. A common version portrays three regional units: a "European" bloc, dominated by Germany and the European Union, with a sphere of influence stretching through Eastern Europe to parts of the Middle East and much of Africa; an "Asian" bloc, led by China or Japan (or both), extending throughout the

Asia-Pacific to the borders of South Asia; and an "American" bloc under the United States, embracing the entire Western Hemisphere. Under these conditions, attempts by Latin America to seek extrahemispheric alliances would be not only useless, but also costly and counterproductive. Such circumstances might further tempt Brazil to continue its quest for subregional hegemony, which would enable it to assume a position of hemispheric coleadership with the United States.

*Scenario 5: North-South separation.* In this perspective there might develop a "North-North" axis of economic and political cooperation encircling the upper half of the globe—from the United States to the European Union through Eastern (or Central) Europe to Russia and Japan. Capital and commerce would flow freely around this circuit and promote accelerated growth. With a few exceptions, however, the South would be left out. Economic benefits would become increasingly concentrated in the North, resulting in a stark separation between haves and have-nots.[55] As Charles William Maynes once observed, "The key division in world politics is likely to become the North-South divide. The reasons are the relationship between poverty and people and the clash between economics and demographics."[56] Under these circumstances, there would be two dominant options for Latin America: first, to find some way to connect with the North, as Mexico has done through NAFTA; or second, to develop autonomous markets of sufficient size for self-sustaining growth, as Mercosur and/or SAFTA may be about to achieve. These latter efforts might also prompt renewed efforts to forge the kind of "South-South" alliance associated with calls for a new international economic order in the 1970s. Because of its contradictory incentives, a North-South separation around the globe would be liable to create divisions within the region we think of as Latin America.

*Scenario 6: Continuing globalization.* A final scenario, perhaps the most optimistic, envisions progressive and multilateral movement toward a global regime that could establish and uphold widely accepted rules of the game. This benevolent scene is most likely to occur, if at all, in the economic realm—perhaps under the aegis of the WTO, which is preparing to initiate a major new round of trade negotiations within the next few years. Under these circumstances, the most effective tactic for Latin America would be the now missing Option 5. Globalization could thus promote continental solidarity.

Short-term events could also push in this direction. For the future of FTAA, much will depend on the Clinton administration's ability to secure fast-track authority from the U.S. Congress. It seems likely that any such approval will be considerably more binding with regard to labor protection and environmental provisions than the administration's original proposal. It is also widely rumored that the White House might be willing to accept, and perhaps even to seek, a "limited" or "partial" fast-track authority—one that would permit fast-track negotiations with the WTO, but not with Latin America for purposes of FTAA. This would bring a halt to forward progress on FTAA negotiations and greatly complicate the conduct of U.S.–Latin American relations. It might also stimulate continental interest in Option 5. Collapse of a regional initiative might thus provide the impetus for a global solution. This world is not without its ironies.

## Notes

I wish to thank Consuelo Cruz, Jaime Granados, Gilmar Masiero, Shoji Nishijima, and Wilson Peres for constructive comments and suggestions on a previous draft of this chapter, and Carlos Cervantes and Erik Lee for valuable research assistance.

There was a play on words in the quote that opens this chapter, since the phrase *hacer América* ("Make America") means to get rich—usually through a windfall.

1. See Paul Kennedy, "The Future of the Nation-State," in *Preparing for the Twenty-First Century* (New York: Random House, 1993).

2. Joseph S. Nye, Jr., "What New World Order?" *Foreign Affairs* 71, 2 (Spring 1992): 88. See also Samuel P. Huntington, "The Lonely Superpower," *Foreign Affairs* 78, 2 (March/April 1999): 83–96.

3. Such calculations can be significantly affected by short-term changes in data, fluctuations in exchange rates, and alterations in measurement procedures. As of 1995, U.S. GDP was 28 times that of Mexico, 25 times that of Argentina, and 10 times that of Brazil. U.S. GDP per capita was only 3.4 times that of Argentina.

4. Jorge Castañeda, "Latin America and the End of the Cold War," *World Policy Journal* 3 (Summer 1990): 477.

5. On traditional alternatives, see Peter H. Smith, *Talons of the Eagle: Dynamics of U.S.–Latin American Relations,* 2nd revised edition (New York: Oxford University Press, 2000), chs. 4, 8, and 12, esp. pp. 298–303.

6. As confirmed by the central concern of Guido di Tella et al., *América Latina: de la marginalidad a la inserción internacional* (Fundación CIPIE: Santiago de Chile, 1998).

7. Andrea Butelmann and Alicia Frohmann, "U.S.-Chile Free Trade," in Silvia Saborio, ed., *The Premise and the Promise: Free Trade in the Americas* (New Brunswick, N.J.: Transaction, 1992), 180.

8. Bilateral and multilateral negotiations provide policymakers with the opportunity to emphasize quid pro quo concessions, which can make them palat-

able to the public; this is not the case with unilateral liberalization, however, which explains the need for strong political consensus.

9. As Argentina has shown, it is also possible to align oneself with the United States on geopolitical grounds (by steadfastly seeking *relaciones carnales* with Washington, as the foreign minister once quipped). A decade of faithful support for U.S. leadership on foreign policy culminated in President Clinton's bewildering coronation of Argentina as a "major non-NATO ally" in late 1997. It is impossible to fathom what this really means.

10. Nora Lustig, "The Future of Trade Policy in Latin America," unpublished paper (The Brookings Institution, March 1994).

11. See Joe Foweraker, "From NAFTA to WHFTA? Prospects for Hemispheric Free Trade," in Shoji Nishijima and Peter H. Smith, eds., *Cooperation or Rivalry? Regional Integration in the Americas and the Pacific Rim* (Boulder, Colo.: Westview Press, 1996), ch. 9.

12. *Expreso* (Lima), 16 November 1997.

13. In something of an anticlimax, the House of Representatives formally rejected fast-track legislation in September 1998 by a vote of 243 to 180 (with only 29 Democrats in favor, 171 against, and 3 abstaining).

14. Calvin Sims, "Latin America Fears Stagnation in Trade Talks with U.S.," *New York Times*, 19 April 1998.

15. Calvin Sims, "Leaders Advance Free Trade Zone of the Americas," *New York Times*, 20 April 1998.

16. See Sistema Económico Latinoamericano (SELA), *La nueva etapa de la integración regional* (Mexico City: Fondo de Cultura Económica, 1992); Luis Rebolledo Soberón, ed., *Esfuerzos de integración en América Latina* (Lima: Universidad de Lima, 1993); Raúl Grien, *La integración económica como alternativa inédita para América Latina* (Mexico City: Fondo de Cultura Económica, 1994); María Laura San Martino de Dromi, ed., *Integración iberoamericana* (Buenos Aires: Fundación Centro de Estudios Políticos y Administrativos, 1996); and Arturo Borja, Guadalupe González, and Brian J. R. Stevenson, eds., *Regionalismo y poder en América: los límites del neorrealismo* (Mexico City: CIDE, 1996).

17. Saborio, "Overview: The Long and Winding Road from Anchorage to Patagonia," in *The Premise and the Promise*, 16–17.

18. Monica Hirst, "El Mercosur: evolución económica y dinámica política," paper presented at the symposium "Japón y México hacia el nuevo siglo: situación actual y perspectivas del NAFTA," Tokyo, March 1998, 2.

19. Miguel Rodríguez-Mendoza, "The Andean Group's Integration Strategy," in Ana Julia Jatar and Sidney Weintraub, eds., *Integrating the Hemisphere: Perspectives from Latin America and the Caribbean* (Washington, D.C.: Inter-American Dialogue, 1997), 10.

20. See Mario Rapoport and Andrés Musacchio, eds., *La Comunidad Europea y el Mercosur: una evaluación comparada* (Buenos Aires: FIHES, 1993); Eve Rimoldi de Ladmann, ed., *Mercosur y Comunidad Europea* (Buenos Aires: Ediciones Ciudad Argentina, 1995); and Miguel Angel Ciuro Caldani, ed., *Del Mercosur: aduana, jurisdicción, informática, relaciones intercomunitarias* (Buenos Aires: Fundación Centro de Estudios Políticos y Administrativos, 1996).

21. See Hirst, "El Mercosur."

22. As quoted in Félix Peña, "Strategies for Macroeconomic Coordination: Reflections on the Case of Mercosur," in Peter H. Smith, ed., *The Challenge of Integration: Europe and the Americas* (Miami: North-South Center/Transaction, 1993), 195.

23. Patricio Meller, "An Overview of Chilean Trade Strategy," in Jatar and Weintraub, eds., *Integrating the Hemisphere*, 145–146.

24. Ibid., p. 150. As another observer has noted, these bilateral trade agreements with Chile are sometimes seen as "the FTAs that don't matter," since Chilean exports do not compete with locally produced goods in Mexico, Chile, or Venezuela.

25. Mexico concluded a bilateral pact with Nicaragua in late 1997, and negotiations with the "northern triangle" of Central America (Guatemala, El Salvador, and Honduras) are still in progress as of this writing.

26. In fact, all three members of NAFTA—even the United States—stand to have less bargaining power in FTAA negotiations than they would have on NAFTA accessions.

27. See speech by Sir Leon Brittan, vice-president of the European Commission, in Santiago, 1 April 1997: "Europe and Latin America: Partners in a Global Economy."

28. IRELA, "America for the Americans? The Enterprise for the Americas Initiative and European–Latin American Relations," Dossier 31 (Madrid: IRELA, 1991).

29. "Constructing the Free Trade Area of the Americas: An IRELA Briefing" (19 June 1997), 8.

30. EU Commission Communication to the Council and the European Parliament, "The European Union and Latin America: The Present Situation and Prospects for Closer Partnership" (1995), 3.

31. Lest we succumb to exaggeration, however, see "Los españoles prefieren Europa y se olvidan de América Latina," *El País* (Madrid), 8 November 1997.

32. Larry Rohter, "Forget the Maine. Spain Is Back," *New York Times*, 15 February 1998.

33. "Spain and Latin America: A Loving New Embrace?" *Economist*, 15 November 1997.

34. There has been a great deal of speculation about Mercosur's potential place in the world and its relations with Europe. See Ricardo A. Pena and Jorge A. Binaghi, *MERCOSUR: estrategias, oportunidades de negocios y armonización de políticas en un contexto de pensamiento globalizador* (Buenos Aires: Ediciones Héctor A. Macchi, 1994); CELARE, *Relaciones América Latina-Unión Europea: nuevas perspectivas* (Santiago: Centro Latinoamericano para las Relaciones con Europa, 1995); Carlos Francisco Molina del Pozo, ed., *Integración eurolatinomericana* (Buenos Aires: Fundación Centro de Estudios Políticos y Administrativos, 1996); Lincoln Bizzozero and Marcel Vaillant, eds., *La inserción internacional del MERCOSUR: ¿mirando al Sur o mirando al Norte?* (Montevideo: Universidad de la República, 1996); Elena de Luis Romero and Luis Felipe Agramunt, *MERCOSUR: aproximaciones hacia la integración con la Unión Europea* (Santa Fe, Argentina: Universidad Nacional del Litoral, 1996); and Ofelia Stahringer de Caramuti, ed., *El MERCOSUR en el nuevo orden mundial* (Buenos Aires: Fundación Centro de Estudios Políticos y Administrativos, 1996).

35. Hirst comment in Tokyo, March 1998.

36. *Economist*, 6 December 1997, 34–36.

37. See Esperanza Durán, "Mexico's Relations with the European Community," IRELA Working Paper 33 (Madrid: IRELA, 1992).

38. "México y la Unión Europea," *El Economista*, 28 August 1996. The phrase "Geopolitics is destiny" was italicized and in English in the original.

39. *Economía*, 9 December 1997. See also Joaquín Roy, "The Helms-Burton Law: Development, Consequences, and Legacy for Inter-American and European-US Relations," *Journal of Interamerican Studies and World Affairs* 39, 3 (Fall 1997): 77–107.

40. See James F. Smith, "Free-Trade Treaty Sought by Mexico, EU," *Los Angeles Times*, 9 December 1997.

41. See Manfred Wilhelmy and Rosa María Lazo, "La política multilateral de Chile en Asia Pacífico," *Estudios Internacionales* 30, 117 (January-March 1997): 3–35, esp. 4, 35.

42. See Alfredo Barnechea, "¿El fin de la tentación oriental?" *El Comercio* (Lima), 16 December 1997.

43. Ana Covarrubias Velasco, "México: crisis y política exterior," *Foro Internacional* 36, no. 3 (July-September 1996): 477–497, esp. 477. See also Víctor L. Urquidi, ed., *México en la globalización: condiciones y requisitos de un desarrollo sustentable y equitativo* (Mexico City: Fondo de Cultura Económica, 1996).

44. Pedro da Motta Veiga, "Brazil's Strategy for Trade Liberalization and Economic Integration in the Western Hemisphere," in Jatar and Weintraub, eds., *Integrating the Hemisphere*.

45. "Slowly, Slowly," *Economist*, 6 December 1977, 34.

46. In fact, the European role in Latin America has been declining: the European Union took only 17 percent of Latin America's exports in 1996, down from 21 percent in 1990, while the U.S. share increased from 38 percent to 42 percent; ibid., 36.

47. Calculated from data in International Monetary Fund, *Direction of Trade Statistics Yearbook 1997* (Washington, D.C.: IMF, 1997).

48. It might be noted, as well, that Mexico has never been seen by Japanese corporations as one of the ten most promising short-term (3-year) sites for investment; in a 10-year perspective, Mexico made the top ten (in tenth place) in 1996 but not in 1995 or 1997. Keiichi Tsunekawa, "Assessing NAFTA's Effects for Mexico: A Japanese View," paper presented at symposium on "Japón y México hacia el nuevo siglo: situación actual y perspectivas del NAFTA," Tokyo, March 1998, Table 10.

49. "Slowly, Slowly," *Economist*, 6 December 1997, 36.

50. One means of evaluating progress would be through international investment ratings. As of April 1998, not a single Latin American country received an "A" rating of any kind from Moody's Investment Service; Chile, Colombia, El Salvador, and Panama obtained "investment grade" scores (Baa); all others received lower scores. For a more comprehensive (and much more controversial) evaluation scheme see the "readiness indicators" proposed by Gary Clyde Hufbauer and Jeffrey J. Schott, *Western Hemisphere Economic Integration* (Washington, D.C.: Institute for International Economics, 1994), esp. chs. 5–6.

51. See Jorge I. Domínguez's excellent chapter in this book.

52. José Luis León, "Entre Belindia y Bolívar: problemas estructurales e integración en América Latina," in Alonso Aguilar M. et al., eds., *México y América Latina: Crisis-Globalización-Alternativas* (Mexico City: Nuestro Tiempo, 1996).

53. Henry A. Kissinger, *Diplomacy* (New York: Simon & Schuster, 1994), 23–24.

54. Samuel P. Huntington, "The Clash of Civilizations?" *Foreign Affairs* 72, 3 (Summer 1993): 22–49, and *The Clash of Civilizations and the Remaking of World Order* (New York: Simon & Schuster, 1996). For provocative commentary on this thesis see *Foreign Affairs* 72, 4 (September/October 1993): 2–26.

55. To some extent this is already happening, as suggested by trade flows in Table 2.1 and investment trends in Table 2.4.

56. Charles William Maynes, "America Without the Cold War," *Foreign Policy* 78 (Spring 1990): 3–25; with quote on pp. 22–23.

# 3

# Good-bye U.S.A.?

## *Heraldo Muñoz*

There has been a silent phenomenon between the United States and Latin America in recent years. The United States is no longer the dominant variable in the foreign relations of most Latin American countries. Hemispheric affairs no longer are led by the sole initiative of the United States, as occurred throughout the Cold War. In other words, Washington has stopped being the principal reference point in the foreign policy decisionmaking process and in the external actions of Latin American countries.

Latin American nations have been quietly cultivating political and economic partnerships with extraregional powers or blocs like the European Union (EU) or the Asia-Pacific Economic Cooperation forum (APEC). Most important, Latin Americans are looking inward, promoting economic and political ties through integration agreements at the bilateral, trilateral, or subregional levels, guided by a conception of "open regionalism" where market liberalization plays the central role.

Ironically, this phenomenon of Latin American distancing from the United States is occurring at a moment when the United States has become the only world superpower and when it has also become "the" single largest and most influential external force in the Latin American environment, be it in terms of society, education, culture, consumption patterns, lifestyle, or financial systems. A key distinction needs to be made to better understand the precise nature of such contradictory relationships. The weight of the United States in the region differs depending on whether it is viewed from a structural or a "relational power" perspective. In structural terms, it can be convincingly argued that there is no distancing between Latin America and the United States. In contrast, in relational power terms Latin American nations, particularly those of South America, rely less on the United States now than they did in the post–World War II period. While Washington is no longer the main agenda setter in the subregion.

Certainly economic ties between Latin America and the United States are still paramount. But, unlike the past, diminished U.S. political and diplomatic presence in the region cannot be compensated for through structural economic links, mainly because these ties nowadays have practically no state components (like foreign aid), but are essentially private in nature and hence less likely to be influenced by public-sector interests. This situation goes well beyond the "ending hegemonic presumption" argument that already in the mid-1970s foresaw the decline of U.S. influence in Latin America.[1] Moreover, the capacities of all nation-states have been diminished due to the process of globalization, forcing them to share power with supranational, transnational, and subnational entities.

A clear distinction must be made between Mexico, Central America, and the Caribbean, on one hand, and South America, on the other. It is in the latter case where the tendencies toward distancing from the United States are more evident. Nevertheless, most Latin American countries, especially those of South America, when adopting important domestic or foreign policy decisions no longer condition their formulation to a previous calculation of how the United States may react.

In short, the central argument of this chapter is that Latin America, at least in terms of foreign policy transactions, no longer views its present and future as being inextricably linked to the United States. Despite a sober realization that the United States is indeed the remaining superpower and a key external actor for Latin America, there is also the perception that it is not as vital as before, that neighbors in the region and other extraregional partners merit strong attention and energy, and that, in the end, Latin America and the United States can live with a degree of mutual indifference. This realization, in the last analysis, could open the way to a truly modern, mature, and realistic inter-American relationship.

## From Confrontation to Convergence

U.S.–Latin American relations historically have been characterized by confrontation and mistrust. For years, many Latin American governments actually defined their foreign policies primarily by expressing their outright opposition to Washington or, at best, by keeping a safe distance from the U.S. government.

Even when in some cases Latin American nations sought a "special relationship" with Washington, either the lack of interest on the part of the

White House, the U.S. propensity for intervention in the domestic affairs of countries of the region, or the simple denial of support for economic favors led those countries to feel disillusionment and resentment toward Washington.

Disputes between Washington and Latin America often stemmed from opposing views on crucial issues such as trade, foreign investment, and good governance. However, the end of the Cold War, along with the collapse of centrally planned economies of the former Soviet bloc, have changed all this. Today, there is what one high-level U.S. authority called "an unprecedented convergence of values and interests among Latin Nations and between them and the United States," centered on the validation of open markets and political democracy.

A sign of the times is that rhetorical confrontation with the United States has declined. Latin American countries no longer feel constrained by pressures to align with one of the superpowers in an East-West confrontation and are thus much less the target of actions by Washington that are unrelated to their national interests. Some unilateral policies, like the U.S. certification on drugs or the Helms-Burton legislation, face firm regional opposition; but Latin American countries feel more at ease when discussing with Washington issues that in the past were considered highly controversial, such as democracy promotion or combating corruption. Certainly, there is now more than ever before in the past half century a congruence between Washington and Latin America on what constitutes an agenda of shared interests and on how to address it. The great irony is that although the United States and Latin America now share common views on a number of key issues, actual relations have become more distant.

Like it or not, Washington is no longer an obsession or the sole external priority of Latin American governments. In fact, to use a well-known phrase in the history of inter-American affairs, some of them have adopted a kind of benign neglect vis-à-vis the United States.

Washington, on the other hand, is not actively interested in the region and, most important, no longer faces situations that in the Cold War context were routinely defined as major threats to national security. So, the United States still attributes theoretical importance to the area because of its economic potential and its significance for problems, like the narcotics trade that spills over into domestic U.S. politics, and some shared core values. The United States is also more comfortable with Latin America, even viewing, for example, the presence of socialist or left-of-center parties in government coalitions as acceptable, something that historically would have activated mechanisms of overt or covert intervention.

In other words, in a new world context the United States and Latin America have progressively grown apart. This has been a relaxed, silent process of separation rather than an abrupt, purposeful rupture. From the Latin American standpoint, this means that Washington today occupies a smaller space on the international relations radar screen of the region's countries, and that other external signals bid for the attention of Latin American nations.

## Emerging New Horizons

During the late 1960s to the mid-1980s some Latin American states attempted to break away from the U.S. sphere of influence by cultivating political and economic ties with other developed powers, and even with other developing nations. This strategy, known as "diversification of dependency," pointed toward the need to reduce reliance on the United States by expanding external contacts, particularly in the direction of Western Europe. The strategy failed. Although the political elites of Latin America visualized Europe as an understanding and autonomous potential partner that was becoming increasingly interested in the problems of the region, reality showed that European political interests in the region were limited to issues like the Central American peace process and South American redemocratization efforts, while economic ties actually stagnated.

At present, however, a more natural diversification of Latin American external ties has occurred that is slowly building a truly universal mosaic of trade, investment, cultural, and political relations between countries of the region and partners ranging from Europe to the Asia-Pacific Basin.

In March 1997, for example, French President Jacques Chirac visited the Mercosur countries and Bolivia, and while in Brazil proposed, after consultations with other European leaders, the celebration of a presidential summit between the European Union and Mercosur that would be followed by a broader meeting among the heads of state and government of both regions. Although viewed by some observers as a largely rhetorical initiative, the proposed meeting was well received in South America and emerged in the context of a growing competition between the European Union and the United States for the Latin American market. The first Presidential Summit between the heads of state and government of the European Union and Latin America and the Caribbean was held in Rio de Janeiro in mid-1999. Such high-level dialogue reflects the quality relationship that both sides are seeking.

However, real European–Latin American ties lag since, for instance, in proportional terms the Latin American share of European exports declined in the past decade. But more recently between 1990 and 1995, sales to Latin America increased 95 percent, a much higher percentage than the growth in overall European exports, which reached 24 percent. For Latin America, the European Union is currently a key external market rather than a "political alternative," as visualized in the 1970s. In fact, for most South American countries the European Union is the main extrarregional market.

Coincidentally, the European Union signed separate framework agreements on economic and political cooperation with Mercosur, Chile, and Mexico. These agreements are the stepping stones toward more substantial free-trade arrangements between these nations and the European Union. The perception of many Latin American countries is that, from a trade viewpoint, the European market may be more important than the U.S. market because countries of the region already enjoy significant access to the relatively open latter market, while the eventual negotiation of lower trade barriers with Europe—although seen as a difficult task because of agriculture—could signify greater advantages to Latin nations.

European trade with Latin America grew 81 percent between 1990 and 1996, much more than Europe's total trade. On the other hand, Europe is already the principal extraregional market for Brazil, Argentina, and seven other Latin American nations. In fact, many South American countries believe that they will get much better results from a free-trade agreement with the European Union than from a Free Trade Area of the Americas (FTAA) led by the United States. It is estimated that Argentina's GNP could grow 6.7 percent with an integration accord with the European Union and only 0.7 percent with the FTAA, while Brazil's would increase 5.05 percent with the European Union agreement and only 2.08 percent with the FTAA.[2]

The *Economist* stated recently that there is "an invasion of foreign banks and firms in Latin America" but, unlike in the past, this one "is being led by Europeans."[3] In fact, the European Union is presently the largest external investor in Mercosur countries. European investments in the region increased 300 percent in the last decade, reaching over $6 billion a year, half the amount of U.S. investments, but nevertheless an impressive sum if compared to past figures.

Moreover, both the European Union and Latin America share the political perception that it is important to balance the tendency toward a unipolar world after the Cold War. Apparently, the Europeans also wish to recuperate some of the cultural ground they have lost in Latin America.

Latin American governments, in turn, see the strengthening of the European presence in the region not as an alternative to that of the United States, but as a complementary, pragmatic relationship that could also serve as a bargaining chip in hemispheric free-trade negotiations, while the latter could play the same role in regard to the EU free-trade talks.

In recent years the Asia-Pacific region has also strongly emerged to bid for the attention of Latin America. APEC, the governmental organization created in 1989, is attracting growing interest from Latin American countries. Mexico and Chile are already full members. Chile was accepted as the first South American member of the group in November 1994 and has since then played an active role in this organization. Even though the United States and Canada are members of APEC, for Latin America the organization represents an opening to some of the most dynamic, fastest growing economies in the world, including the so-called Asian tigers, plus China, Korea, Australia, and Japan.

Latin American exports to Asia increased 93 percent in the 1980–1990 period, while Asian sales to the region jumped 447 percent in the same span. As an illustration, industrial trade between Southeast Asia and Colombia rose from 4 to 24 percent in 8 years, ranging from the late 1980s to the mid-1990s, while that of Chile went from almost 0 to 21 percent in the same period.

The case of Chile is symptomatic of the newly acquired presence of the Asia-Pacific Basin in the foreign relations of some Latin American nations. Aside from being part of APEC since 1990, Chile belongs to the Pacific Basin Economic Council, an association of business leaders from throughout the Pacific that promotes the expansion of trade and investment through open markets; and since March 1991 has been participating in the Pacific Economic Cooperation Council (PECC), an organization that brings together government authorities, business leaders, and researchers to address key trade and investment issues.

Formed in 1980 at the initiative of the prime ministers of Japan and Australia, PECC has been integrated by leaders of twenty-two Latin American countries, including Mexico, Chile, Peru, and Colombia, which for the first time gathered in Latin America, in Santiago, in October 1997, because Chile held the presidency of PECC from 1996 to 1997. Interestingly, the Santiago meeting of PECC opened a bridge between Latin America and the Asia-Pacific region, a situation underlined by the fact that the three keynote speakers at the meeting were the prime minister of Malaysia, Mohammad Mahatir, the president of Brazil, Fernando Henrique Cardoso, and the president of Chile, Eduardo Frei.

Chile's orientation toward the Pacific region is not merely geograph-ical, it is an economic reality. More than 31 percent of its exports ($5.6 bil-lion) go to Asia-Pacific countries. Although Japan and Korea are its main trade partners, Chile is intensifying its economic ties with such countries as Malaysia, New Zealand, and Australia. The presence of Malaysia in Chile is exemplified by the modern building constructed by the Malaysia South-South Corporation in Santiago to house its growing trade and investment initiatives. New Zealand, in turn, has invested over $1 billion, making Chile the third most important recipient of New Zealand foreign investment. Australia has over thirty enterprises operating in Chile, and between 1990 and 1995 Australian investments in South America (most-ly in Argentina and Chile) doubled to $1.5 billion. Last, there are Chilean direct investments (in joint ventures) in several Asian countries, including Malaysia and China.

Ties have also expanded between Asia-Pacific countries and Mercosur. Several meetings have taken place at the ministerial level between Australia and New Zealand with the Mercosur nations. One indicator of Australian interest in the South American bloc is that its exports to Latin America have climbed an average of 14 percent a year since 1990, double the increase of Australia's total world exports. Brazil has also expanded its presence in Asia. Brazilian trade with Asian partners has grown to almost 20 percent of total commercial flows, and President Cardoso was the first Brazilian head of state to visit Malaysia. Joint ventures between Brazilian firms and Chinese enterprises are another new development in this same direction.

Interestingly, the protocol of Chile's association with Mercosur includes a chapter on Atlantic-Pacific integration through bi-oceanic cor-ridors that aim at exploiting Chile's potential as a bridge between South America and the Asia-Pacific region. In the meantime, Chile, Brazil, and other Southern Cone countries have been working to make viable efficient multimodal connections between the Atlantic and Pacific Oceans. One study on the bi-oceanic route is being funded by a Japanese government agency through the Inter-American Development Bank.

Latin American countries have expanded their horizons in other direc-tions. Chile, Brazil, Mexico, Argentina, Peru, and Venezuela belong to the G-15, a select group of developing countries from Latin America, Asia, and Africa that has permitted a flexible nonideological forum for dialogue with the developed world on key economic and political issues.

The process of diversification of Latin America's extrarregional ties includes regular Ibero-American Summits of Heads of State and Government since 1991, when the first meeting convened in Guadalajara,

Mexico. Six summits have taken place since, the last one in Portugal, and meetings have already been scheduled up until 2001.

This mechanism of political dialogue and cooperation has reaffirmed the Ibero-American cultural personality and has afforded a flexible forum for discussions of common problems at the highest level. Interestingly, and as a reflection of the post–Cold War era, the Ibero-American Summits include Cuba but exclude the United States. Whatever the concrete outcomes of these meetings, they have become part of the new external reality of Latin America, underlining the fact that the external radar screen of the region is filling up with new actors and opening wider horizons.

## Changing Economic Dependence

Almost one-fifth of the world's product is exported nowadays. The international trade of goods and services reaches almost $10 trillion annually, and this international trade continues to grow at a faster pace than world production (5.9 percent as compared with 2.7 percent annually between 1990 and 1995). On the other hand, in 1996 the United States registered a trade deficit of about $160 billion, $50 billion of which represented its trade deficit with Japan.

In this context, the name of the game in the United States is to open foreign markets and gain trade surpluses: the health of the U.S. economy increasingly depends on foreign markets. Latin America, therefore, has become a valuable target for U.S. exports because the region, along with Asia, has become a minilocomotive for the world economy. Unlike three decades ago, however, the United States no longer thinks that developing countries should enjoy some protection or advantage, and thus a level playing field is being sought everywhere—even, if necessary, through the application of section 301 of the foreign trade law against countries that supposedly place obstacles in the way of U.S. exports.

But the United States today faces strong competition from other powers that also want to profit from the process of recovery and steady growth that Latin American economies have been experiencing in recent years. The United States still enjoys a clear advantage in the region, although this has been changing, especially as regards South American countries.

Exports from the Mercosur countries (Argentina, Brazil, Uruguay, and Paraguay) to the NAFTA market (United States, Canada, and Mexico) dropped, in percentages as a share of total exports, from 23.9 percent in 1990 to 16.9 percent in 1995. In the same period, intra-Mercosur trade jumped from 6.9 to 20.5 percent. The Andean Group countries' exports to NAFTA countries fell, in the same period, from 49 to 43.8 percent, and even the Central American Common Market nations saw their exports to NAFTA drop, from 45.6 to 38.3 percent between 1990 and 1995.[4] The few exceptions to this clear tendency are related to the weight of geographical contiguity: Mexico, for instance, in the same period increased its exports to the NAFTA from 71.3 to 85.9 percent.

The interesting phenomenon is that nowadays the United States depends to a large extent on Latin America to balance its foreign trade deficit.

In the period 1990–1996 alone, Brazil's share in total U.S. exports rose from 1.3 to 2.0 percent, while that of Argentina, Chile, and Venezuela grew from 1.5 to 2.1 percent.[5] In contrast, Brazilian exports to the United States as a share of total U.S. purchases dropped from 1.6 to 1.1 percent between 1990 and 1996, while the participation of Argentina, Chile, and Venezuela in total U.S. imports in that same period fell from 2.5 to 2.2 percent. In 1997, the United States exported to Mercosur countries the equivalent of what it sold to Russia and China together; but, in contrast, the United States imported from Mercosur nations five times less than what it bought from Russia and China.[6] Moreover, U.S. exports to Latin America grew from $34.5 billion in 1987 to $134.5 billion in 1997, and from 13 percent of all U.S. exports in 1987 to nearly 20 percent in 1997.

U.S. exports to the European Union and Asia grew 23 and 64 percent, respectively, between 1990 and 1996. However, U.S. exports to Latin America accelerated at a rate of more than 140 percent. To Brazil alone, U.S. exports soared from $5.06 billion in 1990 to $12.7 billion in 1996, a 150 percent increase. In 1997 the United States exported more to Brazil than to China; more to Argentina than to Russia; more to Chile than to India; and double the amount to Central America and the Caribbean than to Eastern Europe. It is estimated that soon the United States will export to Latin America double what it will export to Japan, thus generating 1 million jobs.[7] Moreover, according to a top U.S. official, in 2010 U.S. exports to Latin America will be greater than all those sent to Japan and the European Union.[8]

The realization that Latin America is a key market for U.S. exports has led Washington to attempt to secure and expand its position in the region. Negotiations to create an FTAA, born of a U.S. proposal in 1994, are the prime example of that effort. Interestingly, the United States has been the most enthusiastic nation behind this integration project, while Latin American countries have eyed it with caution, conscious that now they have greater bargaining power than when the United States dominated their external trade flows unchallenged.

This realization of the new importance of Latin America explains the White House's frustration over not obtaining from Congress the fast-track authority to engage with confidence in hemisphere free-trade negotiations. This same perception led to modification of U.S. arms policy toward the region—under pressure from U.S. manufacturers that have lost a large share of the regional market, mainly to European competitors—to rescind the general ban on high-technology weapons sales and approve such sales case by case. The risk the United States faces in the region today, according to U.S. Trade Representative Charlene Barshefsky, is that the United States "will leave a vacuum of leadership in the hemisphere," as Latin American countries emphasize their own political and economic integration and strive to achieve a wider diversification of their economic ties. More specifically, a high U.S. official has contended that the lack of "fast track authority cost U.S. enterprises more than US$500 million in exports to Chile that were lost to Canadian and Latin American exporters."[9]

To make things worse from the U.S. standpoint, Washington no longer possesses the instruments that made Latin American countries pay attention in the past. For example, total U.S. economic aid to Latin America and the Caribbean dropped from $1.8 billion in 1985 to $687 million in 1996. The U.S. government's capacity to make donations to other countries is now severely limited and increasingly threatened. After the 1997 budget-balancing agreement, Washington's total official development assistance fell from $9 billion to less than $8 billion, thus provoking, according to one source, "a reduction of the U.S. contribution to less than 15 percent of total world economic assistance, with the consequent decline of U.S. influence in multilateral institutions."[10] In any case, in Latin America U.S. aid is now irrelevant, and where it does exist, it concentrates on the small nations of the Caribbean and Central America. By contrast, the European Union has turned into the principal contributor of foreign aid to Latin America with $2.2 billion per year.[11]

Of course the significance of these data should not be overemphasized. Economic disparity between Latin America and the United States has probably increased over the past decades, and overall economic ties between the region and the U.S. market are still paramount. Our central point is that although the regional market has become increasingly interesting for the United States, and while the U.S. market is still vital for many Latin American countries, the region no longer sees its present and future as inevitably dependent on the United States.

## A Renewed Regionalism

Part of the reason why Latin America today pays less attention and is less oriented toward the United States than in recent decades is that the region is engaged in a dynamic process of integration and cooperation of unprecedented proportions.

The recovery from the sharp contraction experienced in the 1980s as a result of the debt crisis meant not only that in the 1990s Latin America became the fastest growing market in the world for U.S. goods and services. Intra–Latin American trade also boomed. Between 1990 and 1996 intraregional trade mounted at an annual rate of 16 percent, doubling the rate of expansion of total world trade. The dynamism of intra–Latin American trade in the 1990s is among the highest in the world, comparable only to intra-Asian trade.

In the 1990s, Latin America has seen unilateral trade liberalization initiatives, together with the revival of half-forgotten preferential trade agreements—such as the Andean Group and the Central American Common Market—and the implementation of new and bold integration processes. In essence, import substitution strategies have given way to outward-oriented trade regimes. At the same time, hemisphere-wide economic convergence has been deferred due to the intensification of Latin American regional, subregional, and bilateral ties. As an illustration of this, at the 1998 Santiago Summit of the Americas, President Clinton watched as a mere spectator as Latin American presidents took advantage of the occasion to sign various integration and crime-fighting agreements.

Without a doubt Mercosur, created formally in 1991, has been the prime example of the new successful regionalism in Latin America, seeking to constitute a common market with free circulation of goods, services, capital, and labor, and having already established a customs union in 1995. Trade within Mercosur is an indicator of its success, having jumped from $4.1 billion in 1990 to $20.3 billion in 1997. As a percentage of its members' global trade, Mercosur's volume rose from 14 percent in 1992 to 25 percent in 1997.

Beyond these exploding trade linkages, Mercosur is a strategic integration process that involves political, cultural, and security dimensions with their corresponding institutions. Moreover, Mercosur actually emerged in the late 1980s based on a historic rapprochement between Brazil and Argentina, two countries with a long history of tension and rivalry.

Mercosur has created such a strong convergence among member countries that it now commands all other foreign policy priorities, particularly between Argentina and Brazil. A recent poll revealed that the majority of Argentinians prefer Brazil as an economic and political partner over the United States. Furthermore, the poll showed that, for the first time in history, Argentinians prefer a foreign policy alliance with Brazil in the context of Mercosur more than with any other country.[12] Asked which nation should be their priority in foreign policy, 54 percent of the Argentinians polled chose Brazil, while only 13 percent indicated the United States.

Behind these changing perceptions are solid data demonstrating a strong economic integration between the two South American countries. In 1997 Brazil bought more than a third of total Argentine exports ($8.2 billion). In fact, Argentina exported more to the Brazilian state of São Paulo ($3 billion) than to the United States ($2 billion). On the other hand, Brazilian dependence on the Argentine market is less marked: in 1997 Brazil sent exports worth $6.7 billion to its southern neighbor, which represented 12.7 percent of its world exports. However, the "quality" of Brazilian exports to Argentina should be noted: most of the recent increase in Brazilian exports is in manufactured products. Between 1996 and 1997 manufactured products sent from Brazil to Argentina more than doubled, while exports of manufactures to the United States stagnated, those to the European Union fell by 2 percent, and those to Asia dropped by 19 percent.[13] Moreover, Brazilian sales to Mercosur countries as a whole surpass 20 percent of total exports, and 77 percent are products with high value added, compared with 30 percent sent to the European Union and only 16 percent to Asia.

This dynamic process of integration has led one high Brazilian official to assert that the Brazilian identity is changing. "Increasingly Brazilians," in the words of that official, are "fully and strongly identifying themselves as South Americans," with Mercosur as the axis.[14] Culturally, economically, and politically, therefore, Brazil sees its future tied to Mercosur and, more broadly, to South America.

In other words, like Brazil and Argentina most countries in South America, thanks to a vigorous process of regional integration, are making their neighbors priorities in foreign policy agendas and not, as in the past, the United States. For Argentina and Chile, for example, what happens today with the Brazilian economy probably matters just as much as what occurs with the U.S. economy. Unlike any other time in the past, South American countries today want their subregional partners to be stable and prosperous.

Another important change in the region is the emergence of new, flexible, and pragmatic forms of regional cooperation. The new scenario of redemocratization, along with the processes of economic reform and modernization of the state, has become a factor of unity and convergence among Latin Americans countries. Thus, contacts and informal discussions among chiefs of state and government to analyze critical common problems and suggest solutions to them have multiplied noticeably. This approach of informal multilateral diplomacy and direct contact among Latin American leaders to collectively manage international problems has intensified the salience of the region.

South American leaders now meet a minimum of five times a year to discuss common problems in such frameworks as the Rio Group Presidential Summit (once a year), the Mercosur Presidential Summit (twice a year), and the Ibero-American Summit (once a year). In the past, hemispheric presidential summits were convened by the United States mainly to control communism and social movement challenges (since World War II remarkably few: Panama, 1956; Punta del Este, 1967; Miami, 1994; and Santiago, 1998), but today, particularly since the 1980s, Latin American leaders meet with flexible agendas and a no-nonsense work approach, consolidating personal relationships, allowing network building among national bureaucracies, and promoting further cross-border ties.

Moreover, Latin American countries are effectively tackling regional problems that in the past depended on U.S. political will for their solution. For example, there is the collective approach, with strong Latin American leadership, to the defense of representative democracy that has evolved from questionable unilateral actions by the United States.

The Rio Group, for example, stressed in its 1987 Acapulco declaration that democracy was a key component of the constitution of the group. Later it condemned attempted coups in member countries and even suspended from its deliberations two members, Panama and Peru, due to incidents that illegally interrupted democracy.

Likewise, when a coup was attempted in Paraguay by General Lino Oviedo in April 1996, Mercosur led by Brazil and Argentina reacted quickly, condemned the attempt, and warned about its eventual consequences to Paraguay in the economic bloc, thus playing a vital role in impeding the overthrow of the democratically elected government of President Juan Carlos Wasmosy. As a consequence Mercosur issued the "Presidential Declaration on Democratic Commitment in Mercosur," which allows for various degrees of suspension from the economic bloc of a member-state government that takes power through a coup d'état. This text was converted into an actual treaty protocol obligation at the Mercosur Presidential Summit of August 1998 and must now be adhered to by any future member in the integration scheme.

In this same vein, the Declaration on the Defense of Democracy by the XI Summit of Heads of State and Government of the Rio Group, held in Asuncion in August 1997, stated that in case of any alteration to the rule of law or a rupture of the constitutional order, the group's secretariat would immediately convene a meeting of foreign ministers to deal with it. Various observers have stated that in the attempted upset of the democratic order in Paraguay in 1996, the strong declarations by Mercosur countries (especially Brazil) condemning such attempts were fundamental in saving Paraguay's democracy.[15] If democratic institutions in Latin America are more firmly rooted than in the past, it is due partly to the new regional activism and to the fact that Latin American countries focus more and more effectively on their own problems without seeking extraregional assistance.

Finally, the renaissance of regionalism in Latin America is not solely a government-level phenomenon. Regional parliaments, such as the Parlatino in Brazil, have become relevant actors in regional affairs, while at the same time political parties like the Christian Democrats, Social Democrats, and Liberals expand their regional activities in the framework of their respective party internationals.

The private sector is actively involved in the construction of new roads, electric connections, and oil and gas pipelines crossing the borders of South America as never before. In addition, a new pattern of direct investments of South American companies in neighboring countries is sweeping the region.

Chilean businesspeople, for instance, have invested more than $7 billion in Argentina in sectors ranging from electricity, to supermarkets, to wineries. Similarly Chilean investments in Peru, Uruguay, Bolivia, and Colombia continue to expand. In Brazil, the explosion of Chilean direct investments made Chile in 1996 the third major world investor, behind only the United States and France, with $977 million applied that year basically in the industrial and energy sectors.[16] Argentinian enterprises are likewise crossing the Andes to do business in Chile. A major gas pipeline now supplies Argentinian gas to central Chile, while an oil pipeline reaches the southern coast of Chile from oil deposits in southern Argentina. Many new bi-oceanic corridors have been opened by joint decision of both countries to facilitate trade and tourism, whereas in the past they were closed because of mutual suspicion.

In addition, new technologies have not only brought the world closer together, but have also multiplied links among Latin American nations. Millions of new telephone connections tie the region, and regional television channels, newspapers, and other media have sprung up in unprecedented numbers. For example, the weekly *Gazeta Mercantil Latinoamericana*, produced in Brazil, is published simultaneously in several Latin American nations in both Portuguese and Spanish. Thus Latin American private interactions are at an all-time high.

This growing network of businesses and private contacts that interrelates the region is leading entrepreneurs to be more interested in their neighbors' stability than ever before. Mistrust and relative isolation have given way to confidence and interdependence. South American businesspeople do not look only to the North for economic opportunities but increasingly see their future in the South where, among other things, they can be more competitive.

## Conclusions and Some Caveats

I have argued that a quiet phenomenon of relational delinking has been going on between the United States and Latin America. The United States, unlike a few decades ago, is no longer the undisputed external priority of Latin America, especially of South American countries.

Unlike in the past, few countries of the region seek to establish special relationships or exclusive political and economic alliances with Washington. Instead, there is a certain perception that the United States does not view South America as a priority, particularly in a post–Cold War context; but since Latin American nations no longer depend primarily on the United States for trade and assistance, such indifference is now mutual. For the first time in a long while, foreign ministries and local leaders are not distraught or even disappointed at the evident fact that the United States does not have a coherent policy toward Latin America, not even a broad strategy to deal with the region. After all, Latin American nations do not face particularly grave problems or conflicts that may require U.S. involvement.

All that being said, it should be noted that the United States is and will continue to be a key actor in the foreign relations of Latin America. Although export dependence on the United States has fallen in recent years and intraregional trade has boomed, there remains an asymmetry in hemispheric trade. For example, although exports from the United States to Mercosur countries represent 3 percent of its total exports, Mercosur sales to the United States represent 15 percent of the bloc's total sales. Likewise, the United States, although facing strong competition from other regions, continues to be the principal source of foreign investment in Latin America.

Despite the remarkable economic transformations of the last decade, Latin American nations still face important problems that hypothetically could make them more vulnerable to U.S. influence. Even with economic stability and the resumption of growth, Latin America continues to show the most unequal distribution of income in the world. Disenchantment with the reform process and a return to populism are threats not to be dismissed. Additionally, sluggish export performances on the part of some countries, low savings rates, and external shocks like the Asian crisis could force Latin American countries to rely once again primarily on the United States.

Trade and investment flows could be reversed by a severe world crisis, thus exposing the marked structural asymmetry of Latin America vis-à-vis the United States. Moreover, continued globalization will probably deepen structural ties between the United States and the region, as can be perceived in the shaping of Latin popular culture through MTV, Disney, and other similar expressions.

It is unlikely, however, that the dependence pattern of the 1960s or 1970s would be re-created even under the most pessimistic assumptions. Although U.S. popular culture has triumphed everywhere, and certainly in the region, Latin America today has a new presence in the United States Salsa outsells ketchup in U.S. supermarkets, high-quality Chilean wines are beginning to displace German, Spanish, and Italian wines on elite tables, and Isabel Allende sells more books than many well-established U.S. authors. Also, while it is true that CNN dominates cable news, today Latin Americans have options they did not have only a decade ago, such as the Mexican cable news network Alianza Latinoamericana of ECO that covers the entire region. Likewise, although an external crisis could indeed produce setbacks in the regional integration processes, it is unlikely that the more invisible interconnections through gas and electric lines or the phenomenon of Latin investments in other regional countries would be affected. A recent report reveals that the so-called multilatinas, the Latin American conglomerates that have expanded through a growing presence in neighboring countries, were an unknown phenomenon 20 years ago and are not likely to go away.[17]

Evidently, the delinking phenomenon between the United States and Latin America refers essentially to foreign policy actions and ties and applies principally to South America. Mexico, Central America, and the Caribbean still exhibit the intensive patterns of trade and political ties with the United States derived from history and geographical contiguity. For example, the overriding objective of the foreign policies of the English-speaking Caribbean countries is to obtain from Washington "parity" treatment regarding NAFTA or, at least, improvement of the Caribbean Basin Initiative Program.

Nevertheless, even though the economic importance of the United States for Latin America is still very high, the fact is that the pursuit of market-oriented policies and liberal reforms in practically all Latin American countries has turned inter-American trade, investment, and financial ties into truly private-channel relations with little or no influence from government policies or preferences. Not even the Helms-Burton extraterritoriality measures have discouraged many important private enterprises in Latin America from doing business with Cuba, a situation that would have been unthinkable in the not too distant past. Nor did efforts by the Clinton administration to see Colombia's President Ernesto Samper ousted succeed. He completed his term—despite the fact that in July 1996 he had his U.S. tourist visa revoked and that Colombia was denied U.S. certification for combating the drug trade from 1996 to 1998—probably because, unlike in the past, structural ties did not easily serve U.S. diplomatic pressure.

In sum, the United States and Latin America have grown apart in recent years, without noise and with little regret. Clearly, this is a healthy process that could lead to the emergence of a mature and mutually advantageous relationship without traumas. In any case, things are not the way they used to be two or three decades ago in inter-American relations, and they will certainly never be the same again.

## Notes

1. See Abraham Lowenthal, "El fin de la presunción hegemónica," *Estudios Internacionales*, 37 (January-March 1977), 45–67.

2. *O Estado de São Paulo*, 20 July 1997, D-2.

3. *Economist* article reproduced in *Gazeta Mercantil*, 11 July 1997, 12.

4. ECLAC figures based on official data.

5. U.S. Departament of Commerce, "U.S. Exports to the World," U.S. Embassy to Brazil, 1996.

6. *O Estado de São Paulo*, 27 March 1997, A-9.

7. Figures cited by José Miguel Insulza in *Ensayos sobre la Política Exterior de Chile* (Santiago: Editorial Los Andes, 1998), 183.

8. Thomas McLarty, Special Assistant to U.S. President, quoted in *Gazeta Mercantil*, A-6.

9. Charlene Barshefsky quoted in *Veja*, 21 May 1997, 119.

10. Carol Graham and Michael O'Harlon, "The Good Intentions of Humanitarian Aid," *Foreign Affairs* (Brazilian edition, *Gazeta Mercantil*, 19 July 1997, 20).

11. *O Estado de São Paulo*, 20 July 1997, B-1.

12. See poll results in *Jornal do Brasil*, 20 December 1997, 11.

13. Celso Pinto, "A dependência Brasil-Argentina," *Folha de São Paulo*, 26 February 1998, 7.

14. Ronaldo Mota Sardenberg, secretary of Strategic Affairs of Brazil, *O Globo*, 31 May 1997.

15. See declarations by José Luis Simón in *Jornal do Brasil*, 28 April 1996, 20; Arturo Valenzuela in *La Nación*, 7 June 1996; and "Tudo pela Democracia," *Isto É*, 19 June 1996, 102–103.

16. Heraldo Muñoz, "Capitais chilenos no Brasil," *Folha de São Paulo*, 12 May 1997, 3.

17. See "Empresas latinas se toman el continente," *El Diario*, Santiago, 10 August 1998.

# 4

## Strategies for Global Insertion: Brazil and Its Regional Partners

*Thomaz Guedes da Costa*

In the conclusion to James Rosenau's book on turbulence in world politics, the author offers several possible scenarios for the future of the international system.[1] Rosenau argues that these scenarios would result from the structural evolution of global interactions combined with the complex dynamics of individual and collective behaviors of political actors, as they forecast the future, select strategies, and make decisions in order to achieve short- and long-term interests amid the turbulence of these post–Cold War years. At a subregional level, one can certainly profit from Rosenau's suggestion that the international system stands at a crossroads of state-centric, sovereignty-bound actors and the sharing of norms for the pursuit of integration on a global scale. However, his approach offers little insight into the individual behavior of countries or societies that will, eventually, result in this "complex dynamic" or the respective consequences that will move the structure of world politics toward either integration or fragmentation. Since Francis Fukuyama's declaration that the world system had reached "the end of history," one finds contradictory results in every corner of policy evaluation and claims that question the inevitability of the ideological evolution of the governance of mankind into the Western liberal democratic form.[2] Nevertheless, decisionmakers are now coping with the intellectual and political challenges of shaping future scenarios, while they address today's socioeconomic and security crises.

Practitioners and theorists of foreign policy are exploring explanations of what are and what accounts for the strategic choices of Latin American countries in what seems to be a new framework of internal politics and external relations regarding the global system. This puzzle is inviting to many: to investors who need to decide where to bet their money, or decisionmakers who must strike balances in their public policies. The following analysis aims to respond to the question of what is Latin America's potential role in world affairs, considering the region in a global context and taking into account current debates in the field of international relations.

Addressing this question from the perspective of the South requires two basic assumptions. The first regards the nature of the "new" globalization of world politics and how it shapes the internal politics of countries, especially newly formed democracies. I agree with the editors in assuming the rapid expansion of politics under broad systems of negotiation and legitimate rule, at both national and international levels, and such features as the internationalization of the economy, the spread of political values based on Western liberal ideology, and changes in the global geophysical environment that affect human conditions and institutional settings.[3] However, I propose two caveats. The first is that it is questionable whether the globalization process is in fact a clear break with the past, both in terms of international politics based on power and the nature of the internal political process in nations based now on democracy and the legitimacy of rulemaking. The second regards what type of new order will give structure to the coming international system. Will it be more conducive to cooperation? How will it manage conflicts? How will it shape relations among actors with distinct interests, degrees of power, and strategic choices?

This second assumption involves the validity of "Latin America" as a unit of analysis in terms of a subregion in the global system. I want to argue that "Latin America" as a unit of analysis has validity only in perceived opposition to the United States. A historical review of efforts toward a constructive, multilateral, regional policy would reveal that the region has not developed a uniform identity in world politics. Even in recent debates on the proposal for a Free Trade Area of the Americas (FTAA), the response of Latin America—as an entity—to the idea of a new, hemisphere-wide framework for commercial relations has been lukewarm.

However, the idea that societies and polities south of the Rio Grande form a unity remains strong in the minds of many academics in Washington and the United States, as well as among nationalist figures in the region. Thus, "Latin America" is commonly portrayed as a single actor, a synthesis of these various nations' interests, political perspectives, and preferential strategies for foreign policy, closer together in nature than they are with those of the United States and other nations overseas. Entities such as the OAS; historical instances of agreement on issues such as World War II, and Cuba and Castro; and a history of struggle against the dominance of the United States feed the unity image. Washington would seem to prefer that there be more coordination among countries in Latin America so that it could define a broad, effective bilateral interaction between itself and the region. However, any collective Latin American "identity" is weakened by the diversity among the nations of the region in terms of their domestic politics, size, location, economic scale, resources, and capabilities, as well as among their different strategic preferences.[4] This desired (by some) integration of identity may someday be possible, but as yet there is too little substance behind the concept to define any unity for practical analytical purposes.

Nevertheless, even while questioning its validity, the adoption of the concept is necessary to address the given theme of Latin American relations with the United States and the rest of the world. This chapter hopes to contribute to this debate by focusing primarily on the strategic behavior of Brazil as a significant actor in defining a Latin American posture in world politics, and the effects of Brazil's interactions in both the regional and global systems.

The central argument is that Brazil (and perhaps other nations in the region), facing the uncertainty of globalization, has adopted a strategy of "pacing and hedging." Brazil prefers to move gradually and with caution in expanding regional cooperation in order to gain time to establish a general sense of unity and direction for the country and its neighbors in the international arena. At the same time, Brazil must hedge its strategy against possible negative effects in the future. All this while the nation copes with difficult adjustments in its internal politics, tries to increase its capacity to promote its interests abroad, and works to improve its relations abroad and to secure cooperation that is lasting and stable within the turbulent process of globalization.

To address Latin America's role in world politics, I examine the impact of recent major changes in domestic politics and their influence on issues related to the search for stable democratic governance. Many Latin American nations share the recent challenges of implementing democratic and economic reforms. The complexity of the adjustment processes and the imbalances they produce in Brazil's heterogeneous local societies (in terms of social and economic conditions) often result in contradictory responses, many of which are antagonistic to these democratic and free-market economic models. My analysis also includes the effects of new initiatives regarding confidence-building measures and overtures for regional and subregional integration in global politics. Efforts to solve historical conflicts and disputes are changing political attitudes, generating new incentives for cooperation, and producing a variety of initiatives for subregional integration. Finally, this chapter examines how Latin America insinuates itself into the strategic thinking of the United States and into world politics as a whole. Brazil is the focus of this analysis, a reflection of the nation's unusual scale as a political unit in Latin America and its potential capacity to act both in concert with and separate from its neighbors.

## Domestic Politics and the Impact of Globalization

The revival of democratic regimes in the Latin American region has already produced significant changes in the conduct of local politics, decisionmaking processes and strategies, and international interactions. The demands of regional democratization—including economic reforms, institution building, and the need to improve income distribution and create jobs—can be contradictory to a nation's long-term foreign policy goals, such as the need to link local development with export production, attracting investment capital, expanding technological sales, encouraging foreign manufactures and service suppliers, granting property and intellectual rights, and controlling monetary exchange.

### Democratic Rule and Liberal Reforms

The establishment of a democratic regime in Brazil in 1988 created new grounds for political rule, and reshaped the national economic model and social relations. The advancement of liberal ideals and the reform of representative institutions have created new channels for interest articulation and policy responses. Increasing participation by social actors and special-interest groups through voting and lobbying has forced the state to modernize, encouraged the development of a market economy, and enhanced vertical and spatial social mobility. In many ways, this weakening of the traditional autarkic, oligarchic, and patrimonial forms of government and the emergence of a modern representative democracy have left Brazil to cope with the dilemma of matching democratic rule with the withdrawal of the state from the control of the daily lives of its citizens.[5] In many ways, new opportunities have appeared for the self-promotion of the rights and benefits of individuals and groups, particularly in economic and social affairs. However, frustrations with timing and costs, and the unintended consequences of partial decisions, have produced popular dissatisfaction with the democratic process and demands from some groups, especially socialist ideological groups, for a return to an authoritative, state-based reallocation of resources.

Since the early 1990s the upper middle class has dominated the political elite in Brazil, as in other Latin American countries, and has created a common perception of the inevitable evolution of the international system toward integration by market forces, cross-cultural trends, and common technological matrices. The Brazilian political elite has accepted that its country is in a period of historical transition within the structure of world politics, especially in matters concerning relationships among the major powers. This transition becomes important when Brazilians observe that many other countries are undergoing significant shifts in their internal political regimes.[6]

World War II changed the international power structure from a multipolar to a bipolar system, introducing a struggle of ideological, geopolitical, and nuclear-military dimensions between the two superpowers and their respective camps. The recent collapse of the Soviet Union, the demise of several Marxist-socialist-oriented regimes, and the drive for the globalization of the world's economy and opening of markets commenced another transition period in world politics and have had marked effects on Brazil. Brazilians perceive that important forces are at work in world politics that have a direct impact not just on relations among the major actors, but also on smaller or weaker actors in every region of the globe. The potential shaping of a multipolar world system and the repercussions of economic interdependence and integration suggest that new interests and patterns of relations, and a new thematic agenda have arrived on the scene.[7] Everywhere in Latin America, there is both an acceptance of these changes as well as growing uncertainty about their consequences for individuals and larger political units. This dilemma demands a shift in each country's international political position toward strategies that can profit from global forces while hedging against negative impacts.[8]

The acceptance of these changes supports the position that Brazil should attempt to take advantage of new opportunities and rethink how to cope with the projection of its national interests regionally and overseas for socioeconomic and political gains. Policymakers are perplexed, however, by uncertainty regarding the true destiny of the international system, more so than from doubts about what road Brazil should take in its long-term foreign relations.[9] As the late Ambassador Paulo Nogueria Bastista said, Brazil must find its way—either in a New World order or a New World chaos.[10]

The idea that the United States now commands hegemony in world politics is mitigated by the perception that the world is tending toward the formation of stronger subregional economic blocs, many of which are likely to contribute to the shaping of a new global regime. Brazilian policymakers debate the optimal course for economic integration and participation in a global market, at the same time as they respond to internal demands for the preservation of national values and the protection of existing power structures and privileges. The ramifications of a unified Europe, a potential challenge from an Asian group or from China, and continued inequality between the North and the South mix with local demands for social and economic rights and benefits, better income distribution, and the full exercise of political rights. Brazil's society and its leadership are compelled to reexamine values and preferences that traditionally have shaped the country's foreign policy.[11]

Brazil is in the middle of an era of change in regard to its constitutional framework and rules for economic management and political decisionmaking, a process that started formally with the new constitution of 1988.[12] The current exercise of democracy reveals the influence of traditional political chiefs, the debilities of existing institutions, and the fast learning curves of new actors now able to participate in the political process. A redistribution of political power among interest groups, political parties, and NGOs has created new alliances and introduced into the national agenda a general reexamination of political values, preferences, and exigencies.

The constitution of 1988 reinforced the political role of the national congress, giving this institution new prerogatives in policy formulation, legislative definition, and allocation of budgetary resources. In fact, the 1988 constitution gave new powers to the Brazilian congress to counterbalance the hegemony of the executive and fortified the states against the control of the federal government. This shift now permits many segments of Brazilian society to observe and influence better national decisions. The new regime shifted the state's center of gravity away from the executive office to the political market represented by the congress. Now, representatives are key players who participate in the decisions in all agendas, including foreign policy and national security, which have traditionally been restricted to the Ministry of Foreign Affairs, the military, and the office of the president.[13]

## Strategic Shifts in the Area of Security

Since democratization, Latin American countries have not achieved stable political regimes with sustainable models for confronting the new challenges of globalization. Despite the implementation of the 1988 constitution, Brazil has not been able to produce a coherent national strategy with wide popular support. Since the establishment of the new democratic regime, Brazil has struggled, without apparent success, with the need for constitutional reform, against inflation and recession, and against despair over the nation's lack of government ethics. Brazilian society has not arrived at a consensual agenda for national security, nor is it prepared to provide direction toward a new national strategy.[14] Up to now, all that has emerged are individual decisions that challenged the conceptions that commanded Brazilian strategic thinking during the Cold War.

Throughout the period of military government there was a notion that national security had to be supported by increasing internal capabilities through the expanded use of endogenous resources, taking advantage of the international exchange of capital and technologies, and with rigid central planning.[15] In this model, the aim was to provide for rapid economic development, exploiting natural resources and generating a modern industrial force with growth rates superior to those of other countries. The dedicated application of the model was expected to result in a higher standard of living for all Brazilians. According to the model, in a few decades Brazil would be able to modernize its economy, escape from underdevelopment, and reinvent itself as an industrialized, developed country, able to sit side by side with other powers to participate in the major decisions of world politics. Internal growth plus a growing presence in external markets would permit Brazil to secure, with its own resources, a high degree of political independence, sovereignty, and ample mobility in dealing with other countries and international crises.

This aim was simultaneously promoted and undermined by Brazil's external dependence on foreign capital, resources, and technologies, as became apparent during the oil crisis of 1979 and the debt crunch of the 1980s. If until the late 1970s Brazil was perceived as a "rising power," even able to become the sixth largest economy in the world, after the mid-1980s the country began to show its managerial deficiencies in controlling public spending and providing for socioeconomic equality.[16] It is no wonder that many Brazilians view the 1980s as a "lost" decade, with continued high inflation, shrinkage in the GNP, an inability to manage its foreign debt, underemployment, and a rise in the concentration of wealth. This combination of factors provoked a crisis in the military model, with society demanding new bases for economic management and political participation. After 1993, with enhanced economic and democratic stability, Brazil was able to open further its internal market to foreign capital and investment, to privatize public enterprises, to pursue regional economic integration, and to accept the rules, attitudes, and values of international regimes as a road to greater participation in the world system.

Until the 1980s, the autarkic model dominated national politics, and encouraged other thinking that aimed to meet the aspirations of the dominant oligarchy for increased national power. But this desire of the dominant national elite, then led by the military, for national expansion and state-directed modernization did not resonate among the large, silent segments of society. Brazil's effort to increase its national capabilities was supported by the notion that it was necessary to reduce internal vulnerabilities and deter aggressors, both regional and global, from using coercion against Brazil in international disputes. General interests, such as safeguarding national borders or natural resources, were part of this discourse. However, even during the Cold War common Brazilians did not feel threatened by the East-West confrontation, nor did they develop a perception that their country was threatened to the degree that strict defense measures would have to be undertaken to provide for security. This lack of agreement regarding national security shifted quickly in the 1980s as democracy and the forces of globalization arrived.

Whether because of its broad geographic features, its physical detachment from the major points of friction in international politics, or its traditionally peaceful relations with its neighbors, there is no concrete evidence that Brazil suffers any clear or present foreign threats to its national security.[17] Nevertheless, globalization has introduced a different notion of security or insecurity that demands a new strategy. The 1997 Asian financial crisis was a demonstration to Brazilians of the power of global capitalism and how lightning-quick fluctuations of investments and savings can destabilize the world economy. In particular it demonstrated the vulnerability of developing economies, such as Brazil's, in the face of such turbulence.[18] Wars in the Middle East, from 1967 to 1991, had disturbing and harmful consequences for Brazil's foreign trade, especially regarding the supply of oil needed for a petroleum-based transportation network. Every oil price shock in the international market pushed inflation to ever higher levels. In every global crisis, the Brazilian government has been surprised by events, and has shown itself incapable of organizing preventive measures to minimize their impacts or of taking corrective measures to reduce recurrent shocks.

In the 1990s other events shook Brazil's tranquility. The Brazilian government had never taken as a high priority the protection of its citizens living abroad. However, the increasing numbers of migrants leaving the country and Brazilian companies operating abroad have created disturbing situations for the authorities. For example, during the Gulf War of 1990–1991 thousands of Brazilian workers were trapped by the hostilities inside Iraq, making the Brazilian government awkwardly aware of its inability to promptly evacuate them. In 1992, with the revival of the Angolan civil war, the Brazilian Air Force had to rescue nationals working in that country, as local groups began to threaten the lives of Brazilians working on projects contracted with the Luanda government.

The Amazon region has also become a focus of concern for the Brazilian government. Taking advantage of Brazil's extensive and uninhabited border, drug traffickers have found new paths to push their products out of Bolivia, Peru, and Colombia toward large consumer markets in the United States and Europe. Illicit air traffic and river boating have become objects of national programs to control regional movements of craft and people.[19] The permeability of Brazil's borders, especially in the Amazonian region, has become a permanent concern. Regional threats to Brazil's national interests include the potential for violence to spill over from internal conflicts in neighboring countries, particularly Colombia, people prospecting mineral resources in the middle of the jungle, the smuggling of drugs or people across borders, and the localized depletion of biodiversity that results from the extensive illegal exploitation of regional resources.

### Internal Adjustment to Economic Insecurity from Globalization

As is the case in many other countries in the Americas in this new phase of regional and global interactions, a new sense of insecurity has arisen domestically regarding Brazil's foreign policy. Unlike the threat of a foreign aggressor, which typically unites a national community, this insecurity is based on a broad and unclear perception that globalization (cultural, economic, and environmental) will harm many individuals, segments, regions, or groups because of their incapacity to act in a new competitive environment. Thus, globalization has become a central theme on the national agenda and a controversial rationale for policy decisions. Under current liberal efforts at modernizing the Brazilian state, the country displays what George Soros views as the deficiencies of capitalism. The effects of globalization increase popular demands, especially by those who perceive they are threatened by it, for remedial measures and new social services, at the same time that the state's ability to respond to those demands is reduced by the process of government downsizing, including privatizations and the reduction of subsidies in the market economy, conducted under the watchful eyes of taxpayers/voters who demand effectiveness in the new democratic regime.[20]

Domestic factors and disputes tend to increase pressure on decisionmakers regarding the impact of the internationalization of the economy. The enhancement of democratic rule allows political reactions from a variety of social sectors (which can be significant in number as well as political articulation) against the redistribution of wealth and power that is partly a consequence of economic globalization. Ironically, these political reactions can threaten the democratic rule that allows them voice. The key problem is that in the short run the economy does not grow as fast as the increase in the number of young citizens entering the labor force plus older individuals being displaced from jobs.

This problem is aggravated by the fact that large segments of the Brazilian population and that of other Latin American countries are uneducated for modernity and unprepared to live in the competitive environment of liberal globalization. In 1990, about 45 percent of the Brazilian population had only primary education or less. Twenty percent of the adult population that is available for the workforce is illiterate.[21] From 1990 to 1996 industrial productivity increased by 17 percent, while the labor force was reduced by 14 percent.[22] The Brazilian federal government reacted with programs to promote employment opportunities. These include the Generation of Employment and Income Program, which offers quick credit to small businesses from employment insurance funds; the Labor Qualification Plan, which provides competitiveness training for individuals and employees (which aimed to reach up to 20 percent of the labor force between 1996 and 1999); and the Family Agriculture Strengthening Plan, which offers financing to support small farmers. However, the erosion of the spending power of the middle class is a key factor in political instability and social turmoil. The rapid expansion of public and private debt has resulted in a high transfer of income in the form of interest to the rich, and the income disparities between skilled and unskilled labor have created a new class conflict.

But how can a nation enact policies to generate new wealth and to improve the distribution of income if the dominant political actors are undecided about the nature of the new economic model? This dilemma is apparent in the deadlock over what type of model of science and technology Latin American countries will adopt in the near future. Following Auguste Comte's view of science and technology as the determining force in modern society, the withdrawal of ideological disputes, the decline in the potential of primary-product-exporting economies, and the value of information all combine to force Latin America to move into the modernization process and find competitive niches. If science and technology shape the structure of development, then decisions about investments in the field of science and technology must be made quickly to match the decisions of those societies that have already set out toward a new-age economy based on intellectual capital and services. In fact, new forms of domination (and liberation) for Latin Americans may lie in the quality of the choices individuals, groups, firms, and countries will make in this regard.[23]

Latin American societies differ in what they perceive to be the implications that globalization holds for their nations. Profits and benefits go to shareholders in select investor countries, and to either those individuals associated with foreign operations in developing countries or their local partners, or to others who are able to shift into the new productive "paradigm." But many stakeholders (those who suffer the negative consequences or who risk losing what they gained in the preglobalization model) are, in the short run, a source of social problems. Less developed countries, such as Ecuador, Bolivia, Suriname, Honduras, or Guatemala, are particularly at risk because of the relative difficulty they face in competing with the larger powers of the global economy. The long-term benefits of the model of liberalized global economics, as praised by economists from the developed world, must balance the severe, short-term negative local effects in the region. Some form of compensation is necessary to gain the acceptance and address the costs that liberalization demands of many individuals in Latin America—otherwise these individuals are likely to look to the past, to models of social rebellion and state-run economies as solutions for their despair. This is a potential scenario for Brazil, domestically, as it is globally for the nations of the South. The gap between rich and poor nations has also increased with internationalization. Latin America's average per capita income is now one-fourth that of the industrialized countries in the North, contrasted to one-third in the 1970s.

## A Strategic Preference for Regional Confidence Building and Integration

### Accommodation with Argentina: A First Step Toward Regional Integration and Competitiveness

Unlike in its relations along its Amazon borders, with poor communications, a scarce population, and little formal trade, the policy of pursuing regional integration in the Rio Plata Basin aspires to improve local relations, reinforce confidence building, bolster the competitiveness of the Brazilian economy, and strengthen Brazil's capacity to interact with other economic blocs. Integration in the Rio Plata Basin has initiated a new political process, designed to overcome the shadow-play of local disputes between Brazil and Argentina for international prestige. As a result, trade between the two countries increased rapidly in quantity and diversity in the early 1990s. A major objective of Brazil's foreign relations in this period was to develop increased transparency in the area of security and improved coordination of its commercial relations with Argentina. That strategy's success led to the establishment of an economic union among Argentina, Brazil, Uruguay, and Paraguay, a subregional unit that has become the cornerstone of Brazil's strategic outlook at the end of this century.[24] The expansion of economic relations in the region, deepened by growing trade and communication links, shows that Brazil has opted for a national strategy of interdependence in its relations with Argentina. Although the main plans and targets established between the two countries are mostly economic, a new partnership has been formed in scientific, military, technical, social, cultural, and political terms, which reinforces the process of political-economic integration and joint coordination in world politics.

In addition to the trade interests that drove the economic aspect of these bilateral relations, two other objectives were essential to making this new construction possible. First, in the 1970s the resolution of disputes over the exploration of the water resources in the Rio Plata Basin paved the way for future interactions. This bilateral regime for the exploration of natural resources has been in the building for over 50 years, with official meetings, memoranda of understanding, and treaties. The mutual accommodation finally has freed both countries from a nagging source of potential disputes. The understandings that this partnership brought has mitigated the aggressive geopolitical visions about these resources and neutralized the impact of nationalist claims. Over the years, successful diplomacy and driving business initiatives overcame traditional antagonisms and each country's desires to exploit unilaterally these resources for electric power generation. Managed cooperatively, the Rio Plata Basin provides a further benefit, with the integration of national waterways for intermodal international transportation.[25]

The rivalry over nuclear power between Brazil and Argentina in the 1970s has been replaced by a system that simultaneously provides bilateral mutual confidence and assurances to third parties. Since the end of the 1940s, Brazil's nuclear policy had been framed by the "prisoners dilemma."[26] On the one hand, Brazil had engaged in a regional race against Argentina in acquiring nuclear weapons technology, and on the other, it challenged the Non-Proliferation Treaty (NPT) as unfair and discriminatory in its prescription for arms control. Brazil's reluctance to fully abide by the Tlatelolco Treaty of 1967 and other measures for the national development of the nuclear technologies indicated that Brazilian authorities felt that they could lose, in both arenas, if they abdicated efforts to fully acquire nuclear technologies.

In its interaction with Argentina, Brazilians saw to some extent a mirror image of their own situation. Brazilian strategists had perceived Buenos Aires as developing a nuclear program to increase Argentina's international status and political force, just as Brasília had sought to do in the 1960s. As for relations with the NPT, a robust interpretation supposes that Brazil's strategic thinkers did not want to accept a vision of a "frozen" distribution of world power based on nuclear weapons, with some countries allowed to have them and others not. Such a scenario was unacceptable to a country that was aiming to become a key player in international politics.

One widely accepted hypothesis of why Brazil eventually changed its nuclear policy argues that the growing interdependence between Brazil and Argentina and between Brazil and the leaders of the NPT changed Brazilian national opinion about the role and utility of nuclear weapons, even in the face of an uncertain future. Another relevant explanation holds that with the establishment of democracy and greater civilian control, the dominant international norm in terms of nonproliferation began to command Brazil's nuclear policy.[27]

Brazil's strategic cost-benefit analysis regarding its shift in nuclear policy is difficult to model or demonstrate, in that the analysis had to address a multilayered context of relations with Argentina, the United States, and the broader world community. I want to argue that the rivalry between Argentina and Brazil in this century does not show any signs of being a conflict without some means for accommodation. The two nations never saw military conflict as unavoidable, despite their sometimes severe nationalist postures. Even in moments of mutually perceived positioning for regional hegemony by the two countries, one finds no conflict situation that would require military means.[28] Strategists had to consider that if nuclear weapons would make a difference in the regional equation, they would also have significant negative strategic repercussions globally. The acquisition of nuclear weapons could in fact have increased the insecurity of both countries, creating negative impacts in other areas of their bilateral and multilateral relations. On the other hand, the gains from cooperation and reciprocity, which allowed an escape from the nuclear security prisoner's dilemma, were estimated ultimately to be greater—and evidently are.

Since the agreements for cooperation in the use of nuclear technology signed between Brazil and Argentina in Buenos Aires (1980) and in Iguaçú (1985), the exchange of technology as well as the systematized transparency of both programs has increased. A new regional regime was established under the Brazilian-Argentine Agency for Control and Accounting of Nuclear Materials. As George Lamazière and Roberto

Jaguaribe have argued, the compatibility of internal controls associated with democratic governments and international management have brought Brazil closer to the NPT regime, as the country adopted international comprehensive safeguards under the Quadripartite Agreement signed with Argentina and with the International Atomic Energy Agency (1991).[29] Both Brazil and Argentina have definitely abandoned programs for weapons of mass destruction and given assurances to others—but this does not imply that Brazil will sign the NPT. Although one could argue for some potential benefits or sympathy that could result from such a move, Brazil would be abandoning the principle of sovereign equality among states that it has cherished traditionally in its foreign policy. However, as a new international regime takes over, Brazil moved in 1997 to abide fully by nonproliferation rules under both the NPT and the Tlatelolco Agreement.

Is regional integration in the Rio Plata Basin an inexorable process? As long as it is led by decisionmakers who have lived in the two historical periods—before and during the growth of Mercosur (Portuguese: Mercosul)—doubts and uncertainties will remain. But as the common benefits of cooperation multiply and spread throughout these national communities, the stakes increase for a potential rupture in the integration process. Segments of both societies will suffer under the changes wrought by integration, and the process will pass through periodic conflicts of interest and setbacks. However, since there is no fundamental dispute worth a return to the past or against continued interdependence, one can be optimistic, even if the process is moving at a slower pace than some would wish.

## Latin America's Role in World Politics

Until the late 1990s, the countries of Latin America were perceived solely in terms of their cultural differences, their raw materials and commodities, and their marginal markets for investment. Today some countries, particularly those with major populations and markets such as Brazil and Mexico, attract attention also for their potential to disturb the world economy if one or more of them fails to meet its obligations or becomes an unacceptably high-risk actor due to economic mismanagement or to a perceived incapacity to adjust quickly to new international circumstances. Here I want to argue that regional integration, relations with Europe, and dealing with the United States in a strategic perspective are key elements of Latin American strategies for insertion into the international system.

### Mercosur as a Strategic Step Toward
### Hemispheric and Global Integration

One way for Latin American countries to gain visibility and bargaining power on global issues is to increase their presence through integration initiatives. The development of Mercosur/Mercosul both strengthens regional bonding and functions as a springboard for the region to gain ground in global competition and markets. This works both for the larger countries, such as Brazil, and the smaller countries, such as Paraguay and Uruguay, which can follow a piggyback strategy of gaining from general subregional growth and enhancement. It is irrelevant whether the motive for regional cooperation is trade- and service-related or more that of achieving greater presence in hemispheric affairs. The fivefold growth in trade between Argentina and Brazil in less than a decade is evidence enough of the common benefit from both types. These bilateral gains and the larger global objectives are met simultaneously through the strategy of strengthening Mercosul. In addition, the implementation of new regional policies is now intrinsically involved with Mercosul's relations with the Free Trade Area of the Americas (FTAA) and with the expansion of trade, investment, and technological transfers with the European Union.

In the traditional Latin American view, Mercosul and Brazil's regional policy are far from Simon Bolivar's dream of Latin American integration based on common bonds of culture and political interests.[30] If the Bolivarian concept were dominant today, then integration would follow patterns of sociocultural preferences, which patterns would only be likely if the public sector provided the critical investments to bind the integration. In reality, the current drive for integration in the Americas follows a pattern of increasing economic exchange driven by the demands and opportunities of the market, within both Mercosul and NAFTA.

The failure of the Andean Pact to advance its integration is evidence of this contrast. The lack of perceived economic space for a win-win situation undermined common political or strategic goals. These national markets basically compete with one another more than they complement one another. The project also has suffered from a context of mutual mistrust. These factors have led member countries, so far, to sustain strategies that pursue individual gains from protectionist measures.

As we consider Brazil's strategy for coping with globalization, namely dramatic neoliberal economic reforms to make the economy more competitive in global markets, it is clear that this leaves Brazil significantly vulnerable. International indices show that Brazil's economy ranked between thirty-fifth and forty-fifth in terms of competitiveness among countries in the 1990s. The country lacks competitive advantage in key aspects of the modern economy, such as telecommunications, computers, pharmaceuticals, transportation, tools, and other capital goods. Industries based on the intensive use of high technology continue to prefer to buy packages from abroad rather than from local providers. Since state-run science and technology industries have been privatized, local innovators must seek new markets abroad to make up for the absence of what were once large local consumer markets.

The development of Mercosul has improved Brazil's ability to compete globally. For both Brazil and Argentina the commercial results have been impressive. Mercosul's GNP grew 3.8 percent from 1991 to 1996, as compared with the world's average of 2.9 percent.[31] Within the subregion, 202 million people form a market with a $991 billion GNP and an increasing potential for growth as new groups of consumers are brought into the consumer market as a result of successful economic policies. Within a decade, internal trade has increased tenfold to $82.2 billion—growing 9.8 percent in 1997 alone—while world commerce increased by 7.0 percent.

According to Brazil's strategic perspective, there is conceptual compatibility between regional arrangements and the global drive for liberalization, under the scheme of the International Trade Organization. Brazil has argued that its strategic focus aims for "open regionalism" as a building block for a global trade regime based on greater liberal principles.[32] In the debate in the Western Hemisphere about possible structures for a common market, decisionmakers in Brazil (and many of its neighbors) are unsure of the wisdom of engaging in an open-trade area that includes the economic powerhouse of the United States.

Brazil's performance in the world market is promising, although it is clearly still vulnerable to competition, severe volatility, and international crises. In 1997 Brazil's exports of manufactured goods remained stable at 55 percent of total sales. The export of basic products stood at 27 percent, led by raw sugar and soybean oil. In general, there was a high degree of concentration on a few products—iron ore, coffee beans, soy flour, soybeans, and shoes—which comprised 23 percent of all sales. Mercosul was the most important market for Brazilian manufactured products (28 percent); the United States was second (21 percent). Internally, dynamic emerging export industries included food and beverages, auto parts and transportation in general, petrochemicals, mining, telecommunications, pulp and paper, wood, leather, and grains.

Latin American countries, and Brazil in particular, prefer to develop a negotiation strategy that will result in postponing decisions on international or regional integration in order to provide more time for their economies to increase in competitiveness and adjust to the levels of their key partners. Some countries, and not just those with smaller and less developed economies (including Brazil, for instance), are afraid that severe adjustment costs in the short term will not match the promised gains in the long term. Exports and the attraction of investments in a free-trade zone are the greatest motivating factors for embarking on the FTAA project. However, the economic displacement of a large portion of the population, within the context of economic and political turbulence and reforms, causes uncertainty about how to carry out such a plan.

In the negotiation and implementation of an integration proposal, each country has to manage its shortcomings and mitigate negative impacts on many national sectors that are less competitive than those of partner countries. Internally some geographic region or a sector, such as agriculture or food processing, may argue against the free-trade arrangement due to short-run losses stemming from their lack of comparative advantage. For Brazil and for Mercosul, these complex internal political matters must be confronted before going to the bargaining table. For Brazil, industrial sectors that produce consumer and capital goods, such as the automotive, tool, computer, and electronics goods industries directed at internal consumption, would have greater advantage from association with the United States through the FTAA. On the other hand, primary-goods exporters, including the agricultural industries, as well as industrial sectors, are more likely to benefit from a liberalization agreement with the European Union and Asian countries.[33]

Another key point is that Brazil as a global trader must aim to maintain a certain balance in the geographic distribution of its trade. In 1997, of its total exports, it shipped 20.6 percent to North America, 22.9 percent to Latin America Integration Association (ALADI) countries, 26.8 percent to the European Union, and 16.4 percent to Asia. The pattern of imports was very much the same. Imports of manufactured goods from all sources increased in the past years to 12–15 percent, while 8–12 percent was from NAFTA countries.

### A Bargaining Triangle: Latin America, the United States, and Europe

Close relations between Europe and Latin America are a historical, cultural, and economic two-way street. Some specific instances are revealing. A Brazilian or Mercosul move for liberalization and integration with the European Union would substantially increase agricultural exports of both grains and meat. European direct investment in the privatization process in Brazil or in large industrial parks with access to Latin American consumers, as seen in the automobile, entertainment, and food industries, produces a situation that Felix Peña called a "natural triangle" for bargaining among Mercosul, the European Union, and the United States.[34]

Politically, the attractiveness of tighter ties with Europe has two substantive elements, especially since many in Latin America are skeptical about the implementation of the FTAA. First, interdependence with Europe would help to balance the region's historical asymmetry in its relations with the United States. Unsure of Washington's commitment to hemispheric commerce, Latin American countries began to distance themselves from bilateral negotiations with the United States, as seen in the early days of NAFTA. Mercosul is a viable anchor for policy coordination, something that does not please U.S. diplomats. Joining a free-trade area with Big Brother can be risky. The option that Mexico took would appear to have dramatic costs for South American nations, as Peter Smith describes in his chapter of this book. In fact a preferential trade agreement with the United States that excludes the European countries is likely to increase the dependence of the region on the United States because it would concentrate trade bilaterally. As Guadalupe González makes clear in her chapter, NAFTA membership has led to significant trade diversion toward the United States, at the relative cost of trade with Europe.

Second, Latin American countries are also subject to the drive of European nations' promoting their own current and future commercial and investment interests in the Western Hemisphere.[35] This factor gives value and viability to the strategy of using European interest as leverage for such countries as Brazil and Argentina in bargaining jointly with the United States. What benefit does the United States provide to South American countries that Europe could not match? As Brazil's President Fernando Henrique Cardoso pointed out, "The greater the trade competition between the United States and Europe, the better for us, since it lowers prices. The fact is that today Brazil has the United States as its main commercial partner. But the European Union, as a whole, imports and exports a little more than the United States. . . . [W]e are anxious to increase our commerce. In relation to the United States, we have greatly expanded. But, unfortunately, we are accumulating deficits."[36] Thus, this strategy adds a European card to the "consolidation of Mercosul and preparation for the FTAA."[37] It is important to note that in 1997 Mercosul's total trade was 25 percent with Europe, 18 percent with the United States, 22 percent within Mercosul, and 8 percent with other Latin American countries (ALADI).[38]

Finally, in regard to the benefits of relations with Europe, countries will pace their decisionmaking and policy implementation in response to developments in the Millennium Round of the International Trade Organization. In the process of consolidating and improving Mercosul, decisionmakers will have to understand how the FTAA will overlap in the future with proposals coming from the WTO's new rounds of global negotiation. Those new ideas and especially the pace of negotiation may depend significantly on the establishment of a free-trade agreement between Mercosul and Europe. First, this agreement can be perceived in itself as part of strengthening Mercosul to bolster trade with Europe. Second, it may then produce an added incentive for the United States to negotiate friendlier, shared terms for the implementation of FTAA.

## Facing the Inevitable: Bargaining with the United States

Brazil's relations with the United States must be viewed in the context of Mexico's decision to join formally with North America, and Argentina's expressed desire for "carnal relations" with the global superpower. Clearly, the nature of a nation's relations with the United States is of paramount importance in determining a strategy for insertion into the international system.

Regarding Brazil there is a pattern of uneasy exchange with the United States. The perceived significance of these tensions depends on the type of lens one uses to observe the impact of Brazil's strategy on the United States and both countries' frustrations in their respective responses to particular political demands. Brazilians argue that their country's caution in opening up its economy is based on the fragility of its producers in competing with external products. The United States, however, wishes to increase its largest bilateral trade surplus, which is with Brazil ($6.28 billion in 1997—60 percent greater than in 1996, 60 percent of Brazil's total imbalance—of $9.37 billion surplus in trade with Latin America, with the exception of Mexico). This has been Brazil's largest deficit with the United States in nine years.[39] U.S. exports are largely capital goods, particularly telecommunications and computer-related equipment. The fastest growing import is aircraft for both countries, reflecting Brazil's continued competitiveness in commuter aircraft and the expansion of Brazilian carriers into the international market.

Bickering about market conditions produces criticism at both ends. Americans complain about the slow pace at which the Brazilian government is opening its internal market, and Brasília is critical of Washington's protectionism. Brazil argues for the reduction of U.S. trade barriers against Latin American agricultural exports (it also protests formally against European protectionism).[40] Again, this bilateral picture, as for any other country in Latin America, must be seen also in light of the multilateral proposal for the FTAA. These contrasting demands and perspectives create ambiguity. It is not easy to imagine a specific, short- or medium-term solution to this bilateral pattern with the United States or to picture these bilateral relations contributing to larger multilateral goals in a global environment marked by the reduction of all tariffs and other barriers to trade.

Washington's reluctance to negotiate obscures the view of the road ahead. Unfortunately, fast-track ability for the president of the United States to negotiate trade agreements with Latin America will not come soon. This puts at risk the credibility of U.S. initiatives, both bilateral and multilateral, until the president is granted broader and more flexible powers of negotiation. Latin Americans are skeptical of the results from the Washington political process because the society in the United States is clearly unconvinced of the value of further free-trade agreements with Latin America. U.S. interest groups maintain protectionist positions, even while they condemn similar measures in other countries.

The uncertainty of Washington's internal decisionmaking and leadership regarding hemispheric trade explains why countries such as Brazil prefer to slow the process of FTAA negotiation and work to promote cooperation with other Latin American countries in creating an agenda for hemispheric trade. Formal negotiations for the FTAA will start in 2005. The preparation phase of the arrangements is now under way with periodic meetings of heads of state, one of the most recent being the Summit of the Americas in Santiago in April 1998.[41] These meetings define the format, rules, and terms of reference for each negotiation front that collectively form the basis for a future free-trade area. The FTAA process, based on smaller meetings that deal with specific items or agendas of substance, is intended to "slice the sausage" into topic areas such as services, government purchases, conflict resolution, agriculture, intellectual property rights, subsidies, antidumping, compensatory measures, and competition policies. The active participation by major Latin American countries is essential and has been effective in reducing the influence of the United States, which would be much more powerful if these negotiations were carried out on a bilateral basis, case by case.

## Conclusion

If one wishes to consider Latin America as a political unit for analysis, either because of its common history in international politics or because its countries as a group face the United States in a complex relationship, the region's role in world politics is essentially mixed. On the positive side, Latin America offers diverse opportunities for trade, exchange of services, investments, and markets for all types of products. Its continued growth both in population and in expansion of niches for businesses provides attractive prospects. However, unstable politics, unconsolidated democratic governance, and persistent inequalities produce unwanted consequences for those actors that see the region with positive prospects.

Countries in Latin America must struggle with national options that are not clear and often are contradictory. In search of foreign support for local development, attention must be given to the sources of capital as well as to questions of public credits and investments. In some instances, accepting prescriptions from Washington for political and economic conduct in internal development (and in bilateral and multilateral foreign relations, for that matter) can yield interesting possibilities for some Latin American countries for bolstering their presence in the global system. But for some countries, especially those with the complexity of Brazil, Peru, Mexico, or Argentina, the combination of internal political structures that demand stabilization and development and external incentives for productive growth in a globalized system may not offer sufficient incentives for alignment. Thus, different patterns of negotiation and mutual understanding must be established to accommodate both internal and external forces into an integrated political process. As observed by a U.S. ambassador to Brazil, as Brazil modernizes and the United States develops new strategies for regional outreach, enhancing the U.S.-Brazilian dialogue will be critical.[42] Washington's new strategies may not fit well with those now under way south of its border. In the decisionmaking process in Latin American countries, the strengthening of democratic regimes does not eliminate the broad scope for conflict among countries in the hemisphere, because such strengthening does not necessarily reduce the differences between their individual interests or strategies. Negotiation may be the best road for resolution, but conflict and disputes will mark the process.

In many ways, the specific type and degree of attention that Latin America receives from Washington are clearly defined by internal domestic issues and political flare-ups in the region, especially those that affect markets and investments. The success of regional cooperation in trade, fighting against drug trafficking, and—for what it is worth—a post-Castro Cuba will depend on how countries in the region accomplish each stage of their own internal adjustment and how external confidence building is perceived by the U.S. government and opinionmakers in the marketplace. Nevertheless, the relations between Latin America and its extraregional actors in Europe and Asia may not receive equal attention among Latin

American countries themselves. As witnessed at the recent Summit of the Americas in Santiago, issues are not always sufficiently expressed and strategies are not perceived as sufficient to form the basis for multilateral consensus.

One suggestion presents itself for how Latin American countries can better promote a new pattern of understanding across the region and greater presence in the global system. Every country in Latin America can increase local potentialities by negotiating free trade with Europe, either individually or as a group, while addressing social demands and seeking to meet the actual costs of liberalizing markets, with attention to the short-term social costs of displacement. Interest groups in Latin America, including business and labor associations, can find partners in the United States that demand the further opening of Latin American markets and oppose protectionist advocacy in the United States. Decisionmakers in subregions can reduce the pace of their regional initiatives for integration by slowing the pace of growth and increasing the density of ties. Finally, if nothing else works, Latin American countries will no longer have to worry about going down the drain alone, because if they fail they very well may bring the U.S. and global economies down with them.

## Notes

1. See James N. Rosenau, *Turbulence in World Politics: A Theory of Change and Continuity* (Princeton, N.J.: Princeton University Press, 1990), 443–461.

2. Francis Fukuyama, "The End of History?" *National Interest* 16 (1989): 3–18.

3. On globalization and political change, the main sources for my guidance are R. Robertson, *Globalisation: Social Theory's Global Culture* (London: Sage, 1992); Guillermo O'Donnell, "Estado, Democratização e Alguns Problemas Conceituais," *Novos Estudos Cebrap* 36 (1993); Eric Hobsbawm, *A Era dos Extremos* (São Paulo: Companhia das Letras, 1995); Stephen Gil, "Globalisation, Market Civilisation and Disciplinary Neo-liberalism," *Millennium Journal of International Studies* 24, 3 (1995); Robert Cox, *Production, Power and World Order: Social Forces in the Making of History* (New York: Columbia University Press, 1987); and José Maria Gomez, "Globalização, Estado-Nação e Cidadania," *Contexto Internacional* 20, 1 (January 1998): 7–89.

4. See Joseph Tulchin, "Hemispheric Relations in the 21st Century," *Journal of Interamerican Studies & World Affairs* 39, 1 (Spring 1997): 33–43.

5. The debate about the nature of new democracies such as Brazil points out a dissonance between regimes with economic liberal systems and illiberal democracies in the sense of the authoritative allocation of physical and political resources; see Fareed Zakaria, "The Rise of Illiberal Democracy," *Foreign Affairs* 76, 6 (November/December 1997): 22–43; Adam Przeworski and Fernando

Limongi, "Modernization: Theories and Facts," *World Politics* 49, 2 (January 1997): 31–52; Joseph Tulchin, ed., *The Consolidation of Democracy in Latin America* (Boulder, Colo.: Lynne Rienner Publishers, 1995).

6. See Hélio Jaguaribe, "A Nova Ordem Mundial," *Politica Externa* 1, 1 (June 1992): 5–15; Peter Drucker, "As Mudanças na Economia Mundial," *Política Externa* 1, 3 (December 1992): 17–39; Luciano Martins, "Ordem Internacional, Interdepêndencia Assimétrica e Recursos de Poder," *Política Externa* 1, 1 (December 1992): 62–85.

7. Joseph Nye, "As Transformações no Poder Mundial," *Diálogo* 1, 24 (1991): 2–7.

8. José Alvaro Moisés, ed., *O Futuro do Brasil, a América Latina e o Fim da Guerra Fria* (São Paulo: Paz e Terra, 1992).

9. See Celso Lafer, who was then Minister of Foreign Relations, "Perspectivas e Possibilidades da Inserção International do Brasil," *Política Externa* 1, 3 (December 1992): 100–112.

10. See Paulo Nogueria Bastista, "A Nova Ordem ou Desordem International," *Política Externa* 1, 1 (June 1992): 31.

11. Traditional positions of Brazilian authorities on such issues can be found in Mario Flores (former secretary for strategic affairs), *Bases para uma Política Militar* (Campinas: Editora da Unicamp, 1992); Marcílio Marques Moreira, "O Brasil no Contexto Internacional no *Final* do Século XX," in José Alvaro Moisés, ed., *O Futuro do Brasil, a América Latina e o Fim da Guerra Fria* (São Paulo: Paz e Terra, 1992): 105–122; and Castrioto de Azambuja (as general secretary of the Foreign Relations Ministry), "A Diplomacia Brasileira e a Nova Ordem International," *Gazeta Mercantil,* 2 December 1991, 3. See also Itamar Franco's speech in *Gazeta Mercantil*, 29 December 1992, 3.

12. One of the key debates in congress is about the absence of a cadre of advisers to congressmen and the active participation of pressure groups.

13. The growing influence of congress was seen in the debates on the Quadripartite Agreement. Many senators did not want to accept the full scope of the International Atomic Energy Agency's verification measures. As for controls on the space program coming from the congress, see "Relator decide alterar destinação de verbas para programa espacial," *Gazeta Mercantil,* 23 January 1993, 5.

14. One of the few events to provoke debate in pursuit of a defense policy was a seminar organized by the congressional house of deputies in August 1992.

15. On the military and centralized planning, see Leonardo Trevisan, *Instituição Militar e Estado Brasileiro* (São Paulo: Global, 1987); and Eliezer Oliveira, *As Forças Armadas no Brasil* (Rio de Janeiro: Espaço e Tempo, 1987).

16. On the idea of Brazil's drive to become a major power, see Ronald M. Schneider, *Brazil, the Foreign Policy of a Future World Power* (Boulder, Colo.: Westview Press, 1977); Wayne A. Selcher, ed., *Brazil in the International System: The Rise of a Middle Power* (Boulder, Colo.: Westview Press, 1981).

17. See Thomaz Guedes da Costa, "Percepção de Ameaças do Ponto de Vista dos Militares Brasileiros nas Décadas de 70 e 80," in *Leituras Especiais* (Instituto Rio Branco, 24 December 1992): 8–17.

18. See José Carlos de Souza Braga, "Impasses do Capitalismo Globalizado," *Indicadores IESP* 62 (September/October 1997): 3–5.

19. On issues regarding the Amazon and its security, see Clóvis Brigagão, *Amazônia, Segurança Ecológica* (Rio de Janeiro: Editora Firmo, 1995).

20. See George Soros, "Towards a Global Open Society," *Atlantic Monthly,* January 1998, 20–24.

21. Instituto Brasileiro de Economia, National Census of 1991.

22. See IPEA.

23. For a discussion on the matter of science and technology as new assets for change, see Franco Ferrarotti, "The Industrial Revolution and the New Assists of Science, Technology, and Power," in Federico Mayor and Augusto Forti, eds., *Science and Power* (Paris: UNESCO, 1995), 47–69.

24. The purpose and goals of the treaty for integration between Brazil and Argentina (1988) and the Asuncion Treaty of 1991 are to create political commitments for cooperation and provide the framework for a broad spectrum of policy coordination that goes beyond the economic field. On the subject, see José A. Guilhon Albuquerque, "Mercosul: Integração Regional pós-Guerra Fria," *Política Externa* (September 1992): 112–121.

25. For an analysis of the Rio Plata Basin settlement, see Christian G. Caubet, "Diplomacia, Geopolítica e Direito na Bacia do Prata," *Política e Estratégia* II, 2 (April-June1984): 337–346.

26. See Thomaz G. Costa, "Mixing and Matching Initiatives in Arms Control in South America: The Relationship Between Threat Perception and International Inspections in the Nuclear Field for Brazil," in James Brown, ed., *New Horizons and Challenges in Arms Control and Verification* (Amsterdam: VU University Press, 1994), 235–248.

27. George Lamazière and Roberto Jaguaribe, "Beyond Confidence-Building: Brazilian-Argentine Nuclear Cooperation," in *Disarmament (UNO)* 15, 3 (1992): 102–117.

28. See an interpretation of Brazil's aspiration to hegemony in Paulo Schilling, *O Expansionismo Brasileiro* (Mexico City: El Cid Editor, 1978).

29. See Lamazière and Jaguaribe, 104–110.

30. A similar argument is presented about Europe in Timothy Garton Ash, "A Ordem Liberal Européia em Perigo," *Foreign Affairs* (Brazilian edition) 9 (April 1998): 4–9.

31. CEPAL and the World Bank.

32. Fred C. Bergsten, "Open Regionalism," *Institute for International Economics Working Papers* 3 (1997): 1–18.

33. Instituto Brasileiro de Economia (IBRE/FGV), "Estudo Comparativo mostra vantagens e desvantagens da ALCA," *Gazeta Mercantil* (23 December 1997): A-6.

34. See Felix Peña, "Triangulo natural: Mercosul, Nafta e UE," *Gazeta Mercantil Latino-Americana*, 8 September 1997, 13.

35. This opinion is posed by the Brazilian ambassador to the European Union, Jório Dauster, in "EUA temem parceria do Brasil com europeus," *O Globo*, 14 October 1997, 10.

36. Fernando Henrique Cardoso, "É tempo de ter compreensão da globalidade," *O Globo*, 15 October 1997, 4.

37. Ibid.

38. Brazil's trade with the United States is 17.8 percent (with a growth in 1997 of 1.0 percent); European Community, 27.8 percent (with annual growth of 13.1 percent); Mercosul, 17.1 percent (growth of 23.8 percent); and Asia, 14.6 percent (growth of −1.1 percent). Source: Ministério da Indústria, Comércio e Turismo, Brazil.

39. U.S. Department of Commerce.

40. Steel, orange juice, sugar, tobacco, shoes, and other Brazilian exports suffer losses of $5 billion per year due to U.S. import barriers.

41. For practical purposes, the AFTA initiative started at the first Summit of the Americas in Miami, 1994.

42. See Melvyn Levitsky, "The New Brazil: A Viable Partner for the United States," *SAIS Review* 28, 1 (Winter/ Spring 1998): 51–71.

# 5

# Political Globalization and Latin America: Toward a New Sovereignty?

*Alberto van Klaveren*

One of the hallmarks of the dawn of the twenty-first century is the increasing internationalization of the world in production, trade, investment, finance, technology, communications, culture, and politics. One major consequence of this trend is the increasing salience of the mutual penetration of economic, political, and social forces among the nations of the world.

For a long period Latin America's vulnerability to external factors was seen as a rather exceptional and pathological trait, derived from the level of underdevelopment and foreign penetration that characterized the region. Today, rising levels of global interdependence, the growing role of nonstate actors, and the emergence of public agendas with strong external components, as well as the corresponding decline in the autonomy of and the capacity for control by the nation-state, are normal in the everyday economic and political life of many countries.

The emergence of new and, in many cases, still incipient international regimes has had a direct impact on the countries of the region. The nature of this impact has varied from area to area. Latin America forms a regional subsystem within the global system; its component states share a sense of regional identity, and are perceived as such by external actors.[1] Accordingly, globalization has tended to assume some common traits in the region, also triggering common responses. According to some authors, new forms of regionalism are emerging as political responses to the market-driven process of globalization and the resulting social reactions.[2]

Global interdependence has not been confined to economics. Many countries are witnessing the emergence of "intermestic" issues, consisting of both international and national components and involving both foreign and domestic actors and decisionmaking processes. These issues are occupying an increasingly important role in the new agendas of both external and local actors in the region. They reflect emerging values and inevitably lead to the revision of traditional notions of sovereignty. They also open up new prospects for international cooperation, but can also be new sources of friction.

In the new export-oriented strategies initiated by most Latin American countries, external links are decisive. The region's trade, investment, and financial interdependence with the major economies of the world continues to increase rapidly. Interdependence is often unbalanced and asymmetrical for Latin America, but it is an inescapable reality. The region's economic progress is strongly conditioned by developments in its main trading and investment partners.

As Latin America deepened its international links, it also shifted from authoritarianism to democracy at an impressive pace. Between the mid-1970s and the early 1990s, Latin America moved broadly from authoritarianism of different kinds toward democratic politics (of all the countries in the region in 1976, elected civilian governments ruled only in Costa Rica, Colombia, and Venezuela). In stark contrast to previous decades, Latin America entered the 1990s with almost all its countries governed by civilian leaders chosen in freely contested elections.

Latin America's new democracy is uneven and fragile, and its nations are often far from perfect. Widespread corruption, drug trafficking, terrorism, human rights abuses, political party weakness, institutional backwardness, military interference and predominance, and social tensions continue to pose dangerous threats to democratic governance. The processes of democratization in the region have been somewhat disorderly, lengthy, and complicated, and in some cases there have been recurrent setbacks. But there is no denying that the past two decades have seen a considerable swing toward democratic politics in one Latin American country after another. And the commitment to democratic norms remains broader and stronger than in the past.

In spite of the relative simultaneity between the trends of increased globalization and democratization in the region, the extensive literature on Latin America's democratization has devoted little attention to the links between them. Although the concepts of *dependencia* and "hegemony" long pervaded (almost obsessively) the analysis of almost every aspect of Latin American economic, social, and political development, the impact of external factors on democratic development in the region has not been emphasized. And although a very influential school of thought stressed in the 1970s the strong affinity between the deepening of transnational capitalism and authoritarianism in the region, paradoxically no comparable theoretical effort was developed to explain why quite the contrary took place.[3]

This chapter concentrates on the influence of external factors in the democratic governance in Latin America. Specifically, it suggests some links between the globalization of Latin American economies, polities, and societies and the democratization processes in the region. Although some reference is made to the impact of external factors on transitions to democracy, the emphasis of the chapter is on the effects of globalization on democratic governance in Latin America today. We attempt to determine how the democratic "minimums" already attained have been expanded or restricted by global trends. Finally, the chapter refers to the challenges that political globalization pose to Latin American foreign policies.

Globalization here is considered as a multidimensional process in which the constraints of geography on the economies, polities, and societies of the world gradually recede. According to Roland Robertson, the concept refers "both to the compression of the world and the intensification of consciousness of the world as a whole."[4] It involves the relativization of individual and national reference points to general and supranational ones. Viewed from a domestic perspective, globalization means that external factors, not necessarily localized in one specific center, exert a growing influence on economic, political, and cultural exchanges within countries. It is important to stress that globalization does not mean that the world is becoming a more integrated or harmonious place, but merely that it is a more unified and systematic entity. While events in any part of the world will increasingly have consequences for, or be contrasted to, events in other parts, this relation may not always be positive. Indeed, the world may be riven by conflicts that are far more intractable than the previous disputes between nations. Some of these conflicts may even emerge as a rejection to globalization.

From a different theoretical perspective, Anthony Giddens points to a similar definition:

> Globalisation can thus be defined as the intensification of worldwide social relations which link distant localities in such a way that local happenings are shaped by events occurring many miles away and vice versa. This is a dialectical process because such local happenings may move in an obverse direction from the very distanciated relations that shape them.[5]

Globalization theorists emphasize the increased interdependence and interconnectedness between the constituent economic units of formerly separate societies. In their view, intersocietal exchanges of management, capital, components, finance, labor, and commodities are increasing relative to intrasocietal exchanges.[6] Although traditional political science has been rather reluctant in dealing with these phenomena, the state and the political system too are affected by globalization, and political activity increasingly has external points of reference.

Indeed globalization has had an important impact on Latin American politics. National and even local rhetoric still pervades political discourse, but the main economic, social, and political issues tend to be strikingly similar in most countries. What is more important, the solutions are also analogous. Political actors in the region may not be global players but they are connecting themselves ever more to the broader world. They use foreign ideas; they apply external formulas; they establish transborder alliances with their counterparts in other countries; they engage in regional rather than strictly national political processes; and they respond, either positively or negatively, to foreign stimuli.

International relations theory has gone through many changes as it has adapted to transformations in the shape of international politics. One of the most significant changes has consisted in the shift from an exclusively state-centric focus to one that encompasses relations between economies and cultures. A leading theorist of emerging global interdependence stresses the existence of an increasingly bifurcated international system, consisting of intergovernmental relations that are supplemented by relations between nongovernmental individuals and groups.[7]

This bifurcation has also been evident in the field of democratization. At the level of the state, Latin American governments and their main partners in the Western world have taken an increased interest in the main internal political issues affecting other countries, and they have developed new forms of international cooperation in this sensitive area. These demonstrations of interest have not always been welcome but, despite recurrent public protestations in the affected countries, they now constitute a fact of daily political life.

## External Factors and Democratization

Latin America's governments and its main political forces have traditionally stressed their strong political and cultural affinities with the United States and European countries. Added to the region's traditional belonging to the U.S. and, to a lesser extent, European spheres of influence, this aspiration has laid the basis for an active policy of promotion of democracy and human rights in the region. In fact, Latin America has become the only effective testing ground for international democratic activism in the developing world.[8]

While increasing their political relations with Europe and the United States, Latin American countries have also strengthened intraregional cooperation in democratization. One of the most salient tendencies of the 1980s in the region was the emergence of regional political cooperation among its countries. The Contadora Group and its Support Group played a pioneering role in the Central American peace process. Subsequently, the Central American states initiated the Esquipulas process, which contributed decisively to the pacification of the isthmus and which also played a significant role in the promotion of democracy in some of its countries. In 1987 eight Latin American countries established a mechanism for regional political cooperation, known as the Rio Group. The group, which now includes thirteen permanent member countries from South America and Mexico plus two observer countries from Central America and the Caribbean Community, explicitly stated the defense of democracy as one of its main aims.

Promotion of democracy has become a central element in the external policies of a variety of governmental and nongovernmental actors in Europe and the United States, contributing to the creation of a favorable international context for global democratization.

Under successive administrations of both political parties, the U.S. government since the mid-1970s has frequently expressed its support for Latin America's democratization. Presidents Carter, Reagan, Bush, and Clinton have all stated explicitly that the promotion of democracy is a central aim of U.S. policy in the Western Hemisphere. Washington has employed various instruments to push for what U.S. officials have regarded as movement toward democracy in countries as different as Chile and Haiti, Panama and Nicaragua, Mexico and Paraguay. Although there is no absolute consensus about the effectiveness and consistency of U.S. policy, there is broad bipartisan agreement in Washington that fostering democracy in Latin America and the rest of the world is a legitimate and significant element of U.S. foreign policy, and that the United States can play an effective role in pursuing this aim.

Since the 1970s, a vast array of European governmental and nongovernmental actors started to show increasing concern for democratic progress in Latin America, denouncing gross human rights violations, distancing themselves from authoritarian regimes in such countries as Chile and Argentina, supporting democratic political parties, sending aid to local NGOs, and strengthening relations with the new democratic governments that began to emerge in the region.[9] To be sure, this policy was carried out with pragmatism and due consideration for other more traditional European interests in the region, and political goodwill was not transformed automatically into economic support for new Latin American democracies. Nonetheless, it marked a significant change in European attitudes toward political development in the region, and, more important, it enabled Europe to play a valuable role in Latin America's struggle for democracy.

Originally European-dominated political internationals also adopted active policies toward the region, supporting their Latin American members, recruiting new affiliates, and getting involved in the major external and internal issues affecting the region.

The governments of the United States and of the main European countries, as well as the institutions of the European Union (EU), have used a variety of means—political, economic, diplomatic, and military—to promote democratization in the region. As Samuel Huntington has illustrated in the case of the United States, these means have included declaratory diplomacy by high officials endorsing democratization and condemning authoritarianism; public certification of human rights records in specific countries; economic pressures and sanctions, including prohibitions or limitations on official assistance, trade, and investment; suspension of military aid; negative votes or abstentions with respect to loans by multilateral financial institutions; diplomatic action, including promotion of democratization by activist U.S. and European ambassadors; material support for democratic forces; military action, including the U.S. invasions of Grenada in 1983 and Panama in 1989, and the United Nations–sponsored invasion of Haiti in 1994; and multilateral diplomacy, aimed at mobilizing opposition by the United Nations and its specialized agencies or the Organization of American States (OAS) against notorious human rights violations or mustering multilateral support for democratic reconstruction in Central America or institution building in Haiti.[10]

Many of these government actions have been activated, supported, or complemented by a myriad of European and U.S. NGOs, including political parties and foundations, religious institutions, labor unions, pressure groups, special lobbies, and academics, which got heavily involved in the promotion of human rights and democracy in Latin America. The NGOs articulated and channeled public opinion in their home countries, mobilized political and financial support for their cause, employed their international connections, and established horizontal links with their counterparts in Latin America.

To what extent did these government and nongovernment actions help democratization in Latin America? Most studies correctly underline the

primary importance of internal forces in determining the course and outcome of processes of transition to democracy in the region and elsewhere.[11] However, it is also true that international factors can provide a
supportive context or a nonsupportive one for domestic processes. For
cases in which internal prospects for democracy seem finely balanced,
such factors can tip the outcome in one way or another and in certain situations can even be crucial variables.

The impact of international efforts in favor of democracy in Latin
America obviously has varied from country to country, and it would be an
impossible intellectual task to evaluate precisely the impact in even one
country. However, there is little doubt that external factors have influenced the democratic outcome in specific political situations in Latin
America. As Giuseppe di Palma notes, democracy does not occur in an
international vacuum.[12] Larry Diamond and Juan Linz assert that international factors have had an impact, and sometimes a crucial one, in different Latin American countries.[13] Although there are some examples of
the very direct effect of external factors in favor of democratization—
Dominican Republic (1978), El Salvador (1980), Honduras (1983),
Bolivia (1984), Haiti (1991–1994), Guatemala (1993), and Paraguay
(1996)—the indirect impact of external factors may well be more important in Latin American prospects for democratic governance. As transitions to democracy in such countries as Chile, Paraguay, or Uruguay
demonstrate, international involvement in human rights abuses, external
support for local NGOs and social movements, solidarity with local political parties (which pushed the process of democratization and prepared for
post-authoritarian government), and the power of a wide range of foreign
ideas can make a very important contribution to democratization. External
considerations also played an influential role in persuading the authoritarian elites of the region to introduce democratic reforms and adopt political regimes capable of achieving international legitimization, which were
seen as necessary complements to a market-oriented economy.

External factors can exert powerful influence on internal political
processes by means of a demonstration or snowballing effect.[14] Successful
democratization in one country can encourage democratization in other
countries, especially in a context of geographical or/and cultural proximity, either because the countries face similar realities or because the country
that has democratized is powerful or is viewed as a cultural and political
model. Transition to democracy in one country demonstrates to leaders and
groups in one society the ability of leaders and groups in another society to
bring about the end of an authoritarian system. Democratization in other
countries implies interesting learning processes for the later democratizers.

(Conversely, a successful coup in one country can encourage similar attempts elsewhere: internal violence caused by authoritarian relapses can have negative repercussions in neighboring states.) The tremendous expansion in global communications, the existence of direct links between civil societies of like-minded countries, and global interdependence are increasing the relevance of these demonstration effects.

The Argentine democratization, which was precipitated by a defeat in a foreign war, encouraged democratization in neighboring countries. Democratization in its large neighbor made the restoration of democracy in Uruguay largely inevitable. Bolivia's remarkable path to democratization has been favored not only by strong U.S. and European support but by parallel trends in its larger neighbors. With the exception of Costa Rica, democratization in Central America must be seen more as a regional process than as a succession of national cases. The new democratic wave that encompassed Latin America during the 1980s encouraged democratization in Brazil, Chile, and Paraguay—and earlier democratization in Spain was immensely relevant and influential in Latin America.[15] Even in Mexico, with its long tradition of nationalism and its invariable adherence to the principle of nonintervention, a growing number of domestic actors are using foreign examples and resorting to foreign lobbies to demand political reforms.

The regional rather than strictly national orientation of democratization is reinforced by the link established between regional integration and democratization in Latin America. Transitions to democracy have coincided with, and have been at least in part responsible for, the quest for integration. New subregional integration schemes such as Mercosur and the Central American Integration System are based on the assumption that membership is restricted to democratic governments and that, as in the European case, integration can be seen as a guarantee against coups d'état. The Rio Group was conceived as a club of democratic countries for the defense and promotion of democracy, and, accordingly, it has suspended from its meetings those member governments that have experienced authoritarian relapses.

It would be erroneous to exaggerate the relevance of any individual external factors on democratization in Latin America. Excepting the cases of some small and highly vulnerable countries in Central America and the Caribbean, external factors are usually of secondary or tertiary importance in determining democratic outcomes in Latin America. But the aggregate and cumulative impact of international factors must not be underestimated. Authoritarian relapses are likely to be met by strong international rejection, which can include diplomatic isolation and, more important, economic sanctions. Such diverse countries as Guatemala, Venezuela, the Dominican Republic, Ecuador, or Paraguay have experienced grave and threatening political crises in recent times. Actual or potential international rejection has played a very important role in aborting authoritarian outcomes to these crises. In some cases, the argument can even be made that it was external rather than internal opposition that tipped the balance in favor of democratic continuity.

## International Regimes and Democratic Governance

With the end of the Cold War has come a worldwide validation of human rights, free elections, and democratic politics. This is evident from the former Soviet Union to the Republic of Korea, from Central America to South Africa. To be sure, the international rhetoric about democracy and human rights has frequently masked indifference, tolerance, or even complicity toward less appealing practices. However, there can be little doubt that human rights and democracy have become major issues in international relations, and that they have been placed on the world's agenda.

It can even be argued that a new international regime—that is, an arrangement containing explicit and implicit rules, norms, principles, and decisionmaking procedures applicable to a certain issue area—is emerging for the defense and promotion of democracy in the world.[16] Just as states have been involved in the establishment of universal practices and norms in, for example, the regulation of international trade, the administration and exploitation of the seas, and the uses of nuclear power, so too a new regime is emerging in an area that in much of the world was reserved to exclusive internal jurisdiction. Three general observations must be made in this regard.

First, we are dealing with an emerging regime, a still incipient and nascent set of rules and practices, which have not been defined in very precise terms. This regime is very far from being codified, is characterized by a rather weak implementation, and is subject to many reservations on the part of a relatively large number of individual states, especially in the former third world. The incipience of this regime tends to leave ample room for unilateral behavior by the main actors in the international system and for discrimination with respect to the countries subject to these policies.

Second, this international regime has important regional variants, which can even be identified as regional regimes. The most developed regime in this regard is undoubtedly that of Europe, which possesses a rather effective and enforceable system for the protection of human rights, and where the existence of a democratic political system is a basic pre-condition for accession to the European Union, with all its corresponding economic and political incentives. Although the Americas have not yet built a similarly effective regional regime in this area, serious efforts are being made in a similar direction, as we will see below. In contrast, the whole notion of a universal regime applicable to human rights and democracy is rejected by a large number of Asian and African countries: governments and politicians of many countries of the former third world invoke the relativity of human rights or special political, cultural, or economic conditions to justify singular interpretations in this area. The old argument, so dear to communist regimes, in favor of the primacy of economic and social rights over public or personal freedoms retains its popularity in such important countries as the People's Republic of China, North Korea or, for that matter, Cuba. Some Asian and African leaders tend to denounce the universalization of human rights and democracy as a cultural imposition by the Western world.

Third, official declarations and international instruments in favor of human rights and democracy do not always coincide with observable international behavior. As a leading expert on inter-American relations recalls, from the turn of the century until the 1980s, "the overall impact of U.S. policy on Latin America's ability to achieve democratic politics was usually negligible, often counterproductive, and only occasionally positive."[17] European interest in the Latin American democratization processes is rather recent, and has been pursued with pragmatism and due consideration for other more traditional European interests in the region, such as the promotion of trade, investments, and arms sales. Measures taken by the OAS in the name of democracy have a long but rather inconsistent and not always presentable history. A long list of Latin American dictatorial regimes without any remorse subscribed to many pious declarations in favor of democracy and human rights in the region (in the company of recognized democratic regimes that did not object to this rather awkward association). Nevertheless, the gulf between rhetoric and practice seems to be narrowing in all cases.

In the past, international action in the area of human rights and democracy was limited by a rigid and strict interpretation of the principles of non-intervention and sovereignty, which were generally regarded by the smaller and weaker states as safeguards against interference and pressure by the hegemonic powers. Although almost no government or political leader in the world is willing to renounce these principles, their interpretation has tended to vary substantially during the last decades. International practice increasingly recognizes that international preoccupation or even action in favor of democracy in the world can be an acceptable and legitimate practice in certain circumstances. The evaluation of these circumstances is open to interpretation by political actors and is, in the end, a political decision—but the twin principles of sovereignty and nonintervention have ceased to represent inviolable barriers. This evolution has been facilitated by the essentially dynamic and changing nature of international law, which has never constituted a rigid and unmovable legal order.

Extreme failures of governance are beginning to be treated under the notion of "failed states." This concept is coined by the international community to identify disintegrating or disintegrated societies, characterized by the absence of effective government and minimal standards of political order and economic policy. Somalia, Ruanda, Burundi, and Haiti provide examples of these extreme cases. Paradoxically, representative political elites in those countries have not only requested international armed intervention, but have also pleaded for its prolongation beyond the original mandate.

Democratic government has been a goal of the peoples of the Americas almost since the time of their independence. The principle of democratic governance has been recognized and formalized in numerous regional conference and instruments. But it has not been until the present wave of democratization in the region that this principle has laid the basis for an incipient international regime, supported by a growing number of governmental and nongovernmental actors, including a large number of Latin American countries, their main international partners in the world, the most relevant international organizations, and, last but not least, a growing number of political parties, social movements, and NGOs.

In recent years, the member states of the OAS have taken important steps to foster hemispheric action on behalf of democracy. The OAS General Assembly approved in June 1991 the Santiago Commitment and its associate resolutions on democracy. These documents mandated an immediate meeting of the OAS Permanent Council following the rupture of democratic rule in any country of the Americas, and the adoption of "efficacious, timely, and expeditious procedures to ensure the promotion and the defense of democracy." The Santiago resolutions were pathbreaking in two ways: first, they obligated hemispheric governments to take action against violations of the democratic order anywhere in the region; second, such action was to be triggered solely by events within a country, regardless of international repercussions.[18] The Rio Group, acting as an informal mechanism for political dialogue, consultation, and consensus seeking, has followed a similar path, promoting the principle of democratic legitimacy as a main criterion for international legitimacy in Latin America.[19] According to some authors, these developments constitute a major step toward the emergence of a "right to democratic governance" in the Western Hemisphere.[20] Thus, the principle of democratic government has evolved from a moral commitment to a juridical obligation for the OAS member states.

Certainly, the gap between rhetoric and practice has not been fully bridged in the Americas or, for that matter, elsewhere in the world. It is obvious that not all Latin American states share this new notion. Rather, a significant group of governments prefer, for understandable reasons, to cling to the traditional principle of nonintervention. The case of Cuba is the most obvious in this respect. However, representatives of Mexico, Peru, and Colombia have strongly held to this position, although they have shown an increasing degree of sensitivity and responsiveness to international concern about their internal situations. The peculiarities of political development in these countries explain their reluctance to open up their democratic practices to foreign scrutiny. And the diplomacy of Brazil, a country that seems less vulnerable in this respect, has also shown reservations about international action in favor of democracy.

However, beyond these differences, all Latin American countries are showing an increasing concern for the international legitimacy of their political regimes. Latin America's relatively mild reaction against the U.S. invasion of Panama in 1989 must be seen in this context. There is little doubt that U.S. unilateral military intervention represented a gross violation of a principle of international law. However, the fact that the corrupt regime it removed in Panama lacked any form of international legitimacy made of this episode a rather minor question in U.S.–Latin American relations. In fact, the Rio Group opted not to take sides in the conflict between Panama's dictatorship and the United States and, more importantly, used the case to establish the precedent that democracy is an essential requirement for participation in the Rio Group. Although the threat of international disapproval had little effect on members of the Haitian military who in 1991 deposed the country's first democratically elected president, 4 years later they were finally forced to return President Aristide to power by a formidable international coalition that included the United Nations, the OAS, the United States, and many Latin American and European countries. Significantly, unlike the Panamanian case, Haiti was occupied under a UN mandate.

Similarly, after shutting down the Peruvian congress and the judicial system in April 1992, President Fujimori of Peru responded to demands by the OAS (as well as to general international condemnation) that the democratic process be respected. He formally committed himself to a gradual restoration of democratic procedures, which included elections for a new congress and a constituent assembly, acceptance of OAS monitoring of that election, and agreement to a human rights investigation in his country. In a less dramatic but equally interesting political context, the Mexican government developed a campaign to make its political reforms known abroad, and accepted for the first time the presence of foreign observers in its 1994 presidential elections. Moreover, it does not require a very sophisticated analysis to establish a direct link between Mexican political reforms and the negotiation of the North American Free Trade Agreement (NAFTA). In the Dominican Republic, the Balaguer government opened negotiations with the opposition to prevent imminent international delegitimization after the controversial 1994 elections. International legitimacy has been a fundamental consideration in the slow democratization of Central America. Economic support provided by the international community, represented mainly by the countries of the Americas, Europe, and Japan, to the peace process in the isthmus remains closely associated with the maintenance of democracy.

The new and still incipient international regime for the promotion of democracy has given rise to a new pattern of international electoral monitoring. For James Rosenau and Michael Fagen, internationally monitored elections are not simply instances of local political systems choosing their leaderships, but must be also seen as instances "of global politics, of the international community crossing sovereign boundaries to participate in the internal affairs of states."[21] Although this form of international action represents a mild, unspectacular, and nonauthoritarian expression of this regime, it is a significant indicator of the growing internationalization of domestic politics. In fact, the United Nations and the OAS have monitored a string of elections in such troubled Latin American settings as Haiti, El Salvador, Guatemala, Suriname, Paraguay, and Guatemala—in each case helping to produce a set of results that were generally accepted as fair and legitimate. Even in larger countries of the region such as Chile, Mexico, or Peru, international observers, often acting on the invitation of the host governments and in a strictly personal capacity, perform a new legitimating role in local elections, which has certainly not been foreseen in traditional texts of constitutional law or political science.

International action to foster democracy has its own operational dilemmas. How far can the international community go in defending democracy? How do we reconcile the defense of democracy with the principle of non-intervention? How does the international community define a democracy? How do governments reconcile different policy interests in this regard? How can double standards be avoided in this field?

There are no easy answers to these questions. The same legal instruments that create international obligations in the areas of human rights and support for democracy flatly bar any interference in the domestic affairs of member states. National sovereignty retains its force as one of the great political principles of our times, not only in Latin America but in such countries as the United States or France. Heraldo Muñoz's argument that international action against a government that denies its own citizens popular sovereignty cannot possibly violate the sovereignty of that country is undoubtedly attractive, but the argument has its risks and is open to rather subjective interpretations.[22] Be that as it may, although international action in favor of democracy is still controversial, it seems clear that it is no longer subordinate to or conditioned by the principle of non-intervention. The relationship between both principles is not immutable, and intervention in favor of democracy under certain conditions is already a political reality. It is important to add that the international action that starts to become legitimate in this respect assumes a multilateral character and, in consequence, requires abiding by norms and procedures established for this purpose by global and regional international organizations, as well as by significant international consensus. Precisely these considerations allow the establishment of a clear contrast between unilateral interventionism practiced by the United States in Latin America during a very long period and the United States–led but multilaterally sanctioned intervention in Haiti in 1994. For the same reason, United Nations–sponsored international action or collective action backed by North American, Latin American, European, and even Asian democracies will always be more legitimate than unilateral action from without.

Another dilemma has to do with the concept of democracy that is at the base of this new international or regional activism to foster democracy. I am not referring to the worn-out debate about the value of "formal" democracy, which had such a negative impact in the analysis of Latin American politics, and which in practice served to defend and justify authoritarian regimes of very different persuasions during the 1960s and the 1970s. Rather, the question has to do with the kind of democracy that deserves international support. Several Latin American governments chosen in reasonably free elections tolerate or are forced to tolerate systematic human rights violations in their territories. In some extreme cases, democratically elected governments in the region have been involved in practices of state terrorism. Normally, international instruments for the defense and promotion of democracy have not been applied to these cases. A case could even arise in which a regime guilty of state terrorism, and that feels threatened by internal rebellion, may request the application of these instruments in its favor. International action can also contribute to the legitimization of regimes that, to put it mildly, are not model democracies. According to several critics, including the renowned Peruvian novelist Mario Vargas Llosa, OAS action against Fujimori's *autogolpe* not only failed in its obligation to promote and defend democracy in Peru, but also contributed to the legitimization of some sort of plebiscitary regime in the country. [23]

The Peruvian case also illustrates the difficulty in reconciling different and sometimes contradictory international goals. The objective of promoting democracy cannot be evaluated in isolation from other international interests. As Richard Bloomfield remarks, "None of the principal (external) actors felt that squeezing Peru further on the constitutional question was worth the risk of a further deterioration in the country's internal situation, already desperate in the face of increasing gains by the guerrilla movement *Sendero Luminoso* and the decline of confidence in public institutions."[24]

A similar problem is posed by the question of double standards. Is the emerging regime for the promotion of democracy to be applied to all countries? Or is it a regime that will only be applied when it does not contradict other foreign policy or economic interests? Is the regime applicable to all countries, regardless of their size and regional weight, or it is restricted to smaller and weaker countries, thus questioning the principle of equality of states?

There are no clear answers to the previous questions. Any serious pretension to consolidating a working international regime in the field of democracy and human rights has to address them.

## Globalization and the
## Relativization of Sovereignty

One of the key features of the system of international relations set up by the new nation-states of the nineteenth century was the principle of sovereignty. According to this principle, the state had the absolute right to determine autonomously its own fate for which it set the political arrangements. Under this principle, interference by one state in the internal affairs of another was deemed contrary to international law and the comity of nations. However, increasing globalization is making this principle relative. The existence of worldwide problems, such as the protection of the environment or drug trafficking, have led to the expectation, at a minimum, that national policies must address the common problems of the planet. However, globalization is leading to even more radical developments.

The notion that individual human beings have rights *qua* humans that can be sustained against the sovereignty of the state in which they live represents a radical departure from the nineteenth-century principle of state sovereignty. A wide variety of international conventions, statutes, and declarations are concerned with universal human rights. These normally involve the condemnation of torture; freedom of speech and action; freedom of political association and participation; due process under law; minimum access to health, education, and material welfare; and control of one's own body, especially in reproductive rights. States frequently violate these principles because the conventions offer no means of collective enforcement. However, regional regimes in this area are gradually increasing their effectiveness, the European system being undoubtedly the most advanced to the extent that it allows individual citizens to initiate proceedings against their own governments. Human rights have also been promoted in the Americas. The American Convention on Human Rights, which came into force in 1978, has both a commission and a court, which have been instrumental in improving member governments' observance of human rights, although the system is far from perfect.

But the internationalization of human rights not only has a legal connotation, but has also led to new forms of political enforcement. Extreme and extensive human right violations often meet with widespread global condemnation and frequently with multilateral or bilateral political action. Among the more notable examples are the patchy (though ultimately effective) economic, political, and cultural sanctions against the racist regimes of the former Rhodesia and of South Africa. In Latin America, the case of Chile became a watershed event in the struggle for human rights. Although many other Latin American countries had suffered comparable or even worse levels of repression—not to mention of nations in the Soviet bloc, Africa, or Asia—very few attracted so much attention from the human rights movement as did Chile.

Concern about environmental protection is also leading to the reduction of the sovereignty of states relative to international arrangements. In fact, certain sectors of the planet's environment have been relocated outside the territorial sovereignty of nation-states, being redefined as "global commons."[25] They include, to varying degrees and with varying levels of enforcement, the high seas, seabed fisheries, marine mammals, satellite orbits, the airwaves, the atmosphere, and the Antarctic.

In an increasingly complex and interdependent world, the negotiation, adoption, and implementation of new international regimes are major elements in the foreign policy activity of every state. Globalization requires new multilateral regulatory agreements, addressing very complex economic, political, and social problems that demand cooperative action among states over time. These cooperative efforts take place within a dense and complex web of norms, rules, and practices.

Globalization is also leading to the emergence of new global and domestic actors. A complex world of diverse, relatively autonomous actors has emerged, characterized by their own structures, processes, and decisionmaking rules. These sovereignty-free actors consist of multinational corporations, political parties, transnational organizations, ethnic minorities, religious groups, and the like. Individually, and sometimes jointly, they compete, conflict, cooperate, or otherwise interact with the sovereignty-bound actors of the Westphalian state-centric world.[26] Such sovereignty-free actors as Amnesty International and Greenpeace are able to deploy more resources and have more effective access to world and national public opinion than most national governments.

The action of sovereignty-free actors has been especially evident in Latin America. However, Latin America's incorporation into an increasingly global political culture does not mean its full adhesion to a new political order or to a monolothic ideology. This globalized political culture is chaotic rather than orderly; it is not unified or centralized but connected so that the meanings of its components can be "relativized."[27]

Globalization is, in general, a differentiating as well as a homogenizing process. Insofar as globalization is based on Western modernity, it introduces possibilities for new identities for cultures or groups in the periphery. In Latin America, this has been especially evident in the case of ecological movements, which have followed very closely the model of similar forces in the developed world, and which have enjoyed an unprecedented degree of external political and financial support. Globalization also brings the periphery to the center. It pluralizes the world by recognizing the value of cultural differences and local preferences. In the wake of globalization, many important ethnic movements in countries such as Mexico, Brazil, Ecuador, or Chile have revived very old struggles or have initiated fully new campaigns for the recognition of their rights, often finding more sympathy and support for their cause abroad than in their own countries. Ironically, what is very often viewed as an indigenous reaction to globalization is one of its by-products.

Gender became a political issue in Latin America only after globalization gave impulse to the diffusion of emancipatory ideas, and after the first international meetings on the subject started to propose policies and goals for reducing women's discrimination.

Although hardly new on the regional scene, transnational organizations have become much more numerous and prominent as interdependence has increased and as technology has made it easier for people and institutions to convene and communicate across great distances. With the increase in global interdependence, the number of political instruments available to individual governments and the effectiveness of particular instruments show a marked tendency toward decline.[28] This tendency occurs because of the loss of a wide range of border controls—whether formal or informal—that served to restrict transactions in goods and services, technology, ideas, and cultural interchange. The result is a decrease in the efficacy of policy instruments that enable the state to control activities within and across its borders. States can experience a further diminution in their ability to control their polities because of the expansion in transnational forces and interactions that reduce and restrict the influence particular governments can exercise over the activities of their citizens.

In the context of a highly interdependent global order, many of the traditional domains of state activity and responsibility in Latin America cannot be fulfilled without resorting to international forms of collaboration. As demands on the state tend to increase, it is confronted with a whole series of policy problems that cannot be adequately resolved without cooperating with other states and nonstate actors.[29] Individual states are no longer the only appropriate political units for resolving key policy problems.

States have had to increase the level of cooperation with other states, either in regional or in multilateral institutions. The result has been a vast growth of organizations and regimes, entities that are laying the basis for the management of global affairs. Paradoxically, the international interdependence that has diminished the state's scope and authority in domestic affairs has also been a source of its widening international competence in such affairs. Transnational actors and forces have greatly increased the vulnerability of domestic societies and polities to external influences. But at the same time, states have been forced to develop institutions and adopt policies that increase their ability to intervene in the international flow of goods, services, finance, and persons in order to cope minimally with the internationalization of these areas. Since states' vulnerability to global events and processes seems likely to increase in the future, the formal or informal controls exercised at the global or regional level appear destined to undergo a corresponding expansion.

However, while there has been rapid expansion of intergovernmental and transnational links, the age of the nation-state is by no means exhausted. The territorial nation-state has suffered a decline, but the importance of nationalism and territorial independence and the desire to establish, regain, or maintain sovereignty does not seem to have diminished in recent times. Some of the world's most seemingly intractable regional crises do not escape the pull of sovereignty.

Another clear testimony of the durability of the states system is the reluctance of states to submit their disputes with other states to arbitration by any superior authority. Most countries have not accepted compulsory jurisdiction before the International Court of Justice. Only in Europe is there a clear process of cession of sovereignty to regional institutions. In the rest of the world, including Latin America and of course the United States, the principle of territorial sovereignty in interstate affairs, which was established after the Peace of Westphalia in 1648, continues to dominate.

In sum, globalization is reshaping politics, economics, and social life, but the nation-state continues to command loyalty, both as an idea and as an institution. States still pretend to express and realize their sovereignty through independent action to achieve their goals. But in an interdependent world, only the "largest and most powerful states can sometimes get their way through sheer exertion of will, but even they cannot achieve their principal purposes—security, economic well-being, and a decent level of amenity for their citizens—without the help and cooperation of many other participants in the system, including entities that are not states at all."[30]

## Concluding Remarks Around a Test Case

Setting forth the external influences that are at play in Latin America does not imply that the current scene is exclusively one of full political globalization. There can be little doubt that powerful and transforming dynamics are unfolding on a global scale, but it is equally clear that these dynamics are conceived as existing in continuous tension with a wide array of static forces that press for continuity. National political cultures, the imperatives of geographic circumstance, the constraints of historical experience, the attachment to territories, and the inertia of organizations are still very much features of the Latin American political arena, and they interact with global change in such a way that outcomes vary across time and place. But in acknowledging the elements of continuity, one cannot deny the enormous changes that are under way on a global scale and the increasing impact they have on Latin America.

There is a breach between the objective circumstances that render systems dependent on each other and the subjective interpretation of these circumstances. Cultural traditions, national pride, and many other sociopsychological dynamics can lead to a discrepancy between the way interdependence is assessed by leaders and publics and the way in which its objective foundations are evaluated.

The relativization of national sovereignty unleashes different and contradictory processes. On the one hand, it means increasingly unchecked power in the hands of international and domestic economic and political actors. On the other, it implies the removal of political, economic, and cultural barriers to the emergence of actors and issues that had been repressed.

These tensions have been demonstrated by the detention in London of the former Chilean dictator, Augusto Pinochet, following an extradition request by a maverick Spanish judge, who wished to prosecute him for the crimes of genocide, torture, terrorism, and conspiracy. Despite the protest of the democratic Chilean government, founded on juridical and political arguments, Pinochet has been subjected to a complex judicial process in the United Kingdom to resolve his immunity from accusation as a former head of state, and to determine whether the alleged crimes for which he is prosecuted are grounds for his extradition.

The trial of General Pinochet in London and Madrid has been presented as a watershed case in the globalization of justice. According to this view, individuals are now able to enforce their most fundamental rights against states and state officials before any court in the world.[31] This is by virtue of the principle of universal jurisdiction, which postulates the right of any state to prosecute an individual believed to be responsible for particularly serious crimes, such as torture, under international law.

The idea of universal accountability and responsibility may be deemed very applicable to a small country like Chile. The fact that opinion polls in that country demonstrated a majority of the Chileans favoring a trial in their own country did not seem very relevant to European public opinion.[32] Yet, the general's trial has raised complex legal, ethical, and political issues. From a legal standpoint, it has been disputed whether Pinochet has immunity as a former head of state and, in the absence of an international criminal court, whether it is legitimate for the court of one country to prosecute an individual from another. It is true that the Chilean transition to democracy has been short on justice with respect to the gross human right violations that had occurred in that country. However, Spain, the very country that demanded Pinochet's extradition from Great Britain, has not prosecuted any human rights violation that occurred in its own territory during the long Franco dictatorship. Spanish judges object to a Chilean amnesty law, which was passed in 1978, but have upheld the Spanish amnesty law of 1977.

Ethically, the claims are also mixed. On the one hand, it seems obvious that gross human right violations should not go unpunished. On the other, there is an obvious double standard in prosecuting one former head of state when others responsible for similar crimes remain unpunished and are even received and courted by European and other democratic leaders.[33] Contradictions abound. With an interval of only a few weeks, the French government enthusiastically supported Pinochet's prosecution and welcomed to Paris President Laurent Kabila of the Democratic Republic of Congo, as well as other less-than-presentable African dictators. European governments have shown enormous restraint in prosecuting past human rights violators in Eastern and Central Europe or the former Soviet Union, and have never intended to bring to court a current or former leader of China or any other important Asian country.

Highly politicized human rights trials can have a negative impact on democratic transition processes that are based on very delicate balances between the need for justice and the need for reconciliation. Ethically, legally, and politically, a foreign court is ill-prepared to solve this dilemma. In fact, Pinochet's detention in London revived the worst aspects of polarization among Chileans and placed him back onto the center of the stage of Chile's public affairs.[34]

Democracy and popular sovereignty still reside overwhelmingly in national states. Thus, challenging decisions taken at that level lead to the question of whether there is another, more legitimate right that justifies the overturning of a sovereign choice. Even if one accepts this principle for the sake of the universality of human rights, there is the equally fundamental question of who has the right to engage in such an exercise. The globalization of justice may be a very positive development, provided that particular countries, or their judges, do not take it upon themselves to become the "Rambos" or sheriffs of the world, to quote the former socialist prime minister of Spain, Felipe González.[35] If this happens, we are confronted with a fairly typical example of unilateralism, which has less to do with globalization and much more to do with paternalistic practices that belong to a very old tradition of power politics in the world.

Pinochet's ordeal demonstrates the need for solid, carefully drafted, and nondiscriminatory regional and global human rights regimes. Where to judge human rights violators is a key issue, one that cannot be freely interpreted and adjudicated by any foreign court. The universalization of human rights is a legitimate aspiration, which should be pursued seriously. However, it is still not a reality, and the Pinochet case may very well become unique and highly symbolic, even performing some expiating function for European, and particularly Spanish, consciences.

Whatever its final implications, this case demonstrates also that in the sensitive field of justice a conflict is emerging between claims made on behalf of the state system and those made on behalf of alternative organizing principles of world order. New directions in international law are discernible, but their application is highly selective, patchy, and unilateral. What the Pinochet case highlights is the urgent need for an international criminal court, agreed on in 1998 in Rome, with the active support of a vast majority of states, including Chile.

The rapid growth of the complex interdependence between states and societies requires new institutional arrangements in international society. New global regimes are not likely to emerge quickly with fully developed clarity. Observers may herald their arrival, but such pronouncements stem less from solid analysis and more from aspirations to break with the past and justify the adoption of new policies. Hence, such observers are unlikely to appreciate the delicate and complex processes out of which new regimes emerge.

## Notes

1. G. Pope Atkins, *Latin America in the International Political System,* 2nd ed. (Boulder, Colo.: Westview Press, 1989), 23–50; and Manfred Mols, *El Marco Internacional de América Latina* (Barcelona/Caracas: Alfa, 1985), 79–81.

2. Björn Hettne, "The New Regionalism: Security and Development," in *Regional Integration and Multilateral Cooperation in the Global Economy* (The Hague: FONDAD, 1998), 201.

3. See, for instance, Guillermo O'Donnell, *Modernización y Autoritarismo* (Buenos Aires: Paidós, 1972). For a good version of the now completely outdated debate on the links between authoritarianism and capitalism in Latin America, see David Collier, ed., *The New Authoritarianism in Latin America* (Princeton, N.J.: Princeton University Press, 1979).

4. Roland Robertson, *Globalization* (London: Sage, 1992), 8.

5. Anthony Giddens, *The Consequences of Modernity* (Cambridge: Polity, 1990), 64.

6. Malcolm Waters, *Globalization* (London: Routledge, 1995), 97.

7. James N. Rosenau, *The Study of Global Interdependence* (New York: Nichols, 1980), 3.

8. See Tom Farer, ed., *Beyond Sovereignty. Collectively Defending Democracy in the Americas* (Baltimore: Johns Hopkins University Press, 1996).

9. Alberto van Klaveren, "Europa y la democratización de América Latina," *Nueva Sociedad* 85 (September-October 1986): 134–140.

10. Samuel P. Huntington, *The Third Wave. Democratization in the Late Twentieth Century* (Norman: University of Oklahoma Press, 1991), 93–94.

11. Laurence Whitehead, "International Aspects of Democratization," in Guillermo O'Donnell, Philippe C. Schmitter, and Lawrence Whitehead, eds., *Transitions from Authoritarian Rule. Comparative Perspectives* (Baltimore: Johns Hopkins University Press, 1986), 4; Abraham F. Lowenthal, "The United States and Latin American Democracy: Learning from History," in *Exporting Democracy. The United States and Latin America. Case Studies* (Baltimore: Johns Hopkins University Press, 1991), 278.

12. Giuseppe di Palma, *To Craft Democracies: An Essay on Democratic Transition* (Berkeley: University of California Press, 1990), 183.

13. Larry Diamond and Juan Linz, "Introduction: Politics, Society and Democracy in Latin America," in Larry Diamond, Seymour M. Lipset, and Juan Linz, eds., *Democracy in Developing Countries: Latin America* (Boulder, Colo.: Lynne Rienner Publishers, 1989), 48.

14. Huntington, *The Third Wave,* 100.

15. See Carlos Huneeus, "La transición a la democracia en España: experiencias para América Latina," in Francisco Orrego Vicuña, ed., *Transición a la Democracia en América Latina* (Buenos Aires: GEL, 1985), 165–182; several articles included in Carlos Huneeus, ed., *Para Vivir la Democracia: Dilemas de su Consolidación* (Santiago: Ed. Andante, 1987); and Rafael López Pintor, "Sobre el Cambio Político en España: Lecciones para Demócratas en Transición," in Enrique Baloyra et al., *Lecciones para Demócratas en Transición* (Buenos Aires: Ed. Belgrano, 1987), 143–160.

16. Stephen S. Krasner, "Structural Causes and Regime Consequences: Regimes as Intervening Variables," in *International Regimes* (Ithaca, N.Y.: Cornell University Press, 1983), 2.

17. Lowenthal 1991, 261.

18. Peter Hakim, "The OAS: Putting Principles into Practice," *Journal of Democracy* 4, 3 (July 1993): 40.

19. Alicia Frohmann, "Regional Initiatives for Peace and Democracy: The Collective Diplomacy of the Rio Group," in Carl Kaysen, Robert A. Pastor, and Laura W. Reed, eds., *Collective Responses to Regional Problems: The Case of Latin America and the Caribbean* (Cambridge, Mass.: Committee on International Security Studies, American Academy of Arts and Sciences, 1994), 135.

20. See, for instance, Thomas M. Franck, "The Emerging Right to Democratic Government," *American Journal of International Law* 86, 1 (January 1992): 46–91; and Heraldo Muñoz, "El derecho a la democracia en las Américas," *Estudios Internacionales* 28, 109 (January-March 1995), 58–82.

21. James N. Rosenau and W. Michael Fagen, "Domestic Elections as International Events," in Kaysen, Pastor, and Reed, *Collective Responses to Regional Problems: The Case of Latin America and the Caribbean,* 32.

22. Muñoz, "El derecho a la democracia en las Américas," 15.

23. See Mario Vargas Llosa's comment, included in *The Americas in 1994: A Time for Leadership* (Washington, D.C.: The Inter-American Dialogue, 1994), 24.

24. Richard J. Bloomfield, "Making the Western Hemisphere Safe for Democracy? The OAS Defense-of-Democracy Regime," in Kaysen, Pastor, and Reed, *Collective Responses to Regional Problems,* 19.

25. J. Vogler, "Regimes and the Global Commons," in A. McGrew and P. Lewis et al., *Global Politics* (Cambridge: Polity, 1992).

26. James N. Rosenau, *The United Nations in a Turbulent World* (Boulder, Colo.: Lynne Rienner Publishers, 1992), 20.

27. Waters, *Globalisation,* 126.

28. Robert O. Keohane and Joseph S. Nye, eds., *Transnational Relations and World Politics* (Cambridge, Mass.: Harvard University Press, 1972), 392–395.

29. Robert O. Keohane, *After Hegemony: Cooperation and Discord in the World Political Economy* (Princeton, N.J.: Princeton University Press, 1984).

30. Abraham Chayes and Antonia Handler Chayes, *The New Sovereignty. Compliance with International Regulatory Agreements* (Cambridge, Mass.: Harvard University Press, 1995), 27.

31. Michael Byers, "A Safer Place for All," *The World Today,* January 1999, 4–6.

32. See *Barómetro CERC,* December 1998 (Santiago: CERC, 1998), 181.

33. Alexandra Barahona de Brito, "Getting Away with Murder?" *The World Today,* December 1998, 301.

34. Ricardo Lagos and Heraldo Muñoz, "Pinochet," manuscript accepted for publication in *Foreign Policy,* 1999 (complete at the moment of publication).

35. "Felipe González advierte sobre una 'fractura social' en Chile," *El País* (Madrid), 16 December 1998.

# 6

## Foreign Policy Strategies in a Globalized World: The Case of Mexico

*Guadalupe González*

### In the Middle of the Road

New trends and developments in the post–Cold War world have drastically changed the strategic environment in which Mexican foreign policy has operated. The three most important among these are the emergence of a hybrid structure of global power, the wave of globalization,[1] and the growing importance of international institutions. By the early 1990s, Mexican policymakers made some important policy choices with long-term consequences about the kinds of broad strategies to pursue in relation to global changes. In a sharp departure from its previous inward-looking stance, Mexico chose to encourage—instead of resist—the economic globalization process by introducing a far-reaching program of market-oriented reforms, and later on, by seeking the institutionalization of a formal economic partnership with its previously "distant" big neighbor, the United States, through NAFTA.

The net immediate effect was that, for the first time in this century, market forces and political choices started to reinforce each other in expanding Mexico's rapid integration into the world economy. Between 1980 and 1998, openness of the economy, measured by the share of exports to gross domestic product (GDP), almost tripled from 11 to 31.9 percent, expanding the degree of exposure of the Mexican economy to international markets and the decisions of foreign governmental and nongovernmental actors. In 1998 total foreign trade represented 64.3 percent of Mexico's GDP. Foreign trade and capital became the main engines of economic growth,[2] particularly after the 1994–1995 financial crisis. Consequently, the country began to experience intensely some of the macroeconomic benefits and many of the social adjustment costs of economic liberalization at the same time that the processes of political liberalization and democratization accelerated.

However, as some analysts have pointed out, Mexico got stuck in the middle of the road between the third and the first world.[3] Along with the deepening of market-oriented reforms came the exacerbation of domestic income disparities and the increasing fragmentation of the economy and society. On the threshold of the twenty-first century an accurate description of Mexico is that of an open economy with sharp social inequalities and a liberalizing political community with fragile institutions for democratic stability and governance. Hence, in terms of Soesastro's analytical framework,[4] the main challenge confronting Mexico in the next decade is how to move quickly into a second-order adjustment phase to globalization that entails coping with domestic changes that had come as a consequence of the first-order adjustment process of opening up. From this perspective, the time might be ripe for revising and moving beyond the 1980s and 1990s neoliberal strategic thinking.

This chapter examines Mexico's ongoing process of adaptation to the changing international conditions in the post–Cold War period, from the first-order adjustment programs of economic liberalization to the second-order adjustment strategies for social development and democratic governance. I argue that Mexico's efforts to adapt to the process of globalization of the world economy, and the transformation of the international system after the end of the Cold War, have followed an uneven, disjointed, and contradictory pattern. While Mexican political leaders quickly accepted the consequences of economic globalization by actively undertaking a policy favorable to regional integration and open markets, they have been reluctant to adapt to the security and political demands posed by the post–Cold War international environment.[5] Mexico's partial adaptation can be explained by the different pace of the rapid economic reform on one hand, and the gradual and slow opening of the postrevolutionary political regime on the other. The uneven character of Mexico's liberalization process over the last two decades led political leaders to try to achieve two incompatible goals: the full integration of the country to the international economy, and the isolation of the domestic political arena from external pressures. In particular, I will address the following four questions:

1.  How have the profound changes in the economic and political international environment affected Mexico's strategic options and overall bargaining power? Specifically, I will focus on the effects of two major trends: the wave of globalization in the internation-

al system, and the deepening of unipolarism in the Western Hemisphere within the uni-multi-polar global system.[6]

2. How has Mexico responded to the changing international environment? The purpose here is to identify patterns of change and continuity in the main components of Mexico's new outward-oriented grand strategy: perceived threats, selection of policy instruments, and definition of priorities.[7]

3. What have been the foreign policy consequences of economic liberalization, the first-order adjustment to contemporary global trends? I will focus on the analysis of Mexico's divergent strategies and its pace of adaptation in two key multilateral arenas: international trade negotiations, and global and regional international institutions that work toward an expanded international security agenda.

4. What tasks lie ahead for the full adaptation of the country to the international waves of globalization and democratization?

## The Emerging Post–Cold War International System: A Better World for Intermediate States?

No consensus exists in the international relations scholarly literature about the nature of the emerging post–Cold War world system. The initial optimistic view of an emerging new world order that followed the end of the bipolar system with the collapse of the Soviet Union in the early 1990s has been gradually replaced by a more skeptical view of an uncertain, fragmented, and complex "transitional" international system. Three main features seem to characterize this transition, described by Peter Smith (1996) as the "age of uncertainty":[8] the emergence of a hybrid structure of global power, the globalization of the world economy, and the increased institutionalization of the international system.

The collapse of the Soviet Union led to the emergence of an uneven and multidimensional power structure based on a sharp disjunction between the unipolar distribution of military power on one hand, and the multipolar distribution of economic power on the other. Samuel Huntington has described contemporary global structure as "a strange hybrid, a uni-multi-polar system with one superpower and several major powers."[9] In Huntington's view, the uni-multi-polar system is a transitional stage that followed a short "uni-polar moment" at the end of the fighting in the Persian Gulf, as part of a long-term movement from a bipolarity to a truly multipolar world. This system is clearly not in equilibrium, as evidenced by the fact that all of its powerful actors are less than completely satisfied with the status quo and are pushing in different directions. While some forces in the United States would prefer a unipolar system, the other major powers seem to promote the consolidation of a multipolar one.

What does this mean for intermediate liberalizing countries like Mexico? First, it means the presence of a less predictable superpower. The structural disjunction of global power implies a two-way dynamic. At the same time that the security threats confronting the United States become less acute because there are no credible competitors for the superpower position, the effective use of the two principal tools for advancing U.S. interests—economic sanctions and military intervention—require the support of other major players in the system. Particularly, in the absence of clear and imminent strategic external threats, domestic political factors exert much greater influence on the U.S. foreign policy agenda, so foreign policy outcomes become less predictable. Second, the prospects of leadership voids are greater in the current hybrid system than in the previous bipolar world. Problems of international leadership may follow from the absence of an overarching global threat and its diffusion into multiple regional threats and the increased active role of multiple domestic actors in foreign policymaking. Third, the disjunction of military and economic power at the global level has increased the importance of regional relations and resulted in the emergence of a more regionally differentiated world.[10] This has led to a new wave of regionalism and the revival of regional institutions as key forums for bargaining on economic issues and managing security problems.

In contrast to other regions, the end of the Cold War has had mixed consequences for the Western Hemisphere. While it has deepened the traditional unipolar power structure in the region and lowered the costs of unilateral intervention, it has reduced the strategic stakes necessary for driving the unilateral imposition of a hegemonic regional order. Despite the fact that in the current uni-multi-polar system the United States still enjoys unparalleled capabilities and the ability to act unilaterally, and that this freedom of action is even larger in the Western Hemisphere than in any other region, it is unclear under what conditions the United States would choose to act alone or to seek the cooperation of other countries through multilateral action. The rationale behind this argument is that structural power is always a weak predictor of behavior. As David Lake points out: "States are not driven by international structures to respond in ineluctable ways. They shape their environments through their purposive choices."[11] Other such factors as globalization, institutionalization, and domestic politics play an important role in foreign policy choices.

The second most important feature of contemporary international politics is globalization and its corollary, the growth of economic interdependence. In general terms, globalization can be defined as an increasing level of economic and social interconnectedness derived from both technological change in the communication and information industries, and policy-driven reforms for the reduction of barriers to trade and capital. A clear indicator of the trend toward intensified economic links is the rapid expansion of world trade and the rise in transborder financial flows. Between 1987 and 1997 world trade nearly doubled, and the ratio of trade to GDP rose from 20.6 to 29.6 percent.[12] In the 1980s total net capital flows to developing and transition countries averaged only $10 to $20 billion a year, or around 1 percent of their combined GDP, but by 1997 these flows had jumped to $280 billion, more than 4 percent of the countries' combined GDP.[13]

What are the main implications of globalization? First, globalization entails the increasing exposure of national economies to international markets and, consequently, the increasing competition among liberalizing emerging economies for markets and foreign direct investment. Globalization, then, provides governments with strong incentives for initiating and sustaining market-oriented reforms to reduce the risk of being left out. Second, globalization implies the emergence of a less state-centric and a more pluralistic world. This means that transnational nongovernmental structures, social networks, and processes may have at least the same impact in people's lives as do states. Transnational links function not only as transmission belts that increasingly expose national societies to the influence of events and decisions beyond territorial boundaries, but also as mechanisms empowering a wide range of new actors from individuals, firms, NGOs, and other groups to act effectively and autonomously in world politics. Third, globalization has brought important changes in the global international agenda, mainly the increased salience of economic and social issues (such as trade, finance, human welfare, ecology, human rights, and democracy) vis-à-vis those regarding security and military. In the new global agenda, the boundaries between domestic and international politics become increasingly blurred. In the end, as Charles-Philippe David and Stéphane Roussel have pointed out, the main foreign policy implication of globalization for intermediate liberalizing countries is that their governments, in order to gain international influence and to cope with increased levels of external exposure, must develop "the ability to grasp problems at many levels (local, national, regional, global) and to negotiate with very heterogeneous players that are not necessarily operating within a state framework."[14]

The third major feature of the post–Cold War world is the growing importance of international institutions, with a trend toward hardening efforts to enforce international rules.[15] From the 1970s onward, the world has witnessed a major effort of institution building and institutional reform that has led to the proliferation of formal international organizations and regimes and the emergence of new forms of global governance.[16] An increasing number of specific activities in the international realm have become institutionalized and governed by agreed rules and standards. As a consequence, there has been an expansion of the scope of action of many international organizations. The recent proliferation of UN peacekeeping, democracy-building, and humanitarian missions is one of the most significant signs of the growing importance of international institutions in the management of security issues. In the 1990s, the end of the Cold War and the growth of economic interdependence have deepened and expanded this long-term process of institutionalization, and have generated a series of efforts to revise the codes of conduct, norms, and rules prevalent in the international arena. Even the traditional state-centered notion of sovereignty has been under revision. Robert Keohane has also raised the point that even the great powers such as the United States are relying increasingly on the use of international institutions and rule-based interactions.[17] As a rational alternative to unilateral action, the use of institutional mechanisms may help states solve a wide variety of bargaining problems that hinder the negotiation of mutually beneficial agreements, and therefore ultimately help those states achieve their material interests.[18] International institutions can generate a great deal of high-quality information about the behavior of participants in an agreement, create linkages among issues that facilitate mutually beneficial exchanges, provide coordinating mechanisms or construct "focal points" on which competing actors may coordinate their actions, reduce transaction costs by setting common standards, establish monitoring and enforcing mechanisms (increasing the costs of cheating), and improve states' credibility as reliable partners.[19]

From the perspective of intermediate countries, the current international wave of institutional reform represents both opportunities and challenges. Although the use of effective international institutions may increase those countries' ability to tie the hands of the most powerful actors in the system, it may also entail the legitimization of governance systems that do not reflect the countries' national interests but limit their sovereignty. Under these circumstances the main challenge becomes how to effectively influence the agenda and the direction of current international institution-building efforts.

To identify the range of strategic options that countries like Mexico face at the turn of the millenium, it is important first to conceptualize globalization and institutionalization not as an inexorable drive toward the full internationalization of politics and economics, but rather as dynamic and uncertain processes driven by technological and market forces as well as by political decisions made by governmental and nongovernmental actors. In fact, globalization and institutionalization have been selective and uneven. Not all countries, sectors, and activities have been integrated or regulated at the same pace or depth. The main implication of this conceptualization is that policymakers in emerging economies and transitional regimes have to make strategic choices without having full information about the practical consequences of their decisions or about the true preferences of their counterparts. In a world of imperfect information and uncertainty, nonstructural variables such as perception or leadership skills are as important as structural factors in the analysis of how nonhegemonic or secondary countries respond to global change.

There are three basic interpretations of how these post–Cold War global trends have affected those countries that occupy an intermediate position like Mexico—between great powers and small states—within the international distribution of power: the systemic-structural approach (Smith 1996), the liberal-institutionalist approach to middle powers described by Andrew Cooper, Richard Higgot, and Kim Nossal (1991),[20] and the revisionist realist approach to pivotal states discussed by Robert Chase, Emily Hill, and Paul Kennedy (1999). Each approach makes different predictions about the range of strategic options that the post–Cold War international environment offers to the so-called intermediate states of the Western Hemisphere, and about the expected foreign policy patterns of behavior of this category of states. While the first and third views emphasize the constraints, the second one focuses on the opportunities for the influence of secondary states that the end of the Cold War has opened.

The main proposition of Smith's systemic-structural approach is that the post–Cold War international system provides Latin American intermediate countries with a more narrowing range of strategic options than in previous periods in the history of inter-American relations. Overall, Smith identifies six distinct historical strategic alternatives that Latin American countries have pursued in different periods to promote economic development and counter the hegemony of the United States: collective unification, extrahemispheric protection, subregional hegemony, international law and organizations, social revolution, third-world solidarity, and alignment with the United States. During the present period, some of these strategies have been closed, and the range of options appears to be even more restricted than during the Cold War. First, the end of the East-West confrontation accentuated the unipolar distribution of power within the Americas by reducing the strategic relevance of Latin America in the global arena, and making it no longer possible for the countries in the region to credibly balance the United States through the establishment of extrahemispheric alliances. Second, the increased economic fragmentation of the "developing world" into differing strata eroded the South-South cooperation mechanisms built during the Cold War and reduced the viability of the third-world solidarity option. Third, the collapse of communism in Europe marked the bankruptcy of the revolutionary option and accentuated the discredit of statist polices that followed the 1980s series of debt crises, reducing the range of plausible models for sustainable development. As a result of all these trends, Smith argues that "by the mid-1990s Latin American countries were left with three strategic alternatives: first, they could undertake unilateral attempts to cultivate ties with Europe and Japan as well as with the United States; second, they could construct regional or subregional communities through economic integration; or third, they could align themselves with the United States."[21] At that time, Mexico was the only Latin American country in condition to successfully pursue a strategy of joining with the North.

By contrast, from a liberal-institutionalist perspective, the unexpected end of the Cold War opened new opportunities for the autonomous action and alternative forms of leadership by the intermediate powers.[22] Following Young's analysis on the sources of international leadership, Andrew Cooper develops the argument that the growing importance of nonstructural forms of leadership (i.e., forms not based on leverage derived from preponderant material capabilities to coerce but on technical and entrepreneurial skills to persuade) in a variety of issue areas has increased the importance of secondary players in the international system. According to Cooper, Higgot, and Nossal's model of middle-power foreign policy behavior, intermediate powers constitute a category of countries that have the ability and willingness to adopt an activist, initiative-oriented diplomatic approach to effectively engage the international system through nonstructural forms of influence associated with the skillful use of their diplomatic capabilities, relying on a highly specialized and coordinated professional foreign policy bureaucracy. Middle-power behavior is associated with an inclination toward good international citizenship (pacifism), multilateral activism, coalition and institution building, and mediation. Usually middle powers engage in selective and segmented diplomacy by concentrating their international efforts in some specific issues.

In this view, three post–Cold War developments have worked to reinforce the ability and willingness of middle powers to play a more active role in the international arena. The first is the growth of economic interdependence and its corollary, the relative decline of the United States' resources and willingness to lead. Under conditions of "waning hegemony," the incentives for superpower restraint are stronger and the emergence of leadership voids in a variety of issue areas more likely. An illustration of this logic would be the 1990s shift in U.S. foreign policy toward the promotion of burden-sharing initiatives giving potential allies and middle powers greater freedom of action and more opportunities to adopt leadership roles. The second factor is related to changes in the agenda of international politics, especially the increased salience of economic, environmental, and human rights issues. On one hand, the new global agenda focuses on those economic and social issues that are closer to the long-standing developmental and security concerns of intermediate countries; on the other, with "low" issues increasingly at the center of international negotiations, a variety of internal societal forces more involved in domestic issues with international ramifications may push for a more active participation in international affairs. Finally, the growing importance of international institutions is considered to have broadened the scope for action and the space for diplomatic maneuver of middle powers on a segmented basis.[23]

While this optimistic view about the increased influence for middle powers in the conduct of the global economic and security agendas seems to hold for the most developed and democratic segments of this category of countries (Canada, Australia, Sweden, and Norway), it does not fully capture the strategic dilemmas faced by those other intermediate states that either come from the developing areas of the world or have not yet consolidated themselves as stable democracies.[24] Mexico is an illustrative case of this later segment of intermediate countries that, according to Chase, Hill, and Kennedy's alternative concept of pivotal states, will certainly be playing a critical role in the maintenance of a stable international economic and political order not as the result of their enhanced status and diplomatic skills, but as the unintended consequence of their greater external economic vulnerability and fragile domestic political equilibrium.[25] Pivotal states are defined according to three criteria: (1) they are developing countries; (2) given their size, geostrategic position, population, and economic capacity, they can affect the security interests of the United States and its allies; (3) these are countries under conditions of domestic turmoil facing serious problems of governability and instability.[26]

Chase, Hill, and Kennedy's analytical framework on pivotal states is based on the assumption that in the post–Cold War world the domestic conditions in some areas of the developing world would have an increasing influence on regional and international stability, and would also play a key role in global negotiations on such crosscutting issues as human rights, environmental accords, and population. The pivotal states' framework differs from traditional realist analysis in two aspects. First, it goes beyond a purely systemic approach and incorporates domestic variables into the analysis of foreign policy, and, second, it focuses on the international roles and influence of secondary states rather than on major powers. Although the pivotal states' analytical framework does not address directly the question of these countries' strategic options at the end of the Cold War, some general propositions can be derived from it.

The main policy consequence from this analysis is that pivotal states will require increased focused and sustained attention from the United States in the years to come. Increased U.S. attention may have mixed consequences in terms of pivotal states' bargaining power. On the one hand such attention may mean greater capability to obtain resources and international support for coping with problems of economic and political instability; on the other, it may increase the ability of the major players in the system to extend their influence and impose their preferences on these countries. Therefore the question for these countries, in contrast to the rest of the developing nations, is not how to attract attention and secure resources from the United States, but how to cope with the stronger incentives for U.S. unilateral action. Another implication is that since the strategic importance of pivotal states is mainly defined in terms of the threats they pose to international stability, these countries may be the object of increasing U.S. negative attention and criticism rather than of constructive engagement. The challenge for these countries becomes how to neutralize the increasing potential of negative attention that comes from their "poor" international image as sources of instability, and, in the particular case of Mexico, from the intensification of economic and social interactions with the United States and the growing active participation of domestic actors on a variety of bilateral issues.

How do these different theoretical perspectives capture the Mexican case? The following brief description of Mexico's foreign policy over the past decade offers strong evidence supporting the pessimistic outlook depicted by both the systemic-structural approach and the pivotal states' revisionist realist perspective on the opportunities for autonomous action by secondary states in the post–Cold War era. It is clear that in the case of Mexico the construction of a new outward-oriented grand strategy has taken place at a time of profound economic vulnerability, political instability, and narrowing strategic options outside the Western Hemisphere. Under these circumstances, Mexico has not deployed the kind of strong internationalist activism associated with the paradigmatic model of middle-power diplomacy despite its increasing integration to the international economy. First, in sharp contrast to Canada or Australia, the elevation of economic issues as first priorities in Mexico's foreign policy agenda did not result in the amalgamated conduct of the "trade" and "foreign policy" sides within the same bureaucratic unit, but it led to an increasing compartmentalization and lack of coordination in the decisionmaking process. Hence Mexico's sources of soft power have remained relatively weak. Second, Mexico's internationalism and multilateralism have been erratic and ambivalent. Mexican political leaders have only occasionally defined the country as a middle power with a proactive global focus, and have usually emphasized the idea of a country without national interests beyond its frontiers and with a strong commitment to the primacy of the principle of nonintervention. Contrary to the middle powers' analytical interpretation, the most important changes in Mexican foreign policy took place at the level of bilateral relations, not at the multilateral level. The decision to negotiate an FTA with the United States forced the Mexican government to relax its long-standing commitment to nonintervention at the bilateral level and to deploy a wide range of activities with the purpose of influencing U.S. policies toward Mexico.[27]

However, some theoretical expectations from the middle powers' approach do fit certain aspects of Mexican diplomacy, particularly Mexico's shift from a traditional legalist multilateral stance toward a more selective, segmented, and pragmatic policy of multilateral engagement. The Mexican case also seems to support the middle-power approach's prediction that intermediate states will take greater responsibilities on the international multilateral stage in the context of the leadership void. Mexico has tended to be more actively involved. It has adopted a leadership role in those multilateral areas where either the distribution of power was less asymmetrical (such as in global multilateral security institutions, in contrast to those of the region) or in those periods or areas where U.S. leadership was waning or lacking (i.e., the United Nations during the 1980s, and the international trade negotiations after the formation of the World Trade Organization).

## The Search for a New Grand Strategy
## in the Face of Globalization

Mexican foreign policy's uneven adjustment to globalization has gone through three different stages in the construction of an outward-oriented grand strategy: unilateral opening for diversification (1985–1990), active bilateralism (1990–1994), and partial retreat (1994–1999). During these three periods, Mexico gradually moved from an ideologically driven and politically centered nationalist diplomacy to a more economically focused and segmented pragmatic foreign policy.

Mexico's new grand strategy started as a unilateral and gradual effort for incorporating the country as a full member in the main international economic institutions, particularly the General Agreement on Tariffs and Trade (GATT), as a way to open up new markets for Mexican exports and promote foreign investment. However, Mexico entered into the era of economic interdependence under conditions of extreme vulnerability. The sequence of several economic crises since the mid-1970s, the decline of world oil prices, and the silent de facto economic integration with the United States reduced Mexico's strategic options. The profound liberalization measures undertaken by Mexico after 1982 can be traced to the increasing structural and political problems in the Mexican growth model that began to appear in the late-1960s, the policy failures of President Luis Echeverría's (1970–1976) and José López Portillo's (1976–1982) administrations, and the prolonged economic crisis of the 1980s. This latter crisis resulted in the discrediting of previous statist and nationalist development policies and the ascent of the technocratic wing of the Institutional Revolutionary Party (PRI). The debt crisis forced the wide-ranging economic policy reforms of President Miguel de la Madrid (1982–1988) and Carlos Salinas de Gortari (1988–1994).[28]

In 1982–1983, the first wave of unilateral trade liberalization came as a forced consequence of the financial negotiations with the World Bank and the IMF, and the need to stabilize the economy. In 1984–1985, the Mexican government had to undertake a series of bilateral trade negotiations with the United States over specific issues in response to the adoption of more aggressive trade policies in that country. By the second half of the 1980s, Mexican trade policy shifted toward multilateralism with the accession to GATT in 1986. Over this period of unilateral liberalization, one of the main purposes of Mexico's foreign trade policy was to diversify the country's external markets and sources of capital. On the diplomatic front, Mexico's foreign policy maintained a clear distance from the U.S. regional and multilateral initiatives. In the Western Hemisphere, Mexico's active promotion of the Contadora Group's peace plan for Central America was designed in opposition to the Reagan administration's policies of indirect military intervention in the region. Thus, despite the increasing level of convergence between Mexican and U.S. economic foreign policies, the bilateral relationship was characterized by cycles of diplomatic conflict over various specific issues, such as drug trafficking, undocumented migration, and the Central American crisis.

By 1990, it had become clear that Mexico's diversification strategy was facing definite limits. A second period characterized by an active bilateral diplomacy in North America set up the two pillars of Mexico's new grand strategy: the economic alignment with the United States and the increased institutionalization of the bilateral relationship. As Smith and other analysts have documented, the end of the Cold War closed some of Mexico's strategic options, particularly those linked to the maintenance of the 1980s program of gradual economic liberalization and diversification.[29] Under conditions of increased competition among developing and transitional nations to attract foreign direct investment and penetrate international markets, the urgent need for foreign capital forced Mexico to accelerate its economic reforms and seek the institutionalization of an economic partnership with the United States.

This decision had important foreign policy consequences. First, it forced the Mexican government to concentrate its diplomatic efforts on its relationship with the United States and to engage in a wide range of activities to influence all those political actors that participate in the formulation of U.S. policy toward Mexico. This led to the adoption of a more cautious participation in multilateral forums at both global and regional levels precisely in the period when these institutional mechanisms were being revived by increasing collaboration among the "great powers," and when the institutions themselves were undergoing important processes of reform. A clear illustration of this trend was Mexico's decision in 1991 to decline the candidacy for nonpermanent membership in the UN Security Council for the 1992–1994 period. This was in sharp contrast to its traditional efforts toward the democratization of the organization through reform proposals like the enlargement of the Security Council and the revision of the right to veto.[30] At the regional level the Mexican government began to abandon some traditional positions, such as the active participation in mediation mechanisms like the Contadora Group[31] and open opposition to any form of U.S. intervention. Mexico's position on the U.S. invasion of Panama illustrates this point.[32] However, this shift toward a less anti-American stance was gradual and had some limits. For example, Mexico maintained a defensive position in the issue of OAS reform and blocked any initiative in favor of strengthening the organization's authority to intervene to address human rights violations or the breakdown of democracy. Mexico's active diplomacy focused its attention on other more flexible ad hoc minilateral mechanisms such as the Rio Group, the Ibero-American Conference, and the Group of Three.

Thus, while Mexico's relationship with the United States was consolidated as the core of its diplomatic activities, the government moved toward the diversification of its bilateral relations beyond the executive branch. The purpose was first to secure the enactment of NAFTA and, later on, to enhance Mexico's credibility as a reliable economic partner with an increasingly democratic political system and establish a collaborative relationship with the Mexican-American community in the United States. Besides NAFTA, domestic factors linked to the increased presence of Mexican opposition parties in the United States after the highly contested presidential election in 1988 pushed the Salinas administration to undertake a more proactive, less defensive approach vis-à-vis the United States in order to influence U.S. policy and to counterbalance its political competitors at home. In 1990, the Mexican government established within the Ministry of Foreign Relations a formal Program for Mexican Communities Living in Foreign Countries with the purpose of providing better services to the large number of Mexican citizens in the United States and improving Mexico's general international image. The forty-two Mexican consulates in the United States were reinforced with new personnel, resources, and proactive directives with the mandate of establishing a better relationship with local authorities and communities. Simultaneously, the Trade Ministry established a NAFTA office in Washington and employed a team of U.S. lawyers, lobbyists, and public relations firms. By the time NAFTA was approved in 1993, the Mexican government had spent over $30 million on its pro-NAFTA campaign in the United States.[33] This campaign focused mainly on lobbying U.S. Congress; getting support from business, political, and social leaders of the Mexican-American community; and improving Mexico's image in the United States among the general public.[34]

Mexico's proactive bilateral strategy was complemented by a permanent effort to isolate the free-trade negotiations from other more conflictive issues of the bilateral agenda, particularly drug-trafficking, immigration, and, eventually, foreign policy issues. This strategy entailed two main components. First, there was the institutionalization of the bilateral relationship through the creation of new institutional bilateral mechanisms for intergovernmental consultation. Second was the segmentation of Mexico's policy toward the United States, that is, the segmented management of the bilateral agenda by different federal agencies, mainly the Ministry of Foreign Affairs, the Ministry of Trade, and the Attorney General's Office. The Mexican government's institution-building efforts focused on the expansion of already existent bilateral mechanisms, particularly the U.S.-Mexican Binational Commission (BNC). The BNC was established in 1981 by President Reagan and Lopez Portillo to serve as a forum for regular meetings between cabinet-level officials from both countries to address issues requiring high-level attention. At every level of the two governments—from staff level up to cabinet officials—regular contacts have proliferated over the past 10 years, partly as an outgrowth of the BNC. Between 1990 and 1998 seven new intergovernmental working groups were added, and by 1998 the BNC had fourteen working groups and two subgroups on a diverse and wide range of bilateral issues, from trade and investment to border cooperation, the environment, antinarcotics issues, migration, energy, agriculture, and education.

At the end of the Salinas administration, it was clear that Mexico had been forced by the circumstances to change from a highly protected economy to one of the most liberalized economies in the developing world with average tariffs lower than international standards. The fact that NAFTA integrated a wide range of issues besides free trade, including investment, services, labor, and environmental provisions, facilitated Mexico's later quick integration into the key multilateral economic mechanisms. In just a few years, Mexico became a member of the World Trade Organization (WTO), the Organization for Economic Cooperation and Development (OECD), and the Asian Pacific Economic Cooperation (APEC) mechanism, and the signer of numerous bilateral trade liberalization agreements with the United States, Canada, Chile, Colombia, Costa Rica, Venezuela, and the European Union. In the economy the change has been notable. In only 16 years, between 1980 and 1996, the importance of foreign trade in national output tripled. Starting from around 11 and 13 percent of GDP in 1980, exports and imports rose to 30.9 and 30.0 percent, respectively, in 1996. Today practically one-third of Mexico's output comes from foreign trade. A second important consequence of Mexico's trade opening has been the intensification of extensive exchange with the United States. While in 1970, 57.0 percent of Mexican exports went to the U.S. market, by 1996, they were up to 83.4 percent. In sum, both Mexico's trade dependence (measured in terms of total trade share of GDP) and Mexico's foreign-trade concentration with the United States have constantly increased over the past two decades. On the basis of these figures it is clear that Mexico has entered into the globalization process in asymmetrical conditions, above all through the North American gateway.[35]

A third period characterized by partial retreat started once Mexico had opened its economy and signed NAFTA. The emergence of severe economic, political, and security domestic problems led to a partial restraint and a lower profile in foreign policy issues. Faced with economic and political shocks in the late 1990s, Mexico retreated.[36] During the first year of the Zedillo administration, the Mexican government centered its international efforts on overcoming the serious credibility crisis that resulted from both the 1994 financial collapse and the increasingly conflictive situation in Chiapas in early 1995. Mexico's international image was seriously damaged by these events. Zedillo's first presidential message reflected Mexico's difficult situation after the financial crisis in December 1994: for the first time, the traditional chapter on foreign policy was not read on the occasion of the state of the union address to the Mexican congress.

The credibility deficit forced the Mexican government to deepen its strategy of collaboration with the United States, institutionalization of the bilateral relationship, segmented conduct of the country's external affairs, and active bilateral trade diplomacy. The reestablishment of confidence among foreign investors, the U.S. government, and the international financial institutions became the first short-term priority of Zedillo's administration. To achieve this Mexico focused its attention on the search for a financial rescue package, relying on the U.S. government as its main ally. President Clinton's strong commitment to reestablish Mexico's macroeconomic stability was crucial for the implementation of the 1995 $50 billion financial rescue package despite strong opposition in the U.S. Congress. The need to maintain a "good neighbor" and "reliable partner" image led the Mexican government to adopt a more accommodating position with the United States in other noneconomic issues, such as drug control, immigration, and foreign policy, despite the fact that the U.S. government adopted more aggressive policies for controlling the border and promoting democracy. As Dresser points out, the "only issue over which Mexico challenged U.S. foreign policy during the first three years of the Zedillo term was the Helms-Burton Act." On the Cuba issue, Mexico launched a campaign against the Helms-Burton bill, enacted an antiextraterritorial law, and opposed U.S. efforts to strengthen the blockade and impose new sanctions against Cuba over human rights violations. In 1999, Kosovo became another issue in which Mexico adopted a less accommodating position with the United States. On the other hand, Mexico has maintained its active participation in other multilateral issues where differences with the United States were of minor importance for U.S. foreign policy, such as the promotion of the UN treaty banning nuclear tests.

On the economic front, Mexico moved toward a more active participation in multilateral trade and financial forums, particularly the WTO and the OECD, and reinforced its trade negotiations with the European Union. In 1997, Mexico and the European Union signed the Economic Partnership, Political Co-ordination and Co-operation Agreement allowing the initiation of negotiations toward a broad-based free-trade agreement. Trade talks between Mexico and the European Union have moved slowly due to the many differences over the scope and timing of the agreement. The European position conditions the negotiation of the trade liberalization components of the agreement to a first-stage negotiation of the political and cooperation components. The Mexican position is in favor of simultaneous negotiations of all three components of the agreement: (1) the progressive and reciprocal trade liberalization of goods, services, and investments according to WTO rules; (2) a permanent political dialogue; and (3) intensified cooperation in such areas as science, technology, tourism, agriculture, and the environment. At the same time, bilateral trade negotiations in the Western Hemisphere have moved relatively quickly. By 1999 Mexico had signed seven new broad-based free-trade agreements with other Latin American countries.

In the political realm the increased domestic pressures for democratization since 1994, the proliferation of governance problems linked to the emergence of guerrilla groups, the wave of political assasinations, the militarization of law enforcement operations, and the consolidation of organized crime have compelled the Mexican government to accept the participation of international institutions and foreign actors in some aspects of Mexico's democratization process. The logic behind this was the need to obtain international credibility and legitimacy. In 1994, for the first time the Mexican government allowed the presence of foreign electoral observers. In 1998, the Acteal killings resulted in a wave of criticism from many NGOs about Mexico's human rights record. Mexico's official response was twofold. The secretary of the interior announced the expulsion of various foreign citizens for participating in political activities in Chiapas, increased the requirements for obtaining "foreign observer" visas and visiting Chiapas, and rejected any initiative for the participation by the United Nations as a mediator in the negotiations between the government and the Zapatista movement. At the same time, the Mexican government sought to soften international criticism by announcing its acceptance of the compulsory jurisdiction of the Inter-American Court of Human Rights of the OAS and by creating an office for coordinating relations with NGOs under the secretary of foreign affairs.

How has the policy shift to a formal economic association with the United States affected Mexico's international position? Was Mexico in 1999 in a less vulnerable or stronger position than in the pre-NAFTA period? On the upside, the new strategy has been successful in accomplishing its immediate goals of establishing a strong export industrial sector, attracting greater foreign direct investment (FDI) flows, and securing access to the U.S. market. Between 1994 and 1998 Mexico's participation in world trade increased from 0.82 to 1.6 percent, reversing a long-standing trend of loss of competitiveness since the 1980s. By 1998 Mexico had become the tenth largest trading country in the world and the first in Latin America, accounting for 32 percent of this region's total exports. Today more than 80 percent of Mexico's total exports are manufactured products. Mexican goods have also increased their share in the United States market from less than 7 percent in 1993 to almost 11 percent in 1998. As a result, Mexico has displaced Japan as the second largest trading U.S. partner, just behind Canada.[37] Efforts for attracting foreign capital had also been successful. Between 1992 and 1998 Mexico received up to $61 billion in FDI, and by 1998 it had become the third biggest recipient of FDI behind only China and Brazil, receiving 11.7 percent of all FDI to developing economies.[38] The presence of a highly dynamic and competitive export sector proved to be a key instrument for the rapid recovery of the Mexican economy after the financial crisis of 1994. In sharp contrast to the crisis of the 1980s, when industrial production took almost 9 years to return to its precrisis levels, in 1995 it took less than 2 years for industrial production to return to its 1994 levels.[39] In this case, sustained export performance helped the Mexican economy overcome its most serious financial crash in a remarkably short period. Finally, NAFTA played a major role in the Clinton administration's political commitment to organize a financial rescue package of loan guarantees to assist Mexico in 1995, despite strong opposition in the U.S. Congress, that helped the rapid stabilization of Mexico's financial conditions. Smith explains very clearly some of the consequences of NAFTA:

> For the United States, NAFTA has had a clear political consequence: Washington cannot permit "collapse" in Mexico. The U.S. government, and especially the Clinton administration invested too much capital in debates over NAFTA ratification to permit disintegration of its neighbor. Chaos in Mexico would vindicate opposition to NAFTA, emphasize the fallibility of the Clinton team and throw confusion into U.S. relations with trading partners around the world. Collapse in Mexico has thus become unthinkable in Washington.[40]

On the downside, despite the consolidation of a dynamic export industry and the entry of immense FDI flows, macroeconomic stability and poor economic growth remain serious problems. Economic growth has been erratic and relatively poor in contrast to the performance of the import-substitution model. On average, real GDP growth was 0.1 percent in 1985–1990, 1.5 percent in 1990–1995, and 5.8 percent in 1995–1998. During the whole liberalizing period from 1985 to 1998, Mexico's GDP increased by only 1.4 percent per year on average, a much lower rate than in the three previous decades.[41] Simultaneously, the dependence of economic growth on both U.S. market and international capital flows has deepened. Table 6.1 shows the increasing concentration of Mexico's foreign trade in one single market. In 1997, 87.5 percent of Mexican exports went to the United States, more than ten points above the 73.9 percent in 1990. While in 1990 exports to the European Union represented 10.2 percent of Mexico's total exports, by 1997 their relative importance had declined to 3.9 percent. Between 1990 and 1997 Asia's share of Mexican exports declined from 6.7 to 2 percent. Only Mexican exports to Latin America and the Caribbean maintained a relative participation of 6.0 to 6.5 percent in the period 1990–1997. The vulnerability of the economy to short-term decisions by foreign investors is one of the main problems of Mexico's economic liberalization strategy. Finally, the export-led and foreign investment model of development has not been able to improve the living conditions of large sectors of the Mexican population. Per capita GDP has remained stationary throughout the 1985–1998 economic liberalizing period.[42] Most of the beneficial effects of the export boom have been unevenly distributed across regions and sectors, mainly in the *maquiladora* industry and the northern industrialized states of Mexico. The relatively high imported component of Mexican exports reveals problems for fostering efficient and dynamic production and employment links with those sectors oriented to the domestic market.

From a purely systemic-structural perspective, it is clear that the structural power asymmetry between the United States and Mexico has not been changed by the opening of Mexico's economy or the institutionalization of a formal economic alliance between both countries. The U.S. economy is around twenty-five times larger than the Mexican economy, and the per capita income gap ratio between the two countries is still one to eight. Although Mexico's economic and geopolitical importance for the United States has increased, Mexican dependence on the United States is now greater than ever. These structural disparities are also reflected in attention asymmetries. As Rozental has explained, although the U.S.

**Table 6.1  Mexico's Foreign Trade by Destination, 1980–1997 (% share of trade)**

| Region/Country | Category | Trade with Major Selected Regions and Countries | | | | | | | | | |
|---|---|---|---|---|---|---|---|---|---|---|---|
| | | 1980 | 1985 | 1990 | 1991 | 1992 | 1993 | 1994 | 1995 | 1996 | 1997 |
| North America | Export | 63.9 | 62.1 | 73.9 | 82.2 | 83.2 | 86.2 | 87.7 | 86 | 86.3 | 87.5 |
| | Import | 67.4 | 68.3 | 72.3 | 75.3 | 73 | 73 | 73.8 | 76.4 | 77.5 | 76.6 |
| United States | Export | 63.2 | 60.4 | 73.1 | 79.5 | 81.1 | 83.3 | 85.3 | 83.5 | 84 | 85.6 |
| | Import | 65.6 | 66.6 | 70.8 | 73.9 | 71.2 | 71.2 | 71.8 | 74.5 | 75.5 | 74.8 |
| Canada | Export | .7 | 1.7 | .8 | 2.6 | 2.1 | 2.9 | 2.4 | 2.4 | 2.2 | 1.9 |
| | Import | 1.8 | 1.7 | 1.5 | 1.3 | 1.7 | 1.7 | 2 | 1.9 | 1.9 | 1.8 |
| European Union | Export | 6.6 | 18.2 | 10.2 | 8.1 | 7.6 | 5.4 | 4.7 | 5 | 3.9 | 3.9 |
| | Import | 13.8 | 13 | 12.6 | 13.1 | 13.1 | 12.6 | 11.9 | 9.8 | 9.1 | 9.5 |
| France | Export | 3.6 | 3.6 | 2 | 1.4 | 1.2 | .8 | .8 | .6 | .4 | .4 |
| | Import | 2.6 | 2 | 2.2 | 1.9 | 2.1 | 1.6 | 1.8 | 1.3 | 1.1 | 1 |
| Germany | Export | 1.7 | 1.3 | 1.5 | 1.2 | 1 | .8 | .6 | .6 | .6 | .6 |
| | Import | 5.2 | 4 | 4.5 | 4.6 | 4 | 4.3 | 4 | 3.7 | 3.5 | 3.5 |
| Spain | Export | 7.9 | 7.6 | 5.3 | 2.7 | 2.6 | 1.6 | 1.3 | 1 | .9 | .8 |
| | Import | 1.7 | 1.5 | 1.8 | 1.1 | 1.4 | 1.6 | 1.6 | .9 | .7 | .9 |
| United Kingdom | Export | .5 | 3.1 | .8 | .5 | .5 | .4 | .4 | .6 | .6 | .6 |
| | Import | 2.2 | 2.1 | 1.2 | 1 | 1 | .9 | .9 | .7 | .7 | .8 |
| Latin America and the Caribbean | Export | 6.9 | 5.4 | 6.7 | 4.7 | 5.6 | 5.4 | 4.5 | 5.7 | 6.5 | 6 |
| | Import | 4.2 | 5.2 | 3.8 | 3.8 | 3.8 | 3.6 | 2.7 | 2.5 | 2.4 | |
| Asia | Export | 5.3 | 9 | 6.7 | 3.7 | 2.4 | 2.2 | 2.3 | 2.4 | 2.5 | 2 |
| | Import | 6.3 | 6.5 | 7.7 | 6.4 | 8.4 | 9.5 | 9.3 | 10 | 9.6 | 10.1 |
| Japan | Export | 3.7 | 7.7 | 5.4 | 2.9 | 1.7 | 1.3 | 1.6 | 1.1 | 1.4 | 1 |
| | Import | 5.3 | 5.4 | 5.1 | 3.5 | 4.8 | 5.1 | 4.8 | 4.9 | 4.3 | 5.2 |

*Source:* IMF, *Direction of Trade,* various years.

ambassador to Mexico "is a *personaje* [major player]" with "instant and unlimited access to everyone, and total press coverage, . . . the Mexican ambassador in Washington is not so visible, and the degree of access and press coverage varies."[43] Despite the perpetuation of structural power asymmetries, NAFTA has increased the strategic importance of Mexico to the United States and intensified the dramatic expansion of multiple economic and social links between the two countries. Increased bilateral connections and the fact of an extensive geographic proximity have widened and deepened the "interdependence" component of this highly asymmetrical bilateral relationship. This trend entails higher costs associated with unilateral action for both countries, which in turn may give Mexico some leeway vis-à-vis the United States under certain particular circumstances. In this sense, although NAFTA has certainly tied the hands and narrowed the policy options of Mexico, it has also constrained the policy options open to the United States by increasing the costs of unilateral action, raising the benefits of bilateral collaboration.

### The Foreign Policy Consequences of Economic Liberalization and Political Opening in Mexico

The literature on the effects of economic liberalization and political opening on foreign policy have produced two main predictions: the adoption of external cooperative strategies, and the deepening of engagement with international institutions to manage the effects of growing external economic ties.[44] Liberalizing regimes are expected to adopt strategies of international collaboration within international institutions. The argument is twofold. First, economic liberalization induces a profound transformation in underlying foreign policy preferences toward "an elevation at the national level of goals of economic welfare" and a concurrent move away from ideology to pragmatism. Second, international institutions provide policy credibility to national governments in the face of increased dependence on external economic transactions.

According to Miles Kahler, international collaboration and institutional engagement follow from four internal dynamics induced by economic liberalization. First, national governments may discover that programs of economic liberalization require additional credibility supplied by international institutions. International institutional engagement may serve to bind succeeding governments to a liberal economic program in the face of shifting political incentives. Second, economic liberalization also impels states toward cooperative strategies through strengthening the influence of those domestic institutions (foreign trade agencies and central banks) strongly committed to the economic opening program and already engaged in close relationships with their counterparts abroad, and reducing the foreign policy roles of more traditional nationalist bureaucracies (foreign ministries). Third, at the level of interest groups in society, both the beneficiaries of liberalization programs and those interests threatened by the increase in international competition face strong incentives for seeking the intervention and support of international actors, either from international institutions, foreign investors, or NGOs in order to strengthen their position internally in the foreign policy battles. Fourth, spillover effects from the consequences of economic internationalization in other issue areas will often result in a ratcheting up of international institution building in order to deal with cross-issue disturbances. Simultaneously, all these domestic factors are reinforced by external ones. Economic liberalization also increases the incentives of many key international actors—financial institutions, private investors, foreign governmental agencies, and NGOs—to pay a more intense level of attention to the domestic economic and political conditions of liberalizing countries.

In the case of Mexico, the dramatic shift toward economic liberalization has had an important impact on how Mexican policymakers define the core goals of foreign policy along the lines predicted by Kahler: the emergence of an economic-centered foreign policy, a move toward pragmatism, a strategy of institutionalized bilateral collaboration with the United States, the use of international institutions for credibility purposes, and the decline in influence of the foreign ministry in the decisionmaking process. However, these trends have been slowed down by Mexico's incomplete political opening. Consequently, Mexico has followed a process of slow and uneven adaptation to the new international environment. Therefore, as the following brief description of recent trends shows, Mexican foreign policy is still in a long-term transition characterized by disjunctures and tensions.

## The Primacy of Economics

Economic liberalization led to a change in Mexico's international priorities toward the adoption of a more economically oriented foreign policy and the emergence of a more assertive foreign economic policy. During the past decade, economic concerns linked first to foreign debt negotiations and later to foreign investment promotion, international market access, and international financial volatility became far more central in determining Mexico's international activities than traditional diplomatic and security concerns. Over the past decade Mexico deployed a very active economic diplomacy at the bilateral level whose main purpose has been the creation of a wide network of free-trade agreements that follow the NAFTA model. At the same time, Mexico actively participated in the WTO, pushing a new round of negotiations and looking for bridging the positions of industrialized and developing countries. Mexican initiatives in APEC, UNCTAD, and the IMF have focused on promoting the creation of an early-warning system to avoid financial crises.

### Closer Alignment with the United States

The need to secure access to foreign markets and capital flows forced Mexico to search for new economic allies, mainly in the club of industrialized countries. The Mexican government sought a closer association with the United States and the developed world, and tacitly rejected the idea of defining itself as a third-world country. Mexico entered the Organization for Economic Cooperation and Development (OECD), which meant renouncing participation in third-world mechanisms of representation, such as the Nonaligned Movement. The main advantage of renouncing any preferential treatment as a developing country and joining the club of industrialized nations was the attainment of credibility and a better reputation. Shortly after joining the organization, Mexico received a grade A country risk classification under OECD rules. Mexican political leaders decided to recognize the realities of the market and to institutionalize an economic partnership with the United States, departing from the nation's historical tendency to maintain its distance. For the liberalizing coalition in the Mexican government, signing NAFTA increased the value of maintaining long-term cooperative relations and expanded mutually beneficial links across a variety of issues, thus facilitating further bilateral cooperation between the United Sates and Mexico.

Mexico abandoned the strategy of diversification in favor of institutionalizing its bilateral relationship. In the words of Rosario Green, Mexico's foreign affairs secretary, "Institutionalization of the bilateral relationship is probably the key to managing what is arguably one of the most complex and singular bilateral relationships in the world."[45] We have seen greater institutional collaboration between Mexico and the United States at both the bilateral and multilateral levels in various realms beyond the economic agenda such as drug control policy and migration. At the multilateral level, Mexican foreign policy also moved closer to the U.S. positions. A useful indicator of this is the increased degree of Mexico's voting coincidence with the United States in the United Nations between

**Figure 6.1    Mexico: Voting Coincidence with the United States in the United Nations, 1985–1998 (% voting with United States in each General Session)**

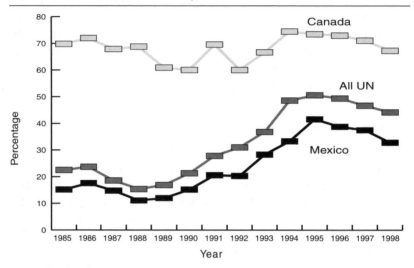

*Source:* U.S. State Department, *Voting Practices in the United Nations. Annual Report,* various years.

1985 and 1998 (see Figure 6.1). However, it is important to point out that by 1998 Mexico's alignment with the United States in foreign policy issues was still the fourth lowest in the Western Hemisphere, after Belize, Antigua and Barbuda, and Cuba. This means that in sharp contrast to the U.S-Canadian relationship, where the economic partnership is complemented by a close strategic alliance, in the U.S.-Mexican relationship foreign policy alignment with the United States still has clear limits. Mexico's position on the situation in Kosovo in 1999, regretting the use of force without the explicit consent of the UN Security Council, as well as its position on Cuba favoring the end of the U.S. embargo, illustrates the limits of Mexico's foreign policy alignment with that of the United States.

### Pragmatism

During the 1990s, Mexico adopted a less ideologically oriented, more pragmatic foreign policy. The decline of nationalist ideology in the economic realm led not only to the acceptance of the liberal trading principles that had been rejected in the past, but also to the promotion of cordial relationships with GATT, the IMF, and the World Bank. Hence, the rise of pragmatism facilitated Mexico's increased, and increasingly necessary, active engagement with international economic institutions. NAFTA also represented another break with Mexico's past official nationalist doctrine.

The decline of nationalist ideology also meant the erosion of Mexico's persistent anti-Americanism in regional and global politics. As Kahler points out, "persistent anti-Americanism disappeared as the logic of economic liberalization reinforced Mexico's economic dependence on its northern neighbor."[46] The gradual erosion of an assertive anti-U.S. foreign policy at regional and global levels gave way to the adoption of a more cooperative relation with the United States. This pragmatic trend is clearly illustrated by the minor nationalist domestic opposition to NAFTA.

## Ambivalent Multilateral Diplomacy

Mexican policymakers have adopted an active economic multilateral policy to gain credibility in the face of increased dependence on external economic transactions, but they have reluctantly accepted the strengthening of a multilateral framework for the promotion of democracy and human rights. In multilateral political forums, Mexico has limited its active participation to such traditional security issues as disarmament and arms controls. As political opening advances in Mexico, greater institutional collaboration in the realm of human rights and democratic promotion (i.e., greater involvement in bilateral or multilateral frameworks for handling human rights issues) may be seen. Up to now, Mexico's strong attachment to the norm of nonintervention and suspicion of the United Nations has hindered Mexico's participation in the OAS programs in promoting democracy.

## Fragmentation of the Decisionmaking Process

Mexico has moved from a highly centralized foreign policy decisionmaking process controlled by the chief executive and the Foreign Affairs Ministry toward a more compartmentalized and fragmented management of its external relations. The Foreign Affairs Ministry's responsibilities have decreased, while foreign trade and treasury agencies have assumed prominent roles in foreign economic policy, eroding the more traditional foreign affairs bureaucracy. The management of the so-called new security issues, such as drug trafficking and transnational crime, has led to the involvement in foreign policy negotiations of new agencies, mainly the Procuraduria General de la República. The main challenge ahead is the coordination of the different subpolicy areas of foreign policy. Mexico is confronted with the challenge of coordinating the nation's foreign policy while incorporating into the policymaking process new domestic institutions. Mexico's sources of soft power are still relatively weak, mainly due to increasing compartmentalization and the lack of coordination that characterize the foreign policy decisionmaking process.

### New Instruments

The need to improve Mexico's international image to attract foreign capital and avoid the internationalization of domestic security problems has impelled the Mexican government to employ a new set of foreign policy tools, particularly in the conduct of relations with the United States. The new instruments range from the launching of numerous public relations programs through cultural programs, the expansion of relations with the foreign press, and the strengthening of the consular network to lobbying in Washington, searching for closer relations with the Mexican-American communities in the United States, and accepting the participation of foreign observers in Mexican domestic elections. The expansion of the public relations dimension of foreign policy represents a break from the past traditional policy of abstention from engagement in the domestic politics of other countries and forging alliances with external actors.[47]

## The Rise of an Active Economic Diplomacy: Mexico and the International Trade Negotiations[48]

Since the early 1980s the rules of the game in international economic relations have changed dramatically. The world economic scene is characterized by a tendency to form regional trade blocs, an acute increase in trade competition, and intensified efforts by all countries to attract FDI. Faced with this economic intensification, with the consolidation of Western European economic integration, and the initiation of a similar liberalizing process in North America between Canada and the United States, Mexico's concerns about economic marginalization have increased. The fear of being left out deepened with the end of the Cold War since the events in Eastern Europe and the dissolution of the Soviet bloc increased the competition for markets and capital. Mexico has responded to these new trends in the international political economy by adopting an aggressive and quick trade liberalization strategy.

However, the shift from import substitution to active export promotion policies was not a planned policy decision but an evolutionary process of adaptation driven by both domestic and international pressures. In terms of the analytical framework developed by Cooper, Higgot, and Nossal, Mexico's changing role in the international trade arena have moved from the reluctant acceptance of others' leadership to the reactive and passive role of follower, and finally to more active forms of followership that increased Mexico's influence in shaping both the timing and the agenda of trade negotiations. The first wave of unilateral trade liberalization (1983–1985) was linked to the financial negotiations with the World Bank and the IMF, and their insistence on dealing with the debt problem through a comprehensive macroeconomic package, of which trade liberalization was an important aspect. Once the trade liberalization had started through the strong conditionality of the international financial institutions, Mexico entered into a period of several short-term bilateral trade negotiations with the United States over specific issues (subsidies, trade preferences, and foreign investment), which lasted until Mexican trade policy shifted toward openness and multilateralism with the accession to GATT in 1986. By the mid-1980s, Mexico's trade negotiation position had changed from a defensive position to a more active participation in multilateral trade negotiations and stronger unilateral trade liberalization. By the end of the decade, most import permits had been dismantled and tariffs had come down to levels comparable with those of developed countries. Mexico was playing an active role in the Uruguay Round negotiations of the GATT and moving toward a closer and more institutionalized commercial relationship with its main trading partner and largest source of foreign capital, the United States.

NAFTA inaugurated a period of "active followership" in Mexico's bilateral and multilateral trade diplomacy. By 1990, after a failed trip to Europe in search of financial support, the Salinas administration precipitated the shift toward an active bilateral trade diplomacy by opening discussions with the United States and Canada on a trilateral free-trade zone. During the NAFTA negotiations, Mexico's main objectives were twofold: (1) to limit the agenda of trilateral negotiations to trade and financial issues; (2) to establish a trade liberalizing schedule that would allow domestic industrial and agricultural sectors to undertake the structural adjustments necessary to increase their competitiveness. Mexico failed in achieving its agenda-setting goals: the approval of the trade agreement was conditioned to the signing of two side agreements on environmental and labor issues, and questions such as the free movement of labor were not addressed. However, Mexico was relatively more successful in setting the liberalizing schedule and defining the nature of the dispute settlement mechanisms. In the end NAFTA adopted a broad scope of action, including major manufacturing sectors, services, government procurement, trade-related investment measures, intellectual property rights, and codified standards that go beyond those negotiated in the Uruguay Round.[49]

The comprehensive nature of NAFTA as a deep integration model paved the way for increasingly active Mexican multilateral and bilateral trade diplomacy. On the multilateral trade agenda, Mexico was the first participant to submit, together with Canada and the United States, a concrete proposal to establish the WTO. During the WTO negotiations, Mexico promoted greater certainty in the context of dispute settlement through the establishment of time limits and the introduction of the quasi-automaticity for the adoption of panel reports. It also supported the maintenance of special and differential treatment for developing countries, primarily with regard to certain procedural issues, and sought to play a highly selective intermediary and consensus-building role between developed and developing countries during the negotiations.

One of the main characteristics of Mexico's trade liberalization strategy is that it has combined unilateral, bilateral, and multilateral elements,[50] initially in a sequential and alternate pattern, but more recently in a simultaneous fashion. The reason behind this multiple-level and mixed-trade diplomacy was the need to obtain quick results to stabilize the economy, restore foreign resources (commercial bank loans and private investment) for financing economic growth, secure access to markets abroad, and lock in the program of economic liberalization initiated by the De la Madrid's administration under conditions of acute financial distress. The credibility of the unilateral liberalization of the early 1980s was subsequently anchored by three further sequential steps: first, the accession to GATT in 1986; second, the negotiation and establishment of NAFTA in the early 1990s; and third, the negotiation of a series of NAFTA-like bilateral trade agreements in the late 1990s. By 1998, Mexico had signed five free-trade agreements that follow the NAFTA model with the following countries in the Western Hemisphere: Costa Rica (1995), Colombia (1995), Venezuela (1995), Bolivia (1995), Chile (1991, 1998), Nicaragua (1998). The Mexican government is currently engaged in active free-trade negotiations with the European Union, Guatemala, Honduras, El Salvador, Belize, Panama, Trinidad and Tobago, Peru, and, more recently, Brazil.

The Salinas and Zedillo administrations considered that a strategy of rapid trade liberalization centered on the United States would not only broaden the access for Mexican exports to foreign markets and stimulate flows of private investment, but would also facilitate the diversification of Mexico's external markets and sources of capital in the long run. The so-called North American gateway to diversification required, however, the deployment of a sustained strategy of bilateral negotiations over free-trade agreements with other Asian, Latin American, and European countries. In sum, the key purpose behind this strategy, as David Mares points out, was twofold: to use the international market to get a better deal with the United States, and to use the country's unique relationship with the United States to benefit from the international economy.[51]

In contrast to other intermediate powers such as Canada, Australia, and Brazil, Mexico did not consistently explore the alternative strategy of seeking and forming coalitions with a large number of countries, such as such as the Cairns Group, the Group of 10, or the Central American Group, to increase its bargaining power in multilateral trade negotiations. Mexico's 1987 initiative to form a group of net food-importing countries proved short-lived as Mexico adopted a more liberalizing domestic agricultural policy by the end of the 1980s. Several factors may explain this tactical choice. First, the fact that Mexico entered late into GATT in order to participate in the Uruguay Round with little prior experience in multilateral trade negotiation meant that it had to adapt to an unknown bargaining arena. Consequently, Mexico's position changed quickly during the Uruguay Round negotiations. As Claudia Schatan documents, Mexico "went from seeking preferences, like any other developing country, to taking a more independent stance that emphasized the country's particular circumstances,"[52] particularly the demand for reciprocal concessions for its previous unilateral trade liberalization. Second, the need to make the position in the Uruguay Round compatible with the goal of joining the North American trade bloc led the Mexican government to move away from the demands of other developing countries, and to adopt a more flexible attitude to the new issues put forward by the United States, such as the protection of intellectual property rights, free trade in services, and flexibility of foreign investment regulations.

A third characteristic of Mexican strategies in the international trade arena complemented the two above bargaining approaches: the rejection of joining or forming rigid coalitions. Unlike the Salinas administration, which had focused explicitly on the goal of transforming Mexico into a full member of the first-world club of industrialized countries, the Zedillo administration has adopted a more flexible stance that recognized Mexico's bridge position between the North and the South and being part of multiple geoeconomic regions. The National Development Plan for 1995–2000 clearly defined Mexico as "a country that requires both selective and flexible" strategic alliances based not on broad general principles of regional or developmental solidarity, but on the identification of topics of common interest, mainly with major emerging nations whose development is comparable to that of Mexico. The premise behind this official strategy was that given Mexico's geopolitical and geoeconomic situation, the country could be transformed into a production platform to get access to several markets, particularly in the Western Hemisphere. In accordance with this view, instead of promoting the enlargement of NAFTA through the accession of other countries into the trilateral framework, Mexico took the decision to actively pursue a series of bilateral and subregional overlapping free-trade agreements with other countries, using NAFTA as a model.

Why has Mexico chosen this course of action? From the Mexican perspective there were several advantages to this approach. First, it permitted moving more quickly and continuing to reap the benefits of trade liberalization at the regional and multilateral level, without depending on the increasingly uncertain leadership of the United States, and sharing the benefits of being the first developing nation reach a free-trade agreement with the United States. Second, it helped to solve some of the problems linked to multilateral negotiations with the participation of a large number of actors, particularly the slow pace and the high transaction costs linked to the multilateral option. Third, it helped to maintain the image of an independent course of action vis-à-vis the United States and to ease the growing resentment and distrust toward Mexico that NAFTA had brought about among other Latin American and Caribbean countries.[53] Finally, this strategy enhanced the international credibility of Mexico's commitment to maintain free-trade and financial liberalization policies, particularly since the 1994 financial crisis and the opening of the political system had eroded the domestic basis of support of the neoliberal coalition. Under conditions of macroeconomic and political instability, the ability of Zedillo's administration to signal a strong and credible commitment to the market-oriented reforms was a key factor in getting the necessary financial support from Mexico's most important trading partners and other OECD members, as well as from the international organizations such as the IMF, the World Bank, and the International Development Bank in order to overcome the 1994–1995 financial crisis.

What are the prospects of regionalization? What is Mexico's most likely role in the future of regional integration? Mexico played a crucial role in both the early-1990s revival and the late-1990s impasse of regional integration in the Western Hemisphere, first as a role model and later as a bridle. Since 1995 the process of regional integration has been facing significant political difficulties. The sequence of virulent financial crises in Latin America and East Asia, as well as the gradual reactivation of the multilateral trade negotiations in the WTO, has slowed the trend toward regionalization after 5 years of continuous advances that had led to the emergence of a complex network of overlapping regional, subregional, and bilateral trade agreements in the Western Hemisphere.[54] In the short run the crises also narrowed the scope of politically viable routes to regional integration. Although regional integration continues to be a primary foreign policy objective for the most important actors in the region, including Mexico and the United States, the 1994–1995 Mexican peso crisis eroded the domestic basis of support for moving ahead the commitment to a Free Trade Area of the Americas adopted at the Miami Summit of the Americas in 1994. In 1997, the U.S. Congress rejected the Clinton administration's long-delayed request for fast-track authority to negotiate the accession of other countries to NAFTA or any other free-trade agreement, creating a leadership void and an impasse in the quest for hemispheric free trade. Since then, it has become increasingly clear that the options of expanding NAFTA or negotiating a hemispheric agreement are not the most plausible paths to regional integration.[55] Consequently, the bilateral approach has gained momentum as the most viable alternative. In the case of Mexico, the uncertain course of multilateral negotiations in the region has certainly strengthened its propensity to rely on a strategy of bilateral negotiations using the NAFTA framework of deep integration as a model. However, the real impact of Mexico's expanding network of trade agreements on the future of regional integration will depend mainly on the performance of the Mexican economy, particularly on its ability to overcome the cycle of macroeconomic instability at the end of each presidential administration.

Despite increasing dissatisfaction with market-oriented reforms, the possibility of a Mexican rejection of NAFTA is limited, and the official commitment to regional integration through the active bilateral promotion of the NAFTA model is still there. Not only does this option seem to be too costly an alternative after nearly two decades of economic liberalization; it also does not constitute an issue in the domestic political debate. The bulk of political forces in Mexico are either pushing for the unilateral adoption of social, industrial, agricultural, and banking policies to compensate those sectors that were the losers in the neoliberal reforms and consolidate a more balanced model of development, or for a negotiated expansion of the NAFTA framework in order to include some of the issues left over from the bargaining table in the early 1990s. While left-wing parties emphasize the need for a "social fund" and an open labor market, the right-wing agenda focuses on the need to improve the level of macroeconomic policy coordination and, eventually, the construction of a monetary union among the three members of NAFTA.

Mexico's international economic policy faces important unsolved questions. The first is that the framework of economic integration formalized in NAFTA fails to address several such key issues as nontariff barriers to trade, macroeconomic policy, compensation mechanisms for development asymmetries, and migration and nationality issues. The neglect of immigration issues constitutes a striking omission, since migration flows and binational labor markets have been the most dynamic and extensive mechanisms of integration between Mexico and the United States. The second pending question is how to move beyond the current highly concentrated pattern of foreign trade in the North American market and gain access to Mexico's second and third most important markets, the European Union and East Asia.

### The Logic of Ambivalent Multilateralism: Mexico's Cautious Approach to the New Global Security Agenda

Mexico has followed an ambivalent multilateral policy. The government actively engages in multilateral negotiations in both economic and traditional security issues while keeping a defensive, low-profile approach in regional matters and in the bargaining processes for the institutionalization of new forms of security cooperation such as peacekeeping operations, the promotion of democracy, and humanitarian intervention. During the liberalizing period, the bulk of Mexico's multilateral activism has focused on two arenas: the economic agenda of Mexican foreign policy, mainly trade and finance, and the traditional security agenda of disarmament, nonproliferation of nuclear arms, and arms control. Mexico has maintained a rather conservative policy on the construction of multilateral institutional capabilities for global and regional collective security. Instead of deepening engagement in formal multilateral organizations, Mexico has looked for potential allies by increasing its participation in multilateral ad hoc groups, such as the Contadora and the Rio Group.

Mexico has followed the pattern of middle-power behavior in terms of the adoption of a clear pacifist and constructive approach. Mexico has also deployed a sustained and intense multilateral activity in the codification of international law and the creation of focal points in various issue areas besides disarmament, such as drug control, migrant workers' rights, and international criminal tribunals. One of the most visible examples of this is Mexico's active role in the multilateral negotiations on the design and implementation of the 1988 UN Convention Against Illicit Traffic in

Narcotic Drugs and Psychotropic Substances. In the first phase of the negotiations, Mexico sought to reach a compromise between the interests of consumer and producing countries by introducing the principles of shared responsibility, reciprocity, and an integrated balanced approach for combating with equal energy the production, trafficking, and consumption of drugs.

Mexico's long-standing commitment to multilateralism has been characterized by a defensive legalist approach rather than a proactive political stance.[56] Mexico, like many other intermediate countries, likes international institutions, prefers multilateral action to unilateral action, and promotes the establishment of formal rules as a way to restrain the powerful. However, current Mexican multilateral policy has been ambivalent in the sense that Mexico prefers some institutions over others. This has led to an uneven or selective commitment to the strengthening of multilateral institutions and multilateralism. While Mexico has followed a pattern of active and assertive multilateral diplomacy in the traditional issues of arms control and disarmament, the country has adopted a passive or critical stance on some of the post–Cold War new security issues, such as peacekeeping operations. Mexico has participated very little in peacekeeping operations. In security issues Mexico has not played a followership role, but instead has acted with defensiveness and reluctance. In the security arena Mexico has emphasized the primacy of global multilateral institutions over regional institutions, about which it has maintained a very conservative policy.

In many very important ways, Mexico's position seeks to reverse (or at least contain) current trends in the international arena. Although there is a trend toward the regionalization of security, Mexico supports an increasingly global management of regional crises. There has been an expansion of the international security agenda to encompass political, social, and environmental aspects, but Mexico proposes a narrower definition of national security. While there has been an expansion of international institutions, Mexico has been against the unrestrained expansion of their powers, particularly the use of force and coercion in enforcing international rules.

In contrast to Mexico's active embrace of internationalism in the economic sphere, Mexican multilateral policy in the international security arena has remained more ambiguous. Mexico responded to the expansion of the new international security agenda, particularly the emergence of the "right of humanitarian intervention" by multilateral institutions, with more reserve and caution than any other Latin American country. Instead of playing a leadership role, Mexico has followed the pattern of a non-joiner. Since the end of the Cold War, Mexico has constantly opposed multilateral intervention, at both the regional and global level, as an instrument for protecting democracy and human rights. Mexico's skepticism and opposition to the use of multilateral institutions for political purposes was in part self-interested as a way to avoid greater external surveillance of its own difficult domestic political transition. The general insistence on the inviolability of the sovereignty and nonintervention norms with respect to political issues also rested on principle and pragmatism. The Mexican government questioned whether foreign interference was either appropriate or productive in intervening to promote democracy, protect human rights, ameliorate the social and human costs caused by the intensification of civil wars, or restore domestic peace. This traditional stance toward the construction of monitoring by international mechanisms to detect human rights violations and promote democracy shows that there were clear limits on the redefinition of Mexican nationalism attempted by Salinas in the economic sphere. In the words of President Zedillo: "We Mexicans do not need or accept foreign tutelage in settling our differences or solving our problems. Mexico's sovereignty is not subject to negotiation, nor will it ever be" (Fourth State of the Nation Report to the Congress of the Union, 1 September 1998).

## Conclusions: The Tasks Ahead

At the beginning of the new millennium, Mexico seems to be on the verge of a second round of strategic policy reforms designed to address pressures from globalization and the risks of hegemonic unilateralism. Various factors push for the introduction of important policy adjustments for resolving serious microeconomic, productivity, and social bottlenecks left unattended by the 1980s and 1990s market-oriented reforms. First, since the beginning, Mexico's grand strategy of openness to the world and economic alignment with the United States had clear limits. The strategy was conceived in purely economic terms as a partial response to some of the challenges posed by the globalization process, mainly the risks of protectionism and marginalization from trade and capital. Many key issues—such as macroeconomic policy coordination, financial instability, technological innovation, transnational labor markets, diffusion of information, migration flows, social inequality, international norms, multiple citizenship, transnationalization of crime—were not addressed by the 1990s neoliberal thinking that promoted the shift of Mexico's development strategy from the import-substitution model to export-led growth. These "other" pending social and political issues are gaining importance for both global negotiations and the national political agenda.

Second, the economic partnership with the United States has also shown its limits. After 5 years of operation, it is clear that although the signing of NAFTA opened a new era of bilateral cooperation and institutional dialogue, collaboration between the two countries remains segmented and the extent of mutual confidence limited. The intensification of police and military migratory controls along the U.S.-Mexican border is a telling indicator of unresolved policy conflicts and the low level of U.S. trust in Mexico. For Mexico, despite the new cosmopolitanism of its foreign policy and the strength of the 1980s and 1990s economic reforms, the asymmetry in the bilateral relationship, the vulnerability associated with proximity and high interdependence, and domestic political constraints have placed severe limits on the extent to which the ruling party can compromise national sovereignty.

Third, the sequence of virulent financial crises in Mexico (1995), Southeast Asia (1997), Eastern Europe (1998), and Brazil (1999) over 5 years has shown the need to implement fundamental reforms in both the international financial architecture and in the fragile domestic financial structures in developing economies and transition regimes in order to prevent, mitigate, and handle the volatility inherent to the operation of unregulated globalized financial markets. As Stephan Haggard has pointed out, the challenge posed by the issue of international financial reform goes far beyond the need to strengthen the IMF's role as the lender of last resort, and includes a broad range of such domestic institutional reforms as eradicating corruption, strengthening central banks and financial regulators, and improving corporate governance and transparency. Consequently, the handling of financial and monetary issues might have long-term spillover effects on issues linked to the ongoing wave of domestic political reforms: rule of law, property rights, accountability, and democratic governability.[57]

Fourth, at the domestic level the process of adjusting to globalization through the implementation of market-oriented policies has been particularly painful, and to a great extent has contributed to the erosion of the social, institutional, and political basis of political stability. The indigenous revolt in Chiapas, the wave of political assassinations, the expansion of organized crime and drug-related violence, and the increased participation by the army in public safety operations are some of the most visible symptoms of the existence of serious governability risks. The real challenge facing Mexican political leaders is not only how to manage growing domestic dissatisfaction with the poor welfare reaped from economic reforms, but mainly how to build up the necessary institutional architecture for democratic governance under conditions of increasing political fragmentation, growing income disparities, and widening exposure to external shocks and competition.

This brief overview of the evolution of Mexico's role and strategies in the trade and security multilateral arenas in the past two decades offers evidence that supports some predictions from each of the three analytical interpretations about the implications of the end of the Cold War for intermediate countries. On one hand, Mexico's recent experience supports the systemic-structural approach and the pivotal-states model argument on the overall reduction of opportunities that intermediate countries in the developing world have for playing an active leadership role in international negotiations. Faced with the need to maintain a cooperative bilateral relationship with its important economic partner and the need to cope with severe economic and political problems, from 1995 onward Mexico has moved to a partial restraint and a lower profile in foreign policy issues. On the other hand, the middle-powers approach seems to explain better Mexico's shift from a traditional legalist multilateral stance toward a more selective, segmented, and pragmatic policy of multilateral engagement. The Mexican case also seems to support the middle-powers approach's prediction that intermediate states will take greater responsibilities on the international multilateral stage in the context of a leadership void. Mexico has tended to be more actively involved and to adopt a clearer leadership role in those multilateral areas where the distribution of power was less asymmetrical (such as the global multilateral security institutions in contrast to the regional security arrangement), or in those periods or issue areas where the leadership of the United States was waning or lacking (e.g., the United Nations during the 1980s, the international trade negotiations after the formation of the WTO, the UN disarmament and arms control agenda vis-à-vis its peacekeeping operation).

In the Mexican case, the increasing importance of multilateral international institutions in the management of the security and the international trade arena has not been automatically associated either with an increase in the number of opportunities for independent and active diplomatic action or with the strengthening of the country's overall bargaining power. The correlation between the extent of institutionalization and the level of active multilateral participation shows no linear trend over time and across issues. Some domestic economic and political factors have played an important role in eroding Mexico's leadership in the post–Cold War multilateral economic and political arenas and in widening the gap between the international and the domestic political agenda. First, the profound economic crisis at the outset of the Zedillo administration in December 1994 not only increased the domestic opposition to deepening the trade liberalization strategy behind Mexico's active participation in the WTO, but also raised doubts about the soundness of the newly reinforced multilateral liberal trade system. Second, the resurgence of political violence, the increasing militarization of law enforcement operations, the institutionalization of corruption, and the deterioration of human rights conditions in Mexico led to an erosion of the country's "good citizen" international image and reputation. The new issues at the core of the international agenda—human rights, promotion of democracy, drug trafficking—were precisely the most sensitive and divisive issues in the Mexican domestic political agenda.

## Notes

1. For the purposes of this chapter, globalization is understood as a multifaceted process that goes beyond the economic realm to include the internationalization of politics. The World Bank's definition of globalization as "the integration of trade, finance, people, and ideas in one global market" captures the multidimensional nature of the phenomenon. See World Bank, *World Development Indicators* (Washington, D.C: World Bank, 1999).

2. Other indicators of Mexico's increasing integration into the global economy point in the same direction. The ratio of gross private capital flows to GDP rose from 2.7 percent in 1987 to 3.8 percent in 1997. Gross FDI share of GDP more than doubled between 1987 and 1997, from 0.6 to 1.6 percent. See World Bank, 1999.

3. Jorge Castañeda makes the point that Mexico's economic opening to the world led to the emergence of a "new cleavage cutting across Mexican society. This split separates those Mexicans plugged into the U.S. economy from those who are not." Even some official economic studies have documented the fact that the opening of the economy reduced the integration of several national production chains, increasing the gap between the export-oriented sector and the rest of the economy. See Castañeda, "Mexico's Circle of Misery,"*Foreign Affairs* 75, 4 (1996): 92–105; Denise Dresser, "Post-NAFTA Politics in Mexico. Uneasy, Uncertain, Unpredictable," in Carol Wise, ed., *The Post-NAFTA Political Economy: Mexico and the Western Hemisphere* (University Park, Pa.: Pennsylvania State University Press, 1998), 221–256; Secretaría de Comercio y Fomento Industrial (SECOFI), *Industrial Policy and International Trade* (Mexico City: SECOFI, 1997).

4. Soesastro distinguishes between two kinds of adjustments to globalization. First-order adjustments focus on the opening up of the economy to the forces of globalization through economic liberalization, deregulation, privatization, free-trade, and financial liberalization policies, whereas second-order adjustments entail coping with the asymmetric side effects of economic liberalization and the adoption of policies to rectify the increasing disparities of income and access to

economic opportunities between different groups in society, regions within the country, and large and medium or small enterprises. The most important issues related to second-order adjustments are the reduction of income gaps, raising of labor standards, improvement of the educational system and the bureaucracy, improvement of the country's scientific and technological base, and need for greater political transparency. See Soesastro (1998, 24–35).

5. This argument draws on Guadalupe González and Jorge Chabat (1996). For a systematic analysis of the contradictions between economic and political aspects of the Salinas administration's foreign policy see Chabat, "Mexican Foreign Policy in the 1990s: Learning to Live with Interdependence," in Heraldo Muñoz and Joseph Tulchin, eds., *Latin American Nations in World Politics* (Boulder, Colo.: Westview Press, 1996).

6. This characterization is from Samuel Huntington, "The Lonely Superpower. U.S. Military and Cultural Hegemony Resented by Other Powers," *Foreign Affairs* 78, 2 (1999): 35.

7. In this section I will follow David Mares's use of the notion of grand strategy. In Mares's view grand strategy has three elements: the identification of threats; the elaboration of economic, military, and other means to oppose those threats; and the relative ranking of those means. See Mares, "Strategic Interests in the U.S.-Mexican Relationship," in John Bailey and Sergio Aguayo, eds., *Strategy and Security in U.S.-Mexican Relations Beyond the Cold War* (San Diego: Center for U.S. Mexican Studies, University of California, San Diego, 1996): 20.

8. Peter H. Smith, "Mexico," in Robert Chase, Emily Hill, and Paul Kennedy, eds., *The Pivotal States: A New Framework for U.S. Policy in the Developing World* (New York: W. W. Norton and Co., 1999): 215–243, see also chaps. 9–12.

9. Samuel Huntington, "The Lonely Superpower. U.S. Military and Cultural Hegemony Resented by Other Powers," *Foreign Affairs* 78, 2 (1999): 35.

10. This argument is developed by David A. Lake in "Regional Security Complexes: A Systems Approach," in David A. Lake and Patrick M. Morgan, eds., *Regional Orders. Building Security in a New World* (University Park, Pa.: Pennsylvania State University Press, 1997): 45–67.

11. David A. Lake, *Entangling Relations. American Foreign Policy in this Century* (Princeton, N.J.: Princeton University Press, 1999): 262.

12. World Bank 1999, 319.

13. Malcom Knight, "Developing and Transition Countries Confronting Financial Globalization," *Finance and Development* 36, 2 (1999): 32–36.

14. See Charles-Philippe David and Stéphane Roussel. 1998. "Middle Power Blues: Canadian Policy and International Security After the Cold War," *The American Review of Canadian Studies* (Spring-Summer 1998): 150.

15. Andrew Hurrell raised this point at the seminar, Intermediate States: Strategies in Multilateral Arenas, organized by the Latin American Program at the Woodrow Wilson International Center for Scholars on 13 May 1999.

16. For a systematic analysis of the growing importance of international institutions and the move toward new forms of global governance, see Robert O. Keohane, "International Institutions: Can Interdependence Work?" *Foreign Policy* (1998).

17. Keohane, 1998: 110.

18. The international relations field is divided over the question of whether international institutions matter for world politics, as neoliberal institutionalists suggest, or do not, as neorealists argue. For the purpose of this chapter, I simply document the empirical trend toward the proliferation of international institutions and review the main neoliberal institutionalist theoretical explanations for this trend. Institutionalist theory is best represented by Robert O. Keohane's *After Hegemony: Cooperation and Discord in the World Political Economy* (Princeton, N.J.: Princeton University Press, 1984). Realist scholars have not developed explicit theoretical propositions on this subject.

19. For a review of the vast literature on international institutions, see Lisa Martin and Beth Simmons, "Theories and Empirical Studies of International Institutions," *International Organization* 52, 4 (1998): 729–758.

20. Andrew F. Cooper, Richard A. Higgott, and Kim Richard Nossal, "Bound to Follow: Leadership and Followership in the Gulf Conflict," *Political Science Quarterly* 106 (Fall 1991).

21. Peter H. Smith, *Talons of the Eagle. Dynamics of U.S.–Latin American Relations* (Oxford: Oxford University Press, 1996), 303. Notice that Smith's list of available alternatives at the end of the Cold War does not include the use of international law and institutions. In contrast, middle-power theorists emphasize the role of international institutions as windows of opportunity for independent action by secondary states.

22. The concept of intermediate or middle power is a loose analytical category used by different authors with different meanings. In general, this category has been defined either as a position or as a role. While realists use the concept to describe a particular set of countries that occupy an intermediate position— between great powers and small states—within the international distribution of power, liberal-institutionalists and constructivists tend to define it in terms of a particular set of behavioral characteristics or roles.

23. Andrew F. Cooper, "Niche Diplomacy: A Conceptual Overview," in Andrew F. Cooper, ed., *Niche Diplomacy. Middle Powers After the Cold War* (New York: St. Martin's Press, 1997): 1–24.

24. It should be noted that some authors have challenged the argument that the end of the Cold War has opened new opportunities for the influence of the paradigmatic middle powers. According to this critique, the end of bipolarity has reduced the importance of the traditional bridge-building role of middle powers, and the growing engagement of great powers in multilateral cooperative initiatives is overshadowing the role of the middle powers in those institutions. See David and Roussel, 1998.

25. See Robert Chase, Emily Hill, and Paul Kennedy, eds., *The Pivotal States. A New Framework for U.S. Policy in the Developing World* (New York: W. W. Norton and Co., 1999).

26. Chase, Hill, and Kennedy identify nine developing countries as pivotal: Mexico, Brazil, Algeria, Egypt, South Africa, Turkey, India, Pakistan, and Indonesia. See Chase, Hill, and Kennedy (1999, 8).

27. Rodolfo O. de la Garza and Jesus Velasco, eds., *Bridging the Border: Transforming Mexico-U.S. Relations* (Lanham, Md.: Rowman and Littlefield, 1997).

28. See Guadalupe G. Gonzalez and Stephan Haggard, "The United States and Mexico: A Pluralistic Security Community?" in Emanuel Adler and Michael Barnett, eds., *Security Communities* (Cambridge: Cambridge University Press, 1998): 311–314.

29. Various studies have documented the fact that the signing of a comprehensive free-trade agreement with the United States was not Mexico's first choice. See Smith 1996; W. Frederick Mayer, *Interpreting NAFTA. The Science and Art of Political Analysis* (New York: Columbia University Press, 1998).

30. Mexico has always opposed the existence of the category of permanent members as well as the creation of new permanent seats, whether exclusive or rotational, in order to lead the organization with the argument that this division establishes a discriminatory situation. For a detailed analysis of Mexico's UN policy in the 1980s and mid-1990s, see Olga Pellicer, "México y las Naciones Unidas, 1980–1990. De la Crisis del Multilateralismo a los Retos de la Posguerra Fría," in César Sepúlveda, ed., *La Política Internacional de México en el Decenio de los Ochenta* (Mexico City: Fondo de Cultura Económica, 1994).

31. The new official position in Central America was in favor of the dissolution of the Contadora Group with the argument that it had fulfilled its tasks with the signing of the Esquipulas Agreement.

32. The Mexican government tacitly supported the United States on this issue and distanced itself from one of the most important traditional practices, the Estrada Doctrine on recognition of governments, by making an open statement against General Noriega.

33. See Mayer, 1998, 236.

34. For a detailed analysis of the Mexican lobby in Washington, see Eisenstadt, 1998.

35. See Carlos M. Gonzalez, "Mexico and the North American Gateway to Globalization," *Voices of Mexico* 44 (1998): 44–46.

36. One clear indicator of this is the fact that President Zedillo did not even mention any foreign policy issue either in his first or in his fifth messages on the state of the union.

37. Data from *NAFTA Works* 4, 2 (February 1999).

38. World Bank, 1999.

39. Jonathan Heath, "The Impact of Mexico's Trade Liberalization. Jobs, Productivity and Structural Change," in Carol Wise, ed., *The Post-NAFTA Political Economy. Mexico and the Western Hemisphere* (University Park, Pa.: Pennsylvania State University Press, 1998): 197.

40. Smith, 1999, 217.

41. Between 1951 and 1981 GDP growth rate averaged 6.4 percent.

42. Growth of GDP per capita was –1.1 percent in 1985–1990, –0.4 percent in 1990–1995, and 4.1 percent in 1995–1998. Data from the Inter-American Development Bank, cited by Diana Alarcon, "Mexico's Income Distribution and Poverty Alleviation Policies in Comparative Perspective," paper presented at the conference, Confronting Development: Assessing Mexico's Economic and Social Policy Challenges, organized by the Center for U.S.-Mexican Studies, University of California, San Diego, 4–5 June 1999.

43. Cited in Robin King, "US-Mexico Relations Approaching 2000: Looking Back to Look Ahead," *Occasional Paper Series*, Center for Latin American Studies, Georgetown University, No. 11, 1999, p. 22.

44. Miles Kahler, "Introduction: Liberalization and Foreign Policy," in *Liberalization and Foreign Policy* (New York: Columbia University Press, 1997): 19.

45. Rosario Green's speech at University of California, San Diego, 22 April 1999.

46. Kahler, 1997, 302.

47. For a detailed study of the new instruments of Mexico's foreign policy, see Jorge Chabat, "Mexico's Foreign Policy after NAFTA: The Tools of Interdependence," in de la Garza and Velasco, 1997, 33–47.

48. This section draws heavily on two excellent analyses of the evolution of Mexico's economic liberalization policies since the mid-1980s: Claudia Schatan, "Out of the Crisis: Mexico," in Diana Tussie and David Glover, eds., *The Developing Countries in World Trade: Policies and Bargaining Strategies* (1993); and Organization for Economic Co-Operation and Development, *Trade Liberalisation Policies in Mexico* (Paris: OECD, 1996).

49. For a comprehensive analysis of NAFTA negotiations, see Mayer, 1998.

50. For a detailed analysis of Mexico's multiple trade strategy, see Tussie and Glover, 1993, 225.

51. See Mares, 1996.

52. Schatan, 1993, 87.

53. The resentment from Latin American nations did have practical consequences. For example, Mexico's trade preferences with Brazil, agreed to under the Asociacion Latinoamericana de Integracion (ALADI), lapsed when Mexico joined NAFTA. Under ALADI, no member was allowed to have better trade preferences with a non-member. Brazil led the call for Mexico's expulsion from ALADI. See *Mexico and NAFTA Report* 4 (May 1999).

54. The current status of integration in the Western Hemisphere includes the following multilateral agreements: ALADI, Mercosur, Andean Group, Central American Common Market, Caribbean Common Market, NAFTA, and Group of Three. For a comprehensive analysis of Mexico's role in regional trade integration, see Lopez-Ayllon, 1999.

55. For a rigorous development of this point see Stephan Haggard, "Why Do We Need the IMF?" *IGCC Newsletter* 14, 1 (1998): 6–7.

56. Here I use the concept of multilateralism in the same terms as Ruggie's 1993 definition, as "the search of cooperation or policy coordination on the basis of generalized principles of conduct."

57. See Haggard, 1998.

# 7

## Cuban Foreign Policy and the International System

### *Jorge I. Domínguez*

In October 1997, Fidel Castro and the Fifth Congress of the Cuban Communist Party confidently celebrated their capacity to survive the collapse of the Soviet Union and of all communist governments in Europe and renewed U.S. efforts in the 1990s to bring to an end this long-enduring, embattled Cuban government.[1] They led the only remaining communist regime outside East Asia. And, although many problems afflicted them and the Cuban people, Castro and the party believed that the economy had touched bottom and had begun to recover, that they retained at least the tolerance and perhaps the support of many Cubans, and that they had fashioned a successful international strategy under severe constraints. In this chapter I will focus on the last of these accomplishments.

I will argue that the Cuban government keenly and accurately understood its predicament in the international system: how to survive given that its major allies had collapsed and that prevailing international norms and alignments had turned strongly against it. Behaving as convinced neorealists, Cuban leaders sharply retrenched the scope of their previous foreign policy, adjusted their economy to the new circumstances, and fashioned an institutionalist strategy to counter U.S. power and, collaterally, to obtain information and reduce uncertainty about this new world order. Cuba remains stunningly isolated compared to its international situation before 1989, but its government has crawled back into the international system thanks to its diplomacy and to the adverse reactions of other states to U.S. policies toward Cuba.

Given the constraints that it faced in the 1990s, Cuba's level of international activity is certainly intense. Cuba is vigorously engaged in the UN system. It pursues a complex diplomacy with the European Union. It has developed good relations with Mexico and Canada, the partners of the

United States in NAFTA. It employs its relations with Latin American and Caribbean countries as a means to elude, and preferably to break, U.S. encirclement. Cuba looks for a role among the Caribbean economies in cooperation with other Caribbean governments; Cuba's success in its Caribbean endeavors was probably greater in the 1990s than at any time since the 1959 revolution.

There are three principal differences between Cuba and other Latin American countries in their respective insertion into international affairs. First, Cuba has a highly centralized political system that has been able to block or to contain the impact of globalization on the country. Paradoxically, it has been assisted in this endeavor by U.S. policies to isolate Cuba. Cuba participates little in international trade and investment flows. Cuba is a living museum for obsolete technology. More noteworthy is its equally limited participation, by Latin American standards, in international information flows; Cuba has limited access to the Internet, its telecommunications infrastructure is dilapidated (though being repaired), and its television programming is of poor quality. Second, the same highly centralized political system permits its government to behave as a unified rational actor in the design and execution of foreign policy. The normal influences on foreign policymaking in other countries that stem from the clashes of domestic social, economic, and political interests play a much smaller role in shaping Cuba's international insertion. And, third, since about 1980 the Cuban diaspora in the United States has controlled at times, and influenced at all times, the design and content of U.S. policy toward Cuba. Cuba holds a unique role in the annals of U.S. foreign policy toward Latin America: no other Latin American government must cope with a hostile and influential diaspora within the United States.

## Born-Again Neorealists

In the scholarship of international relations neorealism insists that states are the most important actors in world politics, that their behavior is rational, and that states seek power and calculate their interests in terms of power in the face of an international system that lacks effective centralized authority (i.e., interstate anarchy).[2] The configuration of capabilities helps to shape behavior in the international system. Neorealists, however, accord little explanatory importance to domestic politics.[3]

From its beginning in 1959, the foreign policy of Fidel Castro's government demonstrated a clear understanding of neorealist premises.

Neorealism provides a better general framework to understand the Castro government's foreign policy than other alternatives, even though there are some noteworthy differences, as noted below. Cuba's alliance with the Soviet Union, forged in late 1959 and especially in 1960, was intended to counter the United States. Cuban leaders understood that the survival of their government and, more generally, the bold and broad scope of Cuban foreign policy rested on the bedrock of their alliance with the Soviet Union. The Soviet alliance enabled Cuba to survive the onslaught from the United States during the 1960s, and to launch a program of economic recovery in the early 1970s. From 1975 to 1990, Cuba (median population in those years about 10 million people) sent over 300,000 troops to overseas military missions. Typically, Cuba had 30,000 to 50,000 troops deployed overseas during any given year in that 15-year span. And, unlike U.S. troops in Vietnam and Soviet troops in Afghanistan, Cuban troops won the three wars they went to fight on African soil (twice in Angola and once in Ethiopia). Indeed, Cuba's was the only communist government capable of deploying significant military forces across the oceans and achieving its objectives on the battlefield. The Soviet Union had no more reliable military ally during the Cold War.

Cuban leaders also disagreed with neorealist expectations concerning the practical and analytical role of domestic politics. In practice, the Cuban government understood that the U.S. government cared not just to tame Cuban foreign policy but also to bring down the Cuban government. Analytically, the Cuban government was convinced that it could not counter the United States if it limited the scope of its actions to interstate relations; it was necessary to confront U.S. attempts to crush the Castro government by seeking to undermine or overthrow governments allied with the United States. For over 30 years the Cuban government actively supported revolutionary movements in other countries. It did so not just for the sake of interstate competition but also as part of its overarching ideology—the set of core beliefs that guided the leadership in its ambitious attempts to transform fellow citizens and make the world safe for revolution.[4] As Castro once put it eloquently:

> The imperialists are everywhere in the world. And for Cuban revolutionaries the battleground against imperialism encompasses the whole world. . . . And so our people understand . . . that the enemy is one and the same, the same one who attacks our shores and our territory, the same one who attacks everyone else. And so we say and proclaim that the revolutionary movement in every corner of the world can count on Cuban combat fighters.[5]

Cuba supported both revolutionary movements and revolutionary states against the U.S. government and its allies. In effect, Cuba did not accept the "hard-shell" notion of sovereignty implicit in neorealist analyses.

The Cuban government responded to the collapse of the Soviet Union and other European governments exactly as neorealist scholars would expect. Cuban leaders understood instantly that the structure of the international system had changed—for them the international system had become threateningly unipolar because their archenemy, the U.S. government, still loomed over them but was now unchallenged by a Soviet superpower. Given the changed configuration of power in the international system and the loss of its indispensable ally, the Cuban government therefore simultaneously retrenched across various dimensions of its foreign policy. In September 1989 Cuba completed the repatriation of its troops from Ethiopia (they had been first posted there in 1977).[6] In March 1990, all Cuban military personnel in Nicaragua were brought back to Cuba (they had first arrived in 1979).[7] In May 1991, Cuba's last troops were repatriated from Angola (they had first been deployed in 1975).[8] Also, in 1990 and 1991, Cuba brought home its troops and military advisers from various other countries.

The collapse of the Soviet Union and the European communist world devastated the Cuban economy. Cuban exports of goods and services dropped from about 6 billion pesos in 1989 to 2 billion pesos in 1993. The principal reason for this drop was the elimination of all Soviet subsidies for Cuban sugar exports. Consequently, imports of goods and services plunged from 8.6 billion pesos in 1989 to 2.4 billion pesos in 1993. Cuba had also lost Soviet subsidies for importing petroleum and Soviet financing for Cuba's trade deficit.[9]

Cuba responded to this economic cataclysm by adjusting to the prevailing distribution of world economic power. Cuba reopened its economy to foreign direct investment (FDI). In May 1990, President Castro inaugurated the first hotel built as a joint venture with a foreign partner in 30 years. He announced that Cuba would seek foreign investment to develop its economy.[10] As Vice President Carlos Lage, the chief of the economic cabinet, put it before the twelfth Havana International Fair on 30 October 1994: "We are offering you an orderly country, a coherent and irreversible policy of openness to capital investment."[11]

By the end of 1996 this economic policy reversal had begun to bear fruit. In that year, Cuba exported 3.4 billion pesos and imported 4.5 billion pesos (both in goods and services). Also by the end of 1996, the accumulated stock of FDI in Cuba was about $1 billion, with signed pledges for another $1.1 billion. These investments came from 260 partnerships from 50 countries.[12] These are tiny amounts by the standards of international capital markets, but they are large sums for the small Cuban economy to garner since 1990 despite U.S. efforts to prevent it.

The Cuban government also stopped supporting revolutionary movements. In April 1991 it curtailed all assistance to its longtime ally, El Salvador's revolutionary movement (Frente Farabundo Martí de Liberación Nacional—FMLN), other than political support.[13] Once a peace agreement was signed in El Salvador, President Castro chose a symbolic event to announce that Cuba would no longer support revolutionary movements militarily. He did so in January 1992, while hosting several former high officials of the Kennedy administration (along with Cuban and former Soviet officials) to reflect on the 1962 missile crisis.[14] Henceforth, the Cuban government would continue to resist U.S. efforts to bring it down, but for the first time Cuba would be able to rally international support because its government was no longer seeking to bring down other governments.

Cuban leaders were reborn as neorealists because they adjusted quickly to the changed distribution of international power and because, at long last, they were prepared to recognize, as well as claim respect for, hardshell sovereignty, forgoing intervention in the domestic affairs of other countries in order to demand the same from the United States.

## An Institutionalist Strategy

Neorealists "maintain that institutions are basically a reflection of the distribution of power in the world. They are based on the self-interested calculations of the great powers, and they have no independent effect on state behavior."[15] If so, communist Cuba should have stayed away from international institutions in the 1990s. On the contrary, in the 1990s Cuba followed a strategy of joining new international organizations and adapting its behavior to "fit" into international organizations that are not dominated by the United States.

Absent a superpower partner or, unlike Iran and Iraq, petroleum or other economic resources to maintain a powerful military, international organizations provided Cuba with an option to counter the United States and break out of isolation. Of course Cuba also sought support directly from individual states, but it understood that states might find it easier to stand up to the United States if they were to act in concert. Cuba thought of international organizations as alliances to stiffen the backbone of governments that the United States might otherwise seek to bully. Cuba, therefore, followed an institutionalist strategy principally for neorealist reasons, that is, to counter the United States.

The Cuban government had no doubt that the United States would press its advantage after the collapse of the Soviet Union. But Cuba made a second bet—that Kenneth Waltz, the modern architect of neorealism, would prove right when he described responses to the United States after the end of the Cold War in Europe:

> Unbalanced power, whoever wields it, is a potential danger to others. The powerful state may, and the United States does, think of itself as acting for the sake of peace, justice, and well-being in the world. These terms, however, will be defined to the liking of the powerful, which may conflict with the preferences and interests of others. The powerful state will at times act in ways that appear arbitrary and high handed to others, who will smart under the unfair treatment they believe they are receiving. Some of the weaker states in the system will therefore act to restore a balance.[16]

Cuba did not have to prove Waltz right in his general analysis of the international system; the hunch of its leaders was that the United States, while speaking in the name of liberty and democracy, in conducting its policy toward Cuba would indeed "act in ways that appear arbitrary and high handed to others."

Cuba also followed an institutionalist strategy, to a limited degree, for reasons where neorealism and institutionalism converge. International institutions facilitate the transfer of information, a valuable asset for an isolated country such as Cuba. Moreover, given Cuba's perception that the U.S. government posed a major threat, institutions also reduce uncertainty to some degree because Cuba finds it easier to gauge just how far other countries will support the U.S. government in its conflict with the Cuban government. In some cases, international institutions lower the relative costs of international transactions. And, of course, international institutions also set normative rules for international behavior that are available for use against any misbehaving state, including a superpower.[17]

### Responding to International Isolation

As Cuba entered the 1990s, it suddenly found itself bereft not just of its major allies but also of its principal network of international institutions. The most important international institution for Cuba's economic development had been the Soviet-led Council for Mutual Economic Assistance (CMEA) with its associated panoply of organizations, which had grouped the communist governments of Europe. In 1972 Cuba had become a member and derived important economic and other benefits.[18] This council dissolved as European communist governments tumbled in 1989 and 1990.

On the other hand, communist Cuba had not participated in, nor has it turned to, membership in the IMF, the World Bank, the Inter-American Development Bank, or the OAS, despite occasional exploratory conversations in each case. (Cuba belongs to certain inter-American organizations, such as the Pan American Health Organization, that precede and are not mere creatures of the OAS.) Nonetheless, with its troops repatriated from all corners of the world and with its newly found commitment to respect the sovereignty of all other states, Cuban foreign policy found it easier than in the past to claim membership in various other international organizations to counter the United States and break out of international isolation.

### The Annual Ibero-American Summits

Faced with isolation, Cuba searched for opportunities to participate in international institutions. Spain and Mexico had taken the leadership to call the first Ibero-American Summit, gathering the heads of state and government from the relevant countries of Latin America, including Cuba, and the Iberian Peninsula. The founding meeting was held in Guadalajara, Mexico, in 1991; as host, Mexican President Carlos Salinas welcomed Fidel Castro's presence. These summits have been held every year since then, and President Castro has attended them all.

At the Guadalajara summit Cuba agreed to sign the Treaty of Tlatelolco. This treaty created a Latin American zone of peace free from nuclear weapons. It was endorsed by most Latin American governments, as well as by the United States, Great Britain, France, China, and the Soviet Union, and was formally signed in February 1967.[19] Cuba had refused to sign the treaty, claiming that it would not until the United States changed its policies toward Cuba and, specifically, until the United States pledged that it would not place nuclear weapons at its naval base at Guantanamo and, preferably, until the base was returned to Cuba.[20] By changing its merely symbolic security policies—there had been no nuclear weapons on Cuban soil since the 1962 missile crisis settlement—Cuba signaled its willingness to accommodate some of the policy preferences of the Ibero-American countries. The issues at the Ibero-American summits would hinge on a bargained exchange. How much would the Ibero-American countries press Cuba to democratize? And how much support would Cuba elicit from these countries in its confrontation with the United States?

At the second summit, held in Madrid, in July 1992, the members adopted a strong declaration in support of democracy. Shortly thereafter, the Latin American governments in the so-called Rio Group called on Cuba to liberalize and democratize its domestic institutions.[21] The Castro government's gamble on participating in these summits seemed to backfire, but then the U.S. Congress came to the Cuban government's rescue.

In October 1992 the U.S. Congress enacted the Cuban Democracy Act, whose principal sponsor was Representative Robert Torricelli. The new law prohibited U.S. subsidiaries in third countries from trading with Cuba. The law directly affected many countries that deemed it extraterritorial and in violation of the rules under the General Agreement on Tariffs and Trade (GATT). Speaking the language of democracy, the United States seemed to be acting arbitrarily, injuring the interests of its trading partners. At the Third Ibero-American Summit held in Bahía, Brazil, in July 1993, the Ibero-American leaders alluded critically to U.S. policies toward Cuba while they reiterated their general support for democracy and human rights. This summit set the pattern for subsequent years. Cuba accepted the endorsement of democratic principles at these summits, while, in turn, the member governments criticized U.S. policies toward Cuba.

In March 1996, the U.S. Congress enacted the Cuban Liberty and Democratic Solidarity Act, sponsored by Senator Jesse Helms and Representative Dan Burton. President Clinton, as authorized by the law itself, suspended enforcement of its key feature, Title III. Title III would authorize U.S. citizens and firms to sue in U.S. courts those firms from other countries that "traffic" with Cuba; the law is broadly written to affect most FDI in Cuba as well as trade. This law threatens the interests of other countries much more directly than the Cuban Democracy Act.[22] Once again, speaking the language of liberty and democracy, the United States acted in ways that seemed arbitrary and that injured the interests of its trading partners. The Cuban government capitalized on the potential for international balancing.

At the November 1996 Ibero-American Summit in Santiago, Chile, the countries termed the Helms-Burton Act "a violation of international law" and urged its reconsideration. Argentina had sought to limit the summit to "pluralistic democracies" in order to exclude Cuba but found insufficient support. Mexican President Ernesto Zedillo was the strongest proponent of Cuba's rights at the summit, thereby reinforcing Mexico's historic position with regard to Cuba.[23] The summit did reaffirm its broad support for democracy everywhere. At the November 1997 Ibero-American Summit in Margarita, Venezuela, the governments condemned the Helms-Burton Act and all other "unilateral measures that violate the sovereignty of states," including new bills under consideration in the U.S. Congress. The summit also failed to support a resolution sponsored by Argentina and Nicaragua specifically calling for greater freedom of expression and respect for human rights in Cuba. The summit did endorse yet again its strong general commitment to democracy.[24]

Cuba was greatly assisted by U.S. policy in securing a niche among the Ibero-American governments. Cuba still has no allies among these countries. But it has been able to ignore their democratic declarations at no risk of sanctions because the Ibero-American countries have been alarmed and offended by increasingly aggressive U.S. policies toward its own allies and trading partners in seeking to achieve U.S. objectives in Cuba. These summits have helped Cuba to break out of its political isolation in the aftermath of the collapse of the communist world in Europe and have helped Cuba to resist U.S. pressure.

## The United Nations

In November 1992, Cuba for the first time gained overwhelming support in the UN General Assembly for a resolution condemning the U.S. embargo. This motion passed just days after the U.S. Congress had enacted the Cuban Democracy Act. The following month the General Assembly approved another resolution, also overwhelmingly, calling on the Cuban government to respect the human rights of its citizens. Cuba has ignored UN resolutions on human rights and refused to accept a visit by the special rapporteur appointed by the United Nations to monitor the human rights situation in Cuba.

The enactment of the Helms-Burton Act in 1996 reduced the number of countries that abstained in the voting in the UN General Assembly and increased the number of countries that voted against U.S. policy toward Cuba. In November 1992, 59 countries voted to condemn U.S. policy; 3, including the United States, voted against the motion, while 71 abstained. In November 1997, 143 countries voted to condemn U.S. policy, 3 voted against the motion, and only 17 abstained. U.S. policy served Cuba's balancing purposes admirably within the United Nations as it had at the Ibero-American summits.

Cuba's strategy in the United Nations has emphasized the common cause of many countries in opposing the extraterritorial dimensions of the Torricelli and Helms-Burton acts. Because governments voted to condemn the sanctions inherent in such legislation, they were consequently not inclined to impose additional sanctions on Cuba for not adhering to the human rights enumerated in the Universal Declaration on Human Rights. Once again, Cuba used an international organization to counter the United States and break out of isolation.

## Caribbean Regional Organizations

In the late 1980s, the Cuban government rediscovered that Cuba was an island archipelago washed by the Caribbean Sea, warmed by the sun, and blessed with beautiful beaches. Tourism became a major strategy for international development. Cuba sought to join the Caribbean Tourism Organization (CTO) to share information, learn about common standards, and coordinate policies. Grenada vetoed Cuba's application in 1989. Cuba had not recognized Grenada's governments after the 1983 invasion of that island country by the United States and various anglophone Caribbean forces. In May 1992, Cuba ended its own Cold War in the Caribbean and reestablished normal diplomatic relations with Grenada. (It established diplomatic relations with St. Vincent and the Grenadines in 1993 and with Antigua-Barbuda in 1994, two countries that had joined the United States in the 1983 invasion of Grenada.) A month later Cuba was admitted to the CTO, accelerating Cuba's insertion into Caribbean international relations.[25]

Trade picked up. Nonpetroleum trade between Cuba and the anglophone Caribbean doubled from 1990 to 1992; including petroleum, this trade reached $100 million in 1992, making up about 3 percent of Cuba's total trade in 1992.[26] In December 1993, the Caribbean Community (CARICOM), which groups the anglophone Caribbean states, signed an agreement with Cuba establishing a commission to increase trade. CARICOM created this joint commission despite explicit, public criticism and warnings from members of the U.S. Congress and State Department officials that the United States might retaliate against CARICOM. The agreement would also promote joint efforts in the sugar industry, livestock, and fisheries. The agreement's signing had been delayed because Cuba objected to references to human rights and democracy; in the end, CARICOM yielded on the grounds that such references did not exist in similar agreements reached with other Latin American countries.[27]

Led by the CARICOM countries, the Association of Caribbean States (ACS) was founded in July 1994. The ACS joins CARICOM countries to Venezuela, Mexico, Colombia, and the Central American nations. Cuba joined as a founding member, the first regional economic integration arrangement Cuba had joined anywhere outside the CMEA.[28]

Cuba has rallied CARICOM members to oppose U.S. policies toward Cuba.[29] CARICOM members have come to vote unanimously against

U.S. policy toward Cuba in the UN General Assembly, resist bilateral U.S. pressures on their policies toward Cuba, and on their own raised the Cuba question in their collective summit meeting with President Clinton in 1997. Cuba used Caribbean regional organizations principally to counter the United States, but it also gained from opportunities for broader international economic cooperation consistent with institutionalist expectations. One limitation to this cooperation is that Cuba has become a major competitor in the Caribbean tourism market; by 1996, Cuba hosted 1 million tourists (three times more than it received in the 1950s), more tourists than any CARICOM member but the Bahamas and Jamaica.[30] Nonetheless, Cuban diplomacy has been more successful in the anglophone Caribbean than in any other setting: Cuba has enlisted the political support of Caribbean countries against U.S. policies toward Cuba, it has mitigated the political fallout from increased competition in tourism, and it has expanded trade with the region.

### Constructing Confidence-Building Measures[31]

To prevent an accidental military confrontation, the U.S. and Cuban governments engaged in a number of low-key confidence-building measures in the 1990s.[32] Although many of the specific measures had been contemplated during the Bush administration, their implementation for the most part began in 1993.[33] The two coast guards share some information on search-and-rescue missions in the Straits of Florida. This collaboration has also led to various instances of joint action against drug traffickers; at times the U.S. Coast Guard has provided the information while its Cuban counterpart (Guardafronteras) has arrested the criminals (and, in some cases, has returned them to the United States). On 8 October 1996, for instance, the U.S. and Cuban coast guards collaborated on the seizure of 1.7 tons of cocaine.[34] In general, Cuba has had tough policies against drug trafficking and consumption: in the 1990s, these policies served Cuba well in depriving its U.S. adversaries of a reason to attack Cuba. On the U.S. side, the Justice Department and the FBI have reciprocated, warning against terrorist actions departing from Florida, and have brought would-be terrorists to court.[35] Some confidence-building measures also began in 1993 in and around the U.S. naval base at Guantanamo, including advance notice from one side to the other on military training and small-scale war games.

The most important reason for U.S.-Cuban contact and collaboration has been to cope with the migration flow. In December 1984 the two governments signed a migration agreement. Cuba agreed to take back a specified number of Cubans whom the United States found excludable under its own laws (most had come through Mariel harbor by sea in 1980), and the United States agreed to accept lawful Cuban immigrants routinely. However, the United States typically accepted fewer than five thousand Cubans per year. In August 1994, in response to severe pressures for emigration (including a large-scale riot in Havana), the Cuban government stopped preventing emigration by boat or raft until a new agreement was reached the following month. The United States agreed to take no fewer than twenty thousand Cubans per year; it also reversed decades of U.S. policy by stopping the presumption that Cubans intercepted on the high seas would be automatically considered refugees. The United States would henceforth repatriate nearly all Cubans intercepted on the high seas. This, too, required almost daily collaboration between the two coast guards.[36]

During the 1994 migration crisis, nearly thirty thousand Cubans were held temporarily in camps at the Guantanamo naval base. U.S. and Cuban military authorities developed a constructive relationship in 1994–1995 to deal with this situation. High-ranking Cuban and U.S. military authorities held meetings at the base every 4 to 6 weeks to deal with practical matters. These meetings continued even after the migration crisis subsided; at least one of them was attended by General John Sheahan, chief of the U.S. Atlantic Command.[37]

Both governments continued to collaborate even after the Cuban Air Force shot down two unarmed civilian aircraft, which belonged to the Cuban exile organization Brothers to the Rescue,[38] over international waters on 24 February 1996 and after the U.S. government enacted the Helms-Burton Act. Indeed, bilateral cooperation deepened. Brothers to the Rescue and other Cuban-American organizations staged events on the high seas to confront the Cuban government. For each of these events, both governments set down clear markers for the Cuban-American flotillas headed toward the U.S.-Cuban maritime border.[39] The respective coast guards, supported by the air forces, established close communications. (U.S. Coast Guard officers travel to Havana in advance of each flotilla episode to discuss what each side will do to prevent an incident.)[40]

Both governments have built procedures that have begun to acquire a life of their own.[41] The relationship between the coast guards is professional and regular, and the two governments keep these arrangements free from the contamination of the politicized hostility that otherwise plagues their relations. These procedures are the highest level of U.S.-Cuban official collaboration, but they certainly reduce uncertainty on both sides and communicate information effectively. They reduce the otherwise high transaction costs in U.S.-Cuban interaction, and these procedures feature and exemplify institutionalist reasons for Cuba's institutionalist strategy.

## The Response of the International System

A government's foreign policy is only one element in a state's location in the international system. The actions of other states matter greatly: Cuba's place in the international system cannot be set all by itself. Because Cuba in the 1990s is a particularly weak state, it is a "price taker." The response of other states in the international system to Cuban entreaties, and to those of its U.S. adversary, shaped Cuba's circumstances. Other states resisted U.S. policy toward Cuba, consistent with neorealist expectations, because they believed that U.S. policies injure the states' interests in the international trade and investment system. This is consistent, in turn, with institutionalist explanations because the critics of the United States claimed to defend the very international institutions that the United States has done much to construct and strengthen over time: GATT and the WTO. None of the states that have most confronted the United States over these matters has an ideological affinity with Cuba's government; they have helped Cuba break out of international isolation mainly as a consequence of their objection to U.S. policies.

### The Response of the United States

By early 1992, the United States could have declared victory in its long-standing conflict with Cuba. All of the Cuban international behavior to which the United States had long objected had stopped. Gone were the Soviet-Cuban alliance and Soviet support for the Cuban military; gone were Cuban troops and military advisers from countries near and far; and gone was Cuba's support for revolutionary movements. Not gone, however, was Fidel Castro's government. Contrary to neorealist expectations, in the 1990s the United States came to care deeply about the domestic politics of other countries. And, in the case of Cuba, the U.S. government was seemingly prepared to make the Cuba question more important for U.S. foreign policy than anything else; the two congressional acts of 1992 and 1996 were ready to punish U.S. allies and trading partners over their relations with Cuba.

Three broad factors account for this notably expansive U.S. policy. First, the Soviet Union, hitherto the balancer of U.S. actions, had disappeared. It became easier for the United States to invade Panama (1989) and Haiti (1994) as well as to deploy its forces worldwide to prevent aggression or enforce a peace to its liking. The structure of the international system had changed; the United States found less resistance to its wise actions—and to its foolish actions.

Second, an ideological shift gripped U.S. politics.[42] Begun in contentious partisanship in the 1970s and the first half of the 1980s, by the second half of the 1980s there was political agreement that U.S. policy should defend and foster human rights and democracy. The evolution of U.S. policies in the Americas in the 1980s is a telling case. The Reagan administration began deliberately trashing the Carter administration's human rights policies. The Reagan administration ended pressing long-time dictators in Chile and Paraguay to step down.[43] In 1991, led by the United States and newly democratic Chile, the OAS rededicated itself to actions to defend democratic institutions; the OAS, various Latin American governments, and the United States acted in concert to prevent coups in Guatemala (1993) and Paraguay (1996).[44] The Clinton administration made the enlargement of democracy one of its fundamental tenets. In this political climate, communist Cuba was a pariah state.

Third, right-wing Cuban-American lobbies became better organized. The Cuban American National Foundation (CANF), established in 1981 by Jorge Mas Canosa and others with the Reagan administration's encouragement, made three important contributions to Cuban-American exile politics: it provided a nonviolent instrument for anti-Castro militancy; it channeled financial and human resources into highly focused one-issue political action committees; and it learned to work with U.S. politicians of both major parties.

Cuban Americans had had little impact on U.S. policy toward Cuba before the early 1980s: during the 1980s, CANF's only significant effect on U.S. policy was the creation of Radio and TV Martí. In the 1990s, however, CANF played U.S. politics exquisitely. During the 1992 presidential election, CANF defeated the Bush administration's opposition to a change in Cuba policy by enlisting, first, U.S. Representative Robert Torricelli (D-NJ) and then presidential candidate Bill Clinton to endorse what would become the Cuban Democracy Act. Unwilling to be outflanked on the right, the Bush administration reversed itself and endorsed Torricelli's bill, which passed Congress 2 weeks before the presidential election.[45] CANF proceeded similarly toward the enactment of what would become the Cuban Liberty and Democratic Solidarity Act of 1996. It worked with both Democrats and Republicans. It fought the executive branch. It played the electoral calendar; President Clinton signed the act into law on the day of the 1996 Florida presidential primary. The only difference from 1992 is that Cuba's shooting down of two unarmed airplanes created a political stampede in Congress to support punitive measures against the Castro government.

Yet, as noted previously, the Cuban government, too, played domestic U.S. politics effectively on one key issue: migration. The Castro government understood that a significant portion of U.S. public opinion preferred collaboration with the Cuban government to prevent waves of illegal migrants washing up on U.S. shores. The Castro government obtained noteworthy collaboration from the Clinton administration to block the kind of disorder in Cuba that might generate emigration.

The result of these various factors was a rigid U.S. policy that magnifies Cuba's importance for U.S. policy. The president of the United States was deprived of significant discretion in fashioning policy toward Cuba; punitive policies could be dropped only by an act of Congress. U.S. law mandated harsh penalties on citizens or firms or other countries—mainly U.S. allies and trading partners—if they deviated from the narrow range of conduct that the United States tolerated with regard to international economic relations with Cuba. In practice, however, the content of U.S. policies changed little: U.S. subsidiaries in third countries could not trade with Cuba and some executives of third-country firms with significant investments in Cuba were denied visas to enter the United States. Other punitive policies on third countries were suspended through presidential waiver. Nonetheless, some future U.S. president could let these sanctions be implemented, and this became a source of concern to many governments. Some governments also opposed the injury that U.S. policies caused to a liberal international trade regime. The Latin American and Caribbean countries responded, as we have seen, in opposition to U.S. policy, as did the United Nations. We turn to examine other responses.

## The Response of the European Union and Canada

The European Community had never been a priority on Cuba's foreign policy agenda, although diplomatic and economic relations with its member states had been normal. The relations between them had long been shaped by their respective Cold War alliances.[46] In the 1990s, however, Cuba turned to European countries as a source of trade, direct investment, credit, and tourism, and the newly named European Union began to concern itself with Cuba. The trigger for that concern was not Cuba's severe economic hardship of the early 1990s, and certainly not the prospects for an economic bonanza. It was an attempt to resist the extraterritorial dimensions of U.S. policy toward Cuba.

In September 1993, the European Parliament condemned the 1992 Torricelli law (Cuban Democracy Act), and in September 1994 it called on the Cuban government to enact democratic reforms. Also in 1993, the European Commission created for the first time a humanitarian aid program for Cuba, supplemented by ad hoc measures tailored to Cuban needs and aimed at supporting domestic reform in Cuba. Cuba remained, however, the only Latin American country with which the European Union had not concluded a formal cooperation agreement—even though there were no barriers to trade between Cuba and European countries and Cuba benefited from Europe's generalized system of trade preferences. All EU member states had diplomatic relations with Cuba.[47] In 1995, led by Spain, France, and Italy, the European Commission explored a deepening of its relations with Cuba, in particular the prospects for a formal cooperation agreement. The commission discovered that the Cuban government would agree to no fundamental concessions regarding democratization and human rights. When the Cuban Air Force shot down the two unarmed airplanes in international waters in February 1996, the commission suspended its conversations with the Cuban government over a formal agreement.

The enactment of the Helms-Burton Act in the days that followed, however, mobilized the European Union to confront U.S. policy toward Cuba. The European Union's institutions and individual European governments condemned this U.S. legislation and began proceedings against the United States in the WTO for an alleged violation of international trade law. Faced with a two-part international problem—the confrontation with the United States over Helms-Burton and the failure of its democratizing initiatives toward Cuba—on 2 December 1996 the European Union adopted a "common position" toward Cuba, the first time this high-level procedure was invoked with regard to relations with any Latin American country. The common position codified previous EU policies, although it adopted a stronger commitment to democratization and respect for human rights. The European Union favors a peaceful democratic transition in Cuba; conditions economic assistance and the eventual signing of a formal cooperation agreement to demonstrable democratization in Cuba; commits itself to ongoing dialogue with the Cuban government and with Cuban civil society; insists on strict adherence to the Universal Declaration on Human Rights; urges individual member states to cooperate with Cuba along the lines of economic reform authorized by the Cuban government; and pledges to continue humanitarian assistance with greater emphasis on NGOs. Separately, the European Union has pledged to oppose and contest the Helms-Burton Act.

The Cuban government, having feared worse, was relatively pleased with this outcome for four reasons. First, the European Union continued to contest vigorously U.S. policy toward Cuba. Second, although there was some reduction of humanitarian aid, basic EU policies toward Cuba did not change. Third, the European Union did not constrain the modest aid and credit programs of its member states toward Cuba.[48] And fourth, the European Union rejected some of the proposals of the new center-right Spanish government. Spain had hoped that the European Union would mandate the appointment of a diplomat to each European embassy in Havana to maintain relations with dissidents, require cooperation with the UN special rapporteur for human rights in Cuba, and ask Cuba to grant freedom of travel to its citizens.[49]

Two factors explain the relatively modest changes in EU policies toward Cuba. The confrontation with the United States over the latter's extraterritorial policies constrained European governments that might otherwise press the Cuban government harder over democracy and human rights. And Europeans, in general, believed that confrontation and punishment alone were unlikely to bring about a peaceful democratic transition in Cuba.

Similar factors explain Canadian policy toward Cuba. Before 1990 Canadian-Cuban relations had been typically low-key, emphasizing bilateral trade relations, and most Canadian firms operated in a depoliticized environment. In the wake of the enactment of the Torricelli law, Canada's Conservative Party government strengthened the Foreign Extraterritorial Measures Act to block the effect of the new U.S. law. Most Canadian firms opted to comply with U.S. law, however. In 1994, the new Liberal Party government changed Cuban policy further: Cuba became eligible for official development assistance; Canadian firms would receive trade and investment assistance for their business in Cuba; and the government would support the relations of Canadian nongovernmental, religious, cultural, and academic organizations with their Cuban counterparts. Canada also supported a peaceful transition in Cuba toward more pluralist politics and would channel resources to facilitate it. Appropriately encouraged, Canadian business firms increased their stake in Cuba.[50]

Thus the Canadian government reacted with fury to the Helms-Burton Act, reinforcing the Foreign Extraterritorial Measures Act. Judgments under Helms-Burton could not be enforced against Canadian firms in Canada, and Canadians would be allowed to sue in Canadian courts to recover amounts lost through those foreign rulings. Canada began proceedings against the United States under NAFTA rules and began to coordinate its actions with the European Union and other governments in the

WTO. In January 1997, Cuba and Canada signed a panoply of agreements to foster political, social, and economic collaboration.[51]

Canada sought to engage Cuba to foster changes—the opposite of the U.S. confrontational approach. Compared with the European Union or the Ibero-American governments, Canada took the boldest approach to cooperating with Cuba and countering U.S. policy. In this way, CARICOM and Canada opposed the United States the most, with the Latin Americans and the European Union doing so less markedly. All agreed that the United States had to be contained, and in that outcome the Cuban government found its most important ally in its never-ending battle with the United States.

## Trade Partners

International politics had implications for Cuban trade performance. The collapse of the Soviet Union had resulted in a collapse of the Cuban economy and of the Russian share of Cuban foreign trade. Cuban export capacity in the 1990s was extraordinarily weak, however. Even the value of Cuban exports to market economy countries fell, not just of those to the former communist countries.

In 1996 Cuba exported at least $20 million worth of goods to eleven countries. Of those countries, from 1989 to 1996 Cuban exports to Canada, Italy, Mexico, the Netherlands, and Spain had increased, but the value of Cuban exports to China, France, Germany, Japan, the United Kingdom, and, of course, Russia had fallen. Only the increases to Canada and Spain were significant: from $55 million to $294 million to Canada and from $86 million to $131 million to Spain; most of the exports to the Netherlands were nickel products slated for reexport.[52] In general, Cuba's productive weakness, not U.S. policy, was the principal obstacle to Cuba's trade. In international services, tourism was Cuba's principal export. Its international partner profile was much the same in services as in goods. In 1996 Italy, Canada, and Spain were the principal sources of Cuban tourism, followed by Germany and Mexico; only Italy had gained market share from 1989 to 1996.[53]

Cuba's partner diversification in goods exports was much safer politically in 1996 than in 1989, however. In 1989, the Soviet Union had accounted for 60 percent of Cuba's exports; China, Cuba's second most important export market, accounted for just 4 percent. The respective numbers for 1996 were 26 percent and 7 percent. In 1996, however, Cuba's second most important goods export market had become Canada, accounting for 15 percent of Cuban exports, while the Netherlands (a reexport base) took 11 percent of Cuban exports. Because Cuban international trade is far more politicized than is typical for most countries, this export partner diversification probably reflects a political conception of risk dispersal.

The collapse of Cuban exports made it much more difficult to import. In 1996, Cuba imported at least $20 million worth of goods from thirteen countries. Of those countries, from 1989 to 1996 Cuban imports had increased from Belgium, Canada, France, Italy, the Netherlands, Mexico, and Spain, in each case substantially. Imports from Argentina, China, Germany, Japan, Russia, and the United Kingdom had fallen.[54] On the goods import side, Cuba's partner diversification was also much safer politically, spreading risk even more effectively than on the export side. In 1989 the Soviet Union had accounted for 68 percent of Cuba's imports; the second most important import partner was the German Democratic Republic, with 4 percent of the total. Neither country existed 3 years later. In 1996, Spain and Russia tied as Cuba's most important import partners at 15 percent each; the third was Mexico, accounting for 10 percent; and then tied as well were Canada and France at 6 percent each.

In short, the evolution of Cuba's international trade shows the impact of the economic collapse and the loss of Soviet subsidies. Cuba diversified its trade partners considerably, especially for goods imports. Overall, Cuban trade relations with various countries in the European Union, Canada, Mexico, and China appeared both strong and sound. Russia remained the major export market, and thus a potential source of instability. In particular, trade relations with Canada, France, Italy, Spain, and Mexico countered the United States.

## Conclusions

In the 1990s, Cuba was more internationally isolated than at any time since the revolutionary victory in 1959. Nonetheless, with consummate political skill, the Cuban government broke out of its isolation in some respects, greatly aided by the collateral fallout from U.S. policies toward Cuba. Some governments weighed the costs and benefits of greater international insertion, and at the end of the 1990s Cuba's international insertion was exceedingly limited, so its government desperately sought to increase it. Cuba required much more international investment and trade; its government had no choice but to fashion an international strategy to contain the power of U.S. policies.

The Cuban government responded to the collapse of the Soviet Union and of other European communist governments by retrenching its far-flung foreign policy, adjusting its economy, and designing an institution-alist strategy for international reinsertion. This strategy focused on coun-tries close to the United States, for they were more influential in U.S. pol-icy than the People's Republic of China or post-communist Russia. This strategy sought to reduce Cuba's isolation and find partners to counter the United States, even if these partners had no political or ideological affec-tion for the Cuban government. Although Cuba dealt as well with indi-vidual governments, it believed that international organizations could function as alliances in the face of U.S. bullying. Governments were more likely to resist pressures on them to conform to U.S. policies toward Cuba if they could invoke the principles of international organizations and each other's political solidarity. The rules of international institutions became a source of leverage: if these governments could hang together, they would hang tough.

Cuba's strategy rested on an analytic hunch, namely, that Kenneth Waltz's neorealist analysis of the international system would prove right at least as far as Cuba was concerned. The United States did not disap-point. Speaking in the name of liberty and democracy, the United States adopted policies toward Cuba that seemed arbitrary, perhaps counterpro-ductive, certainly extraterritorial, and clearly adverse to the interests of its allies and trading partners. The latter countered U.S. policy toward Cuba. At first, in response to the Torricelli law, they did so cautiously. Later on, in outrage over the Helms-Burton law, they did so more vigorously.

Cuba pursued an institutionalist strategy principally for neorealist bal-ancing reasons. In so doing, it understood that a key institutionalist insight served its neorealist purposes: the members of international institutions cared about the norms and rules of those institutions. Such beliefs became a lever for Cuba to use to gain those members' support in confronting the United States. Moreover, Cuba's strategy was consistent at times with the expectations of institutionalist analyses. In nearly all cases, this strategy generated valuable information not otherwise available to an internation-ally isolated state and it helped to reduce uncertainty. And in constructing bilateral confidence-building measures with the United States, the trans-action costs of managing this complex interaction were reduced as well.

Other factors played a role. In the 1990s, elections proved important in changing policies toward Cuba in the United States, Canada, and Spain. In the United States, the combination of more effective right-wing Cuban-American lobbies with the expansive ideological shifts and the loss of international constraints on U.S. actions proved powerful at election time. These changes within the United States pulled the Cuban question into the maelstrom of U.S. domestic politics, endowing it with both visibility and rigidity. The United States raised the stakes of its Cuba policy to confront its own allies and best trading partners precisely at the moment when Cuba mattered less for the United States than it had in decades.

Together, the effects of international system balancing and the Cuban David's sling strategy brought about the impossible: on the subject of U.S.-Cuban relations, the United States became at least as isolated as Cuba. Both governments became the target of international pressure to change their respective policies. Although Cuba was rather accustomed to this condition, the United States was not. Cuba eagerly welcomed allies in its decades-old effort to contain the United States. Fidel Castro had not defeated the United States, but he seemed confident that he would outlast the ninth U.S. president who attempted to bring him down.

Fidel Castro cannot outlast every future U.S. president, however. His eventual passing is likely to bring about major changes in Cuba's domestic politics and foreign policy. If Castro's successors manage at first to retain a political system with only modest changes from the one they will inherit, relations with the United States are not likely to improve much. And, absent Fidel Castro's talent and residual domestic and international appeal, this successor government may well be much less effective. This seems, therefore, a transitional outcome pending a subsequent larger change. Such an eventual more significant change is likely to realign Cuba's foreign policy to bring it much closer to the U.S. government. It may turn the Cuban diaspora in the United States into an asset, not a liability, for such a future Cuban government. Under those circumstances, Cuba's insertion into the wider international system may be thinner than in the 1990s (and certainly less so than in previous decades) but the intensity of its engagement with the United States may be much deeper and tighter. The unanswerable question for the time being is whether Cubans wish to embrace the United States or just to give it a friendly but formal handshake. The legacies of Cuba's nationalist past cannot yet be assessed independently of Fidel Castro, but that past is surely likely to weigh heavily upon the future.

## Notes

1. For a summary of Fidel Castro's marathon speech to the party congress, celebrating this accomplishment, see *Granmá*, 9 October 1997.

2. For recent summaries of neorealist views, John J. Mearsheimer, "The False Promise of International Institutions," *International Security* 19, 3 (Winter 1994–1995): 5–49; Stephen G. Brooks, "Dueling Realisms," *International Organization* 51, 3 (Summer 1997): 446.

3. Kenneth Waltz, "A Response to My Critics," in Robert O. Keohane, ed., *Neorealism and Its Critics* (New York: Columbia University Press, 1986), 329. See also Brooks, "Dueling Realisms," 446.

4. See especially Jorge I. Domínguez, *To Make a World Safe for Revolution: Cuba's Foreign Policy* (Cambridge: Harvard University Press, 1989), chap. 5.

5. *Documentos políticos. Política internacional de la revolución cubana*, vol. 1 (Havana: Editora Política, 1966), 83.

6. A. Pérez-Ruiz, "Saludos en la hora cero," *Verde olivo* 9 (1990): 8–11.

7. *Granmá Weekly Review*, 9 June 1991, 13.

8. *Bohemia* 83, 15 (12 April 1991): 33.

9. United Nations, Economic Commission for Latin America and the Caribbean (hereafter ECLAC), *The Cuban Economy in the Nineties: Structural Reform and Economic Performance (Statistical Appendix)*, LC/MEX.R.621 (26 August 1997), Table A.15.

10. *Granmá Weekly Review*, 27 May 1990, 3; 1 July 1990, 1.

11. Carlos Lage, "Discurso pronunciado por el Dr. Carlos Lage Dávila, vicepresidente del Consejo de Estado y secretario del Comité Ejecutivo del Consejo de Ministros, en la inauguración de la XII Feria International de La Habana," *Dossier* (Havana: Centro de Estudios sobre América, 1995), 89.

12. ECLAC, *The Cuban Economy in the Nineties*, 131 and Table A.15.

13. *Granmá*, 18 June 1991, 8.

14. James G. Blight, Bruce J. Allyn, and David A. Welch, *Cuba on the Brink: Castro, the Missile Crisis, and the Soviet Collapse* (New York: Pantheon, 1993), 303. I was present at this meeting and heard the statement.

15. Mearsheimer, "The False Promise of International Institutions," 7.

16. Kenneth N. Waltz, "Evaluating Theories," *American Political Science Review* 91, 4 (December 1997): 915–916.

17. See Robert O. Keohane, *After Hegemony: Cooperation and Discord in the World Political Economy* (Princeton, N.J.: Princeton University Press, 1984), 85–95. Other elements in institutionalist explanations do not fit the Cuban experience in the 1990s. These would include the expectation that institutions would facilitate cooperation, not just ward off trouble or serve as a balancing alliance, or that they would assist in adjusting domestic institutions and procedures to facilitate international cooperation.

18. Domínguez, *To Make the World Safe for Revolution*, 92–104.

19. Michael A. Morris and Martin Slann, "Controlling the Sources of Armaments in Latin America," in Michael A. Morris and Victor Millán, eds., *Controlling Latin American Conflicts: Ten Approaches* (Boulder, Colo.: Westview Press, 1983), 124–126, 138–142.

20. Isabel Jaramillo, "Seguridad y cooperación hemisférica," in Rafael Hernández, ed., *Cuba en las Américas* (Havana: Centro de Estudios sobre América, 1995), 36.

21. Juan Valdés Paz, "La política exterior de Cuba hacia América Latina y el Caribe en los años 90: los temas," *Cuadernos de Nuestra América* 9, 19 (July-December 1992): 27, 130.

22. For the text and the conference report, see U.S. House of Representatives, "Cuban Liberty and Democratic Solidarity (Libertad) Act of 1996," *Report* 104–168 (1 March 1996).

23. For historical illustration, see Ana Covarrubias, "Cuba and Mexico: A Case for Mutual Nonintervention," *Cuban Studies* 26 (1996): 121–141.

24. *CubaInfo* 8, 15 (21 November 1996): 7–8; 9, 15 (13 November 1997): 5.

25. John Walton Cotman, "Cuba and the CARICOM States: The Last Decade," in Donna Rich Kaplowitz, ed., *Cuba's Ties to a Changing World* (Boulder, Colo.: Lynne Rienner Publishers, 1993).

26. Manuel Rúa and Pedro Monreal, "El Oriente cubano y el Caribe: desafíos y oportunidades para el comercio y la inversión," *Cuban Foreign Trade* (Havana) (October-December 1993).

27. Canute James, "Caribbean Community, Cuba Sign Controversial Trade Pact," *Journal of Commerce*, 15 December 1993.

28. Andrés Serbin, "Globalization and Regionalization in the Caribbean Basin: The Challenges of a Sociopolitical Agenda for Integration," in Michael C. Desch, Jorge I. Domínguez, and Andrés Serbin, eds., *From Pirates to Drug Lords: The Post–Cold War Caribbean Security Environment* (Albany: State University of New York Press, 1998).

29. See also a thoughtful article by H. Michael Erisman, "Evolving Cuban-CARICOM Relations: A Comparative Cost-Benefit Analysis," *Cuban Studies* 25 (1995): 207–227.

30. ECLAC, 126.

31. This section draws heavily from Jorge I. Domínguez, "U.S.-Cuban Relations: From the Cold War to the Colder War," *Journal of Interamerican Studies and World Affairs* 39, 3 (Fall 1997): 49–75.

32. For a general discussion of confidence-building measures in Latin America and the Caribbean in the 1990s, see Joseph S. Tulchin with Ralph H. Espach, "Addressing the Challenges of Cooperative Security in the Caribbean," *Peace and Security in the Americas* (September 1997): 1–8; Francisco Rojas Aravena, "América Latina: alternativas y mecanismos de prevención en situaciones vinculadas a la soberanía territorial," *Paz y seguridad en las Américas* (October 1997): 1–15.

33. These paragraphs draw heavily from several confidential author interviews in Washington, D.C., 1993, 1996, and 1997, and Havana, 1996.

34. *CubaInfo* 8, 13 (10 October 1996): 1.

35. *CubaInfo* 7, 16 (20 December 1995): 1.

36. Jorge I. Domínguez, "Cooperating with the Enemy? U.S. Immigration Policies Toward Cuba," in Christopher Mitchell, ed., *Western Hemisphere Immigration and United States Foreign Policy* (University Park: Pennsylvania State University Press, 1992); and author interviews in Washington, D.C., 1997.

37. Confidential author interviews, Washington, D.C., 1993, 1996, and 1997. For criticism of these meetings by some Cuban-American members of Congress, see *CubaInfo* 8, 9 (11 July 1996): 2–3.

38. On 9 and 13 January 1996, Brothers to the Rescue pilots had dropped flyers over Havana, alarming the Cuban government because of a breach of security. On 24 February, at least one of three airplanes piloted by the Brothers penetrated Cuban air space, though none were over Cuban waters at the time of the shoot-down.

39. Larry Rohter, "Ceremonies Honor Fliers Shot Down by Cuban Jets," *New York Times*, 25 February 1997, A12.

40. Confidential author interviews, Havana, 1996; Washington, D.C., 1997; Miami, 1998. On 13 July 1996, on Cuban television I watched the Cuban-American flotilla just outside Cuban territorial waters surrounded by collaborating U.S. and Cuban coast guard vessels.

41. For an argument by a Cuban scholar that the Cuban government seeks cooperation over security issues, see Rafael Hernández, "Cuba and Security in the Caribbean," in Joseph S. Tulchin, Andrés Serbin, and Rafael Hernández, eds., *Cuba and the Caribbean* (Wilmington, Del.: Scholarly Resources, 1997).

42. For a more general discussion of this point, see Andrew Moravcsik, "Taking Preferences Seriously: A Liberal Theory of International Politics," *International Organization* 51, 4 (Autumn 1997): 526–527.

43. Thomas Carothers, *In the Name of Democracy: U.S. Policy Toward Latin America in the Reagan Years* (Berkeley: University of California Press, 1991).

44. Viron P. Vaky and Heraldo Muñoz, *The Future of the Organization of American States* (New York: The Twentieth Century Fund Press, 1993); Arturo Valenzuela, "Paraguay: The Coup That Didn't Happen," *Journal of Democracy* 8, 1 (January 1997): 43–55.

45. Gillian Gunn, "In Search of a Modern Cuba Policy," in Donald E. Schulz, ed., *Cuba and the Future* (Westport, Conn.: Greenwood Press, 1994), 129–133.

46. Wolf Grabendorff, "The Relationship Between the European Community and Cuba," in Donna Rich Kaplowitz, ed., *Cuba's Ties to a Changing World.*

47. Commission Communication to Parliament and the Council, "Relations Between the European Union and Cuba" (Brussels, 28 June 1995), 5–7. See also a free-ranging discussion between Cuban and EU officials and scholars in Instituto de Relaciones Europeo-Latinoamericanas, *Cuba: apertura económica y relaciones con Europa* (Madrid: IRELA, 1994).

48. Instituto de Relaciones Europeo-Latinoamericanas, "La posición común de la UE sobre Cuba: debate interno, reacciones y repercusiones," *Un informe de IRELA*, INF-96/6–CUBA; Instituto de Relaciones Europeo-Latinoamericanas, "Cuba y la Unión Europea: las dificultades del diálogo," *Un informe de IRELA*, INF-96/3-CUBA.

49. On domestic Spanish politics and Cuba, Felipe Sahagún, "Cuba: un asunto interno español," *Meridiano CERI* 10 (August 1996): 4–9.

50. Julia Sagebien, "The Canadian Presence in Cuba in the Mid-1990s," *Cuban Studies* 26 (1996): 143–168.

51. Government of Canada, Department of Foreign Affairs and International Trade, *News Release* (17 June 1996); Government of Canada, Department of Foreign Affairs and International Trade, "Joint Declaration of the Ministers of Foreign Affairs of Canada and Cuba" (22 January 1997).

52. República de Cuba, Comité Estatal de Estadísticas, *Anuario estadístico de Cuba, 1989* (Havana: 1991), 253, 255, hereafter cited by its title only; U.S. Central Intelligence Agency, Directorate of Intelligence, *Cuba: Handbook of Trade Statistics, 1997,* APLA 97-10006 (Washington, D.C.: 1997), 1–3, hereafter cited as CIA.

53. ECLAC, 127.

54. *Anuario estadístico de Cuba, 1989,* 257, 259; CIA, *Cuba: Handbook of Trade Statistics, 1997,* 3–4.

# 8

## Between Vision and Reality: Variables in Latin American Foreign Policy

### *Robert O. Keohane*

The chapters in this book are rich in anecdotal evidence of the impacts of globalization and international integration on the nations of Latin America. There is an aphorism that states that the plural of "anecdote" is "data." In that sense these chapters present data that strongly indicate that a transition—or many transitions—is under way. The natures of those transitions, however, and of the regional and national structures that are both shaping and being shaped by them, are the subject of our critical attention.

In response to these chapters I propose ten theses, five about Latin America—a region with which I am relatively unfamiliar—and five about global issues. My first proposition on Latin America is about economics and politics, and it is that economic integration will only occur if there are strong political reasons to promote it. It is not going to come by itself. As a result, economic integration will be shallow at the Latin American regional level, meaning the region as a whole. It may be greater at the sub-regional level, but we are not in our lifetime going to see a strong Latin American common market on the order of the European Union. The chapters in general seem to agree with this proposition.

I do not agree with the statement that Latin America forms a regional subsystem within the global system. Empirical evidence does not support this hypothesis. Certainly, there are historical and perhaps sociocultural characteristics shared by most of the region, but it has been pointed out before that if you were to map communication routes, airline routes, and trade relationships across the globe, without sticking on national or regional labels, you would not be able to pick out a coherent geographic entity to be called Latin America. Mexico would appear to be entirely North American. In fact, judging by airline connections alone, the entire region would appear tied to North America. There is, therefore, little meaning in speaking of Latin America as a political or economic region.

The chapters repeatedly emphasize the region's heterogeneity and diversity in terms of political and economic systems, levels of development, size, and potential or real influence in the world. Because of this heterogeneity, integration and cooperation thus far has succeeded much more at the subregional than at the regional level. Some of the chapters go on to argue that subregional groupings contribute to regionalism, and will eventually be melded together into a greater regional system. As the European case has shown, this is far easier said than done. The construction of subregional entities does not necessarily foster a larger regionalism. In Europe over the past 5 years the entities have, with the introduction of the European monetary unit (EMU), been pursuing a subregional strategy—seeking deeper instead of wider integration—as opposed to a regional European strategy. This strategy has done little to increase ties with Eastern Europe.

On this point the chapters are divergent: some are internally inconsistent about whether heterogeneity or regional coherence predominates. This seems one of the key questions facing analysts and policymakers of inter-American relations.

My third proposition is that the attention the United States gives to Latin America is relatively scarce and sporadic, except for its peculiar relations with Mexico and Cuba. Major developments in Latin American affairs or inter-American relations rarely break the front pages in U.S. newspapers. In the exceptional case of Mexico, we see through NAFTA a deepening engagement and increasing complexity. U.S.-Mexican relations now require institutional attention on a daily basis in multiple dimensions of high relevance for both nations, including trade, investment, drugs and drug trafficking, crime, and migration.

Regarding Cuba, as Jorge Domínguez points out, the United States magnifies the importance of its island neighbor and shoots itself in the toe. In the toe, I repeat, because whatever occurs with Cuba does not matter much to the United States—or should not matter much—according to the island's size, resources, and political or strategic importance. But what you see in the U.S. posture toward Cuba is perfectly rational behavior: politicians find it worthwhile from a vote-getting perspective to attack Cuba and sponsor anti-Cuba legislation.

My fourth proposition is that U.S.-Latin American relations are characterized by a striking asymmetry in their structural relationship. Ambassador Muñoz's chapter is interesting, but to state that Latin America is more important to the United States than vice versa is an exaggeration.

Interdependence may be increasing, as Ambassador Muñoz states, but this is an asymmetrical interdependence that leaves Latin America potentially much more vulnerable to U.S. displeasure and action than vice versa.

Also I would not be so sure that the private and the public spheres are so separate. If a serious political dispute were to erupt between the United States and a Latin American country, it would sharply affect FDI to that country, its production, and even its trade. The degree of impact would of course depend on the country, but in no case would it be insignificant. But even with those points in mind, lots of space exists for Latin American countries to maneuver in their relations with the United States and other partners because either the United States does not care or its policies are determined by domestic politics. In other words, in the structural sense the United States has the potential to dominate Latin America, but it does not because it does not have a sustained interest in doing so. It is interesting to note that the chapters diverge widely on this issue of the degree and nature of the asymmetry between the United States and Latin America. In my view this diversity of opinion does not draw into question the fact of asymmetry, but it reveals a multiplicity of perceptions regarding the meaning and importance of this asymmetry for the strategic options of Latin American countries.

The last of my propositions on regional affairs is that the political foreign policies of Latin American countries seem to be of secondary importance to them and everyone else. Attention is given mostly to economic policy, even when talking of long-term strategic relations. Fortunately peace has been relatively assured in this continent.

Cuba of course is the exception, but it is the kind of exception that proves the rule. Political foreign policy is still a predominant issue in Cuba because today it is the only country in the region that is a target of attack by the United States. Because the avoidance of such interference from the regional hegemon is the major purpose of Latin American nations' political foreign policies, today when this threat is diminished this area of policy is just not very important to them. In international politics they are takers or receivers of policy, as Alberto van Klaveren argues. Cuba is the exception because in its posture of constant defense against being ostracized and attacked, it cannot afford to be a taker.

Those are my comments on the Latin American side. I also have five theses regarding the global system. The first one is in response to Alberto van Klaveren's question of whether the world is moving toward a concentration or a diffusion of power. My opinion is that during the past 16 years it has been moving toward concentration. Peter Smith gives data that between 1962 and 1982 there was a marked tendency toward diffusion of economic resources throughout the world. I do not believe that trend holds up, however, from 1982 to today. Data show that the United States since 1982 has grown more rapidly than Europe and has certainly been more successful in innovation and generating employment, and since 1988 or 1989 has also been doing much better than Japan. So relative to the other developed countries the United States has reversed that process of diffusion, and of course militarily, politically, and normatively in terms of soft power, the United States is unchallenged.

The period from 1989 to the present is one marked by the greatest degree of single-power hegemony in the world system since at least the 1860s and probably before. I am not sure there has ever been a country as powerful as the United States since the Westphalia Congress of 1648 when the nation-state-based world system was created. The only major contender would be Victorian England.

I disagree with Peter Smith that the current global system is relatively lawless. This is the most lawful system in the history of the world. It is the most orderly, least uncertain international political system since Francis I of France. With the establishment of the World Trade Organization and the legalization of NAFTA and the European Union and other trading blocs, international lawyers are having a field day. They have never been happier—and they are not in general a happy group. They still gripe all the time, of course, but they have never been happier than they are now. Relative to the standard legality of domestic politics in the United States, the international system is not highly legalized, but it is quite legalized relative to the historical standards of international politics and even relative to the legal systems of many states, including Russia and many developing countries. Today's international system is remarkably orderly and regime-governed.

My second thesis is in regard to another question by Alberto van Klaveren, that is, whether or not the trade blocs we see developing today are significant. I do not think that most regional trade agreements are likely to foster protectionism, but I am more concerned about the implications for cooperation in world politics of increasing regionalism.

What is significant about the strengthening of the EU, and the EMU, is the prospect of having two equally strong regions that compete with each other. I am reminded of Charles Kindleberger's comment from 20 years ago that world monetary stability depends upon there being a single stabilizer. There has never been an international monetary system that has functioned well with more than one central reserve currency. So as the European Union develops its own currency there will be more conflict. If the euro and the U.S. dollar coexist with as much harmony as Larry Summers claims to believe, it will be the first time in history.

My last three propositions refer to globalization. In my opinion, analysts should not ignore or underestimate the effect globalization is having on Latin America. If we define globalization as the rapidly increasing movements of goods, services, capital, people, and ideas across state boundaries, coupled with the integration of global production and the globalization of information, then it has to have enormous effects on Latin America.

My first comment on globalization is about institutions. Globalization has occurred within the context of the dramatic institutionalization of foreign policy. Unlike 20 years ago, you cannot talk about foreign policy without talking about international institutions, for better or for worse. I am not trying to glorify international institutions. After all, the IMF made many mistakes in the financial crises of 1997–1999. I am simply stating that today globalization is managed through international institutions.

This comment leads to my second system-wide proposition that Latin American countries are takers, instead of makers, of international policy. They have relatively little influence in international institutions. They will continue to participate in the international institutions, but mostly defensively. As Peter Smith notes, they will not be able to form a consolidated political bloc strong enough to influence the international system. Thinking practically, these regional institutions will not have any incentive to push for overall policies, because they face the reality that they are a small part of the whole world. So they will work to avoid exclusion or isolation or to make certain marginal gains inside international institutions.

My third system proposition is that globalization involves values and the sharing or spread of ideas, an issue largely missing in these chapters. A number of international values or ideas supported generally by the institutionalized system—such as those regarding human rights, reciprocity, and democratization—have had a tremendous resonance with Latin Americans. I am not a Latin Americanist, but it seems to me that the impact of these norms on Latin America—especially the desire not to be excluded from the civilized world as were the Argentine military dictators and the apartheid regime in South Africa—must have played, and continue to play, a large role in the transformation of Latin American domestic politics.

This point is critical because at the end of the last wave of globalization, which ended in 1913, trade flows, capital flows, and migration flows were all reversed dramatically. Proportionally speaking, we did not reach the trade levels of 1928 until 1973. There is no reason to think such a reversal may occur again in the case of another Great War or worldwide crisis of some sort. On the other hand, World War I had much less effect on information flows. Technologically speaking, it is almost impossible to control the cross-border flow of information. These types of flows—of information, norms, culture, and ideas—are less reversible and in my mind tremendously significant.

Globalization, in this sense, is closely related to a phenomenon referred to as "Americanization," which describes the common perception that at least some groups—the younger, mostly—are becoming homogenized in their popular culture. Whether you are in Bangkok or Berlin or Buenos Aires, university students tend to wear blue jeans, eat hamburgers, and listen to the same, mostly American, music. This is a form of what Joseph Nye describes as soft power, which he defines roughly as the ability not to twist arms, but to persuade others to want what you want or to be what you are.

Some of this may be trivial. The importance of Levi knock-offs in Bangkok is certainly debatable. Some of it, however, is certainly not trivial. If it is indeed true, as is often suggested, that people across the world believe that they are not living in a civilized society or that they will not be accepted in the world if they do not have democratic institutions, that belief has definite consequences. They may adopt democratic institutions not only because they believe them superior or useful, but also because they seek the legitimacy that the democracy label bestows.

The example of the U.S.-based Cable News Network is interesting to consider in this regard. The technology of simultaneous worldwide broadcasting is probably not reversible. Similarly, the particularly American-style presentation and tone of these news broadcasts, if they continue to be widely viewed around the world, will likely have some form of long-term influence on news broadcasts and the perception of international affairs worldwide. This technology and the spread of communication and information are not reversible. What is reversible is who controls them. Consider what the Iraq war would have been like if the worldwide broadcast of events had been based in Cairo or Oman instead of in Atlanta. The framing of the issue would have been fundamentally different. The world would have had a very different picture of what was going on than it had with CNN's American perspective. That control, that soft power, is reversible. One can imagine a world in which there still exists this kind of global communication structure, but not with the Americans at the helm. I do not believe this is likely at all within the coming decades, but it is a possibility.

My last proposition is in agreement with Thomaz Guedes da Costa's point that globalization is handled best by domestic policy. If I were advising a Latin American government, I would say simply, "If you get your domestic, economic, and political policies right, you can make globalization work in your favor. If you get them wrong, it is going to work against you." As takers of policy, Latin American countries can not really affect globalization, but they can affect how it refracts on their societies. This is done through economic reform; for instance, Chile's unilateral lowering of its import tariffs, or the privatization of state interests that makes the labor market more flexible. The maintenance of social solidarity is also crucial, so attention must be paid to maintaining the social welfare net and expanding and protecting the benefits and rights of political democracy. Brazil's disastrous devaluation in January 1999 illustrates the costs of getting your domestic politics wrong.

One lesson from the East Asian crisis is that countries like Korea and Taiwan, which had moved through their transitions to democracy by 1997, weathered the crisis better than did their neighbors with less legitimate or stable democratic systems, like Indonesia. Thailand is somewhere on the cusp, but I believe it is evident that there is a significant correlation between a country's degree of democratization and its potential success at handling the pressures of globalization.

One of the striking features of the European case, after all, is that the social democratic countries of northwestern Europe, far from being swallowed by globalization because of their ties with much larger states, have prospered within globalization. Holland and Denmark have performed very well. It is simply not true that globalization inevitably creates some sort of race to the bottom. It certainly does not seem to be the case that globalization is destructive to democracy. To the contrary, well-functioning democracies tend to bounce back best from the shocks of globalization.

# 9

# Beyond Neoliberalism: A Long-Term Perspective on Regional Strategic Thinking

*Ernest R. May*

In reviewing these chapters on Latin American international relations strategies, I am struck by their emphasis on increasing international ties and deepening economic interdependence, mostly among one another but also with Europe or Asia. The attention is on increasing markets, increasing economic competitiveness, and shielding themselves from the interests of the regional hegemonic power, the United States.

This strategy has its costs. There are domestic costs in that as much as a government does this, it limits its capacity to control resources internally. It commits a nation to a certain agreed-upon degree of discipline that limits its ability to direct autonomously its financial and material resources. This is the basic trade-off.

The effect of these limitations, which exist to a greater or lesser extent, depending on the formality of the international agreement, is that you have fewer strategic options. For the sake of maximizing economic returns, governments forgo or make much more difficult the possibility of changing courses in the future, perhaps to follow a different economic model or to respond to changes in the international or domestic environments. With the exception of Thomaz Guedes da Costa's analysis, these limitations are not discussed in the chapters. In some respects this appears to be a case in which economic objectives and models have superseded or have priority over those of politics, at least in the region's international relations. If this accurately reflects a bias or tendency in regional policy-making, that is an important and interesting point.

Another quality of these chapters that I find particularly interesting is their implicit assumption that the orderly, institutionally formalized international environment that Robert Keohane has described, and that facilitates regional economic blocs and the like, is bound to persist.

The point can be made in two ways. First: this international climate following the end of the Cold War constantly reminds me of the mood in Europe and the United States following World War I. There is so much talk about this being a peaceful, cooperative era, in which traditional international hostilities are largely overcome, in which almost all the world shares a commitment to democracy and free-market capitalism, and in which the stock market will more or less continue upward indefinitely. As late as 1930, people were saying these sorts of things as well and were confident that that was so. I am not suggesting that anything similar to the Great Depression is bound to happen, but I believe there is a chance that this euphoria we are experiencing will prove more ephemeral than is often thought.

A second way of making this point is to note that most governments and managers of nongovernmental, international institutions like the Vatican, a drug cartel, or the World Bank typically run their governments or institutions in a regulated, rather predictable fashion closely adhering to long-standing institutional traditions or definitions. Occasionally, however, motivated by a dramatic change in their environment or circumstances, they suddenly become innovative. These chapters present a regulated, orthodox, rather neoliberal approach to international activity and the strategic options of Latin American countries, an approach that seems underpinned by an assumption that the world will remain more or less the same. The primary considerations of these strategies for insertion into the international system seem to be the pursuit of marginal gains or losses, the expansion of trade, increased investment, and economic growth with low inflation. Ultimately, however, to address some of the long-standing, perhaps structural problems that beset these countries, what is required is innovation, a new approach or a new way of thinking.

A potential source of this innovation, or of the change in the region's international or political environment that might bring about such innovation, is the groups in one nation or across the region that are adversely affected by this neoliberalization and globalization. There are lots of people who are paying a high price for this exercise in marginal gains and benefits. It is easy to envision scenarios in which their concerted efforts pressure governments into a reconsideration of overall policy approach or a reprioritization of objectives. Within the current thinking, lacking some visionary political leadership, there is not a clear response to these pressures. There are many constraints on what a country can and cannot do in its fiscal policies, including social investment. A country simply cannot maximize returns to investment in education in the short run. It is also difficult to take serious steps toward progress 20 years down the road because countries have to respond immediately to the pressures of a global economic crisis, or to rein in spending to keep investors interested, or those kinds of concerns. Thomaz Guedes da Costa's chapter discusses this—that with increasing democratization and the dramatic growth of organized civil society groups like the environmental movement, there does appear the possibility of one or many of these groups or popular initiatives taking on more relevance in national or regional affairs. The rise of such popular movements at the local, national, and even international level, based on issues like the environment, human rights, the alleviation of poverty, or other moral issues, could significantly affect regional politics. If so, the contradiction between their objectives and those of the supporters of the neoliberal economic system will not be resolved without some innovation, for better or for worse.

Another possibility for potential change is related to the historical tensions in the region between local and national sovereignty. The enormous discrepancies in average income and various social indicators that exist in Latin American states could make distributional issues a key area of contention in coming decades. Such division does not necessarily fall along geographic lines. We see in Mexico, for instance, that disparities in the social indicators and income levels of various ethnic groups—rural, indigenous peoples relative to others—are a cause of instability. The benefits and costs of increased regional and global economic integration will not be distributed evenly. The tensions caused by these disparities will continue to grow in coming decades. In countries with a history of inequality among various groups and areas, it will require significant political leadership and farsightedness to implement policies that address these divisions.

The authors describe very effectively the options and strategies available to Latin American nations within the current system and under the current ideological and practical constraints. However, they may want to include considerations of what might lie beyond this current menu of policy considerations, in case there is some form of dramatic change in the political or economic environment, either domestic or external. Luckily, a major regional war appears extremely unlikely, but an economic crisis or some other development that shifts the relative powers of various political actors, or creates tremendous pressures for a revision of the prevailing policy model, is not impossible.

It is interesting to note that the end of the Cold War has meant relatively little for Latin America, in comparison with other regions around the world. With the exception of Cuba, the fall of the Berlin Wall seems to have neither altered significantly the major actors in the region nor changed national calculations of their interests or strategic alliances. India and Pakistan, for instance, face an entirely different regional framework for their strategic options, and have had to reexamine long-held balancing and alignment strategies. This has not been true for Latin America, again with the exception of Cuba, a point that merits some consideration.

I agree with Robert Keohane on the importance of looking at norms and perhaps a type of "soft power" when considering Latin America's influence and insertion into the international system. There was a time near the middle of this century when Chile, for instance, was a center for intellectual activity regarding economic development and the international system. The same could be said, perhaps, for the region as a whole when one considers the dependency model that came from the Brazilian sociologist Fernando Henrique Cardoso, and the popularity of Cuba's revolutionary ideology and image across the world. The true degree or importance of such influence is difficult to gauge, obviously, but a good indicator of this is the degree to which a country's policies, norms, or institutions are imitated abroad. If you had asked in the middle to late nineteenth century in continental Europe how Germany was most influential, the answer would have been to look at how the German welfare system and other state institutions were copied throughout Europe. One measure of U.S. influence in recent decades is the extent to which U.S.-style institutions have been copied worldwide, even in places where you would not think a need existed for such an institution. States seem to decide that they must have a film industry, a science ministry, and so on, for little other reason than to gain the legitimacy that seems to come from appearing like the United States. One example of this that arose in our analyses is the attention given to Chile's social security system. If a nation such as Chile develops a reputation for innovative, effective policies that can be replicated abroad, that is a form of legitimacy and a means for gaining if not power, then space in the international system.

# 10

# Toward Innovative Strategic Policies: A Conclusion

## *Joseph S. Tulchin & Ralph H. Espach*

In Chapter 1 we argued that the nations of Latin America currently face a window of opportunity for enhancing their strategic international relations. A number of factors contribute to this opportunity. These include the end of the constraints of the Cold War, the concurrence of democratic rule and free-market economic policies across the region, a relatively distant and noninterfering attitude on the part of the United States, and an increasingly institutionalized, accessible international community. However, recent developments indicate that the relative stability and commonality of interests that characterized hemispheric relations in the 1990s and that represented the window of opportunity for Latin America are increasingly threatened.

Colombia is struggling against a widening guerrilla campaign, rampant crime, and the infiltration of illegal money and arms related to the drug trade into all facets of national life. Venezuela has a new constitution that concentrates power in the hands of President Hugo Chavez. President Alberto Fujimori has seriously undermined the autonomy and capacity of Peru's democratic system. In all these cases, and others, the military is playing a wider role than had been anticipated at the beginning of the 1990s. Across the region government monetary reforms and free-market policies have so far kept inflation in check, but they have not been able to avoid painful crises and have had difficulty generating growth. The economic gains of the 1990s have been unevenly distributed, to the growing frustration of much of the region's population. In many nations, crime, unemployment, corruption, and economic stagnation are taxing the public's patience with their democratic governments. These frustrations contributed in large part to the elections of antiestablishment candidates Hugo Chavez in Venezuela and Abdala Bucaram in Ecuador.

Most Latin American nations remain relatively stable and clearly committed to democratic governance. States are learning to address through relatively transparent and constitutional means problems including social violence and division, corruption, transfers of power, and other difficult areas of democratic life. The drive for expanding trade ties and other forms of regional collaboration bolster democratic and free-market practices. Nevertheless, the optimism that prevailed in the early 1990s has given way to a sober realization that the road to democratic consolidation and economic stability will be long and rocky.

The window of opportunity previously described still exists, but is somewhat diminished. U.S. attention to the region continues to be scant. FTAA negotiations continue, but without fast-track authority the United States has little to offer except rhetorical support. Latin America receives scarce attention or resources from the Department of State or the National Security Council. Brazil and Argentina, for instance, were recently left without U.S. ambassadors for 2 years. The only agency of the U.S. government actively involved in regional events at the highest levels, and with sizeable and growing resources, is the Office of National Drug Control Policy (ONDCP), whose director was formerly chief commanding officer of U.S. Southern Command. As a result, the objectives of the ONDCP mission have growing weight in general U.S. policy. Without any better ideas, the U.S. government continues to attempt to address drug trafficking—and now to assist Colombia in its civil war—by improving the capacity and training of regional militaries and police, while it cuts funding for aid and social programs. In this regard, the hemispheric superpower shows a lack of historical vision and sensitivity that the rest of the hemisphere finds disturbing.

Aside from the issue of cooperation on antidrug operations, the attitude of the U.S. government toward Latin America continues to be characterized by negligence. This could be worse. Since the operation in Haiti in 1994, there have been no threats of invasion or economic embargo (outside of Cuba). Taken in sum, recent U.S. relations with Latin America may not have been as cooperative or creative as one might have hoped, but they have not been as destructive or overbearing as in the past. Unfortunately the nations of the region, although with less interference from the regional hegemon, have failed to produce legitimate, cooperative institutions or mechanisms that might protect them from future turns in the superpower's disposition, or that might protect their national interests more effectively than does the existing hemispheric archtecture. The arrogant tendencies in U.S. policy toward the region—exemplified in unilateral certification and its hard-line stance against Cuba—are largely based on the perception in

Washington that without U.S. oversight or involvement, sooner or later these nations will revert to economic collapse and authoritarian or military rule. In the minds of many officials of the executive branch, or members of Congress and their staffs, there is no compelling argument to behave in a more collaborative or collegial manner. Sadly, the historical record of this century shows that this belief can be self-fulfilling. Looking ahead from the year 2000, the region has an unusual political opportunity to undermine those perceptions by demonstrating that it can manage its own security affairs through cooperation, that it can defend collectively its commitment to democratic rights and practices, and that such collective action is in the interests of the United States. The nations of the hemisphere should work harder to establish multilateral, cooperative institutions—ones that include the United States but are not dominated by it or beholden to it—to replace U.S. guardianship with active, collective responsibility for regional security and stability.

At the global level, the halting march toward international community and the globalization of liberal political values continues. The case brought by the Spanish judge Baltasar Garzon against former Chilean dictator General Augusto Pinochet is a beacon for institutionalists and revived idealists who yearn for an international community of shared values and behavior, and for a robust structure for enforcing those norms. In 1999 Garzon issued another indictment, this time against almost one hundred Argentine military officers allegedly involved in that nation's "dirty war" of the late 1970s and 1980s. These legal actions build upon the momentum generated by the international tribunal at the Hague in Amsterdam, which is trying numerous individuals for war crimes committed during conflicts in the former Yugoslavia and in Rwanda.

Holding individuals accountable in international or foreign courts for crimes against principles of warfare or human rights is both a boost to and a challenge for national judicial systems. These international actions are based on the assumption that the institutions of justice of the nations involved are incapable of protecting human rights violations on their own. In the Chilean case, the arrest of General Pinochet sparked action and reform in Chilean courts. In other cases, however, the process has had a destabilizing effect on local peace and politics, especially in regions still torn by ethnic strife. This type of international, institutionalized activity, if it continues to proliferate, represents a new source of pressure on nations of Latin America with weak judiciary and regulatory systems.

This book argues that the changing structures and increasingly dynamic and interwoven form of the international system demand a revised, broadened approach to strategic planning. For much of the 1990s, Latin American international relations focused on trade relations as part of an agenda of economic liberalization. Some subregions, most notably Mexico, the Southern Cone, and Mercosur members, benefited from trade integration and continue to emphasize the importance of increasing trade as a national objective. Others have had less success, or are suffering from the effects of liberalized trade, in particular the islands of the Caribbean. In no case, however, is increasing trade by itself a sufficient response to the growing pressures of economic and political globalization.

A strategic agenda for the twenty-first century must be multifaceted and innovative. The nations of Latin America must continue to explore options for increased participation in international cooperative efforts and institutions, at the subregional, hemispheric, and global levels. Cooperation can take many forms, from sharing specialists, regional data or information, health workers or doctors; to being outspoken in negotiations; to sending military contingents to join international forces. High-technology research and training are an essential element of the industrialized economies. Private funding for laboratories and universities can be promoted using tax credits and options for state funding. Cultural promotion and exchange, the protection of unique biological or natural resources, increasing tourism, and support for regional films, television, and Internet media are all potential components of a national strategic agenda. Only a broad, nontraditional agenda that is flexible with the shifting demands of internationalized markets is likely to be successful. Ultimately, as Robert Keohane argues, the best defense against the pressures of globalization will be the flexibility and stability that come from effective, responsive democratic governance.

# Suggested Readings

Atkins, G. Pope. *Latin America in the International Political System,* 2nd ed. (Boulder, Colo.: Westview Press, 1989).

Bizzozero, Lincoln, and Marcel Vaillant, eds. *La inserción internacional del MERCOSUR: ¿mirando al Sur o mirando al Norte?* (Montevideo: Universidad de la República, 1996).

Carothers, Thomas. *In the Name of Democracy: U.S. Policy Toward Latin America in the Reagan Years* (Berkeley: University of California Press, 1991).

Chase, Robert, Emily Hill, and Paul Kennedy, eds. *The Pivotal States. A New Framework for U.S. Policy in the Developing World* (New York: W. W. Norton and Company, 1999).

Cooper, Andrew F., ed. *Niche Diplomacy. Middle Powers After the Cold War* (New York: St. Martin's Press, 1997).

Cooper, Andrew F., Richard A. Higgott, and Kim Richard Nossal, "Bound to Follow: Leadership and Followership in the Gulf Conflict," *Political Science Quarterly* 106 (Fall 1991).

Cox, Robert. *Production, Power and World Order: Social Forces in the Making of History* (New York: Columbia University Press, 1987).

Cox, Robert W., and Timothy J. Sinclair, eds. *Approaches to World Order* (Cambridge: Cambridge University Press, 1995).

Desch, Michael C., Jorge I. Dominguez, and Andrés Serbin, eds. *From Pirates to Drug Lords: The Post–Cold War Caribbean Security Environment* (Albany: State University of New York Press, 1998).

Domínguez, Jorge I. *To Make a World Safe for Revolution: Cuba's Foreign Policy* (Cambridge, Mass.: Harvard University Press, 1989).

Dupas, Gilberto, and Tullo Vigevani, eds. *O Brasil e as Novas Dimensões da Segurança Internacional* (São Paulo: Editora Alfa-Omega, 1999).

Evans, Peter B., Harold K. Jacobson, and Robert D. Putnam, eds. *Double-Edged Diplomacy: International Bargaining and Domestic Politics* (Berkeley and Los Angeles: University of California Press, 1993).

Farer, Tom, ed. *Beyond Sovereignty. Collectively Defending Democracy in the Americas* (Baltimore: Johns Hopkins University Press, 1996).

Friedman, Thomas L. *The Lexus and the Olive Tree* (New York: Farrar, Strauss, and Giroux, 1999).

Hartlyn, Jonathan, Lars Schoultz, and Augusto Varas, eds. *The United States and Latin America in the 1990s: Beyond the Cold War* (Chapel Hill: The University of North Carolina Press, 1992).

Higgott, Richard A., and Kim Richard Nossal. *Relocating Middle Powers: Australia and Canada in a Changing World Order* (Vancouver: University of British Columbia Press, 1993).

Huntington, Samuel P. *The Clash of Civilizations and the Remaking of World Order* (New York: Simon and Schuster, 1998).

————. *The Third Wave. Democratization in the Late Twentieth Century* (Norman: University of Oklahoma Press, 1991).

Hurrell, Andrew, and Louise Fawcett. *The Resurgence of Regionalism in World Politics* (New York: Oxford University Press, 1995).

Jatar, Ana Julia, and Sidney Weintraub, eds. *Integrating the Hemisphere: Perspectives from Latin America and the Caribbean* (Washington, D.C.: Inter-American Dialogue, 1997)

Kahler, Miles, ed. *Liberalization and Foreign Policy* (New York: Columbia University Press, 1997).

Kennedy, Paul. *Preparing for the Twenty-First Century* (New York: Random House, 1993).

Keohane, Robert O., ed. *Neorealism and Its Critics* (New York: Columbia University Press, 1986).

————. *After Hegemony: Cooperation and Discord in the World Political Economy* (Princeton, N.J.: Princeton University Press, 1984).

————. "The Big Influence of Small Allies." *Foreign Policy* 2, 1971.

————. "Lilliputians' Dilemmas: Small States in International Politics." *International Organization* 23:2, 1969.

————, and Joseph S. Nye. *Power and Interdependence: World Politics in Transition* (Boston: Little, Brown, 1977).

————, and Joseph S. Nye, eds. *Transnational Relations and World Politics* (Cambridge, Mass.: Harvard University Press, 1972), 392–395.

Kissinger, Henry A. *Diplomacy* (New York: Simon and Schuster, 1994).

Krasner, Stephen S., ed. *International Regimes* (Ithaca, N.Y.: Cornell University Press, 1983).

Lake, David A. *Entangling Relations. American Foreign Policy in this Century* (Princeton, N.J.: Princeton University Press, 1999).

————, and Patrick M. Morgan, eds. *Regional Orders. Building Security in a New World* (University Park: Pennsylvania State University Press, 1997).

Lowenthal, Abraham F. *Exporting Democracy. The United States and Latin America. Case Studies* (Baltimore: Johns Hopkins University Press, 1991).

————. *Partners in Conflict: The United States and Latin America in the 1990s* (Baltimore: Johns Hopkins University Press, 1990).

Mace, Gordon, and Jean-Philippe Thérien. *Foreign Policy and Regionalism in the Americas* (Boulder, Colo.: Lynne Rienner Publishers, 1996).

Martz, John D. *United States Policy in Latin America* (Lincoln: University of Nebraska Press, 1995).

Moisés, José Alvaro, ed. *O Futuro do Brasil, a América Latina e o Fim da Guerra Fria* (São Paulo: Paz e Terra, 1992).

Mols, Manfred. *El Marco Internacional de América Latina* (Barcelona/Caracas: Alfa, 1985).

Muñoz, Heraldo, and Joseph S. Tulchin, eds. *Latin American Nations in World Politics,* 2nd ed. (Boulder, Colo.: Westview Press, 1996).

Neuman, Stephanie G., ed. *International Relations Theory and the Third World* (New York: St. Martin's Press, 1998).

Nishijima, Shoji, and Peter H. Smith, eds. *Cooperation or Rivalry? Regional Integration in the Americas and the Pacific Rim* (Boulder, Colo.: Westview Press, 1996).

Nye, Joseph S., Jr. *Bound to Lead: The Changing Nature of American Power* (New York: Basic Books, 1991).

Pastor, Robert A. *Whirlpool: U.S. Foreign Policy Toward Latin America and the Caribbean* (Princeton, N.J.: Princeton University Press, 1992).

Pena, Ricardo A., and Jorge A. Binaghi. *MERCOSUR: estrategias, oportunidades de negocios y armonización de políticas en un contexto de pensamiento globalizador* (Buenos Aires: Ediciones Héctor A. Macchi, 1994).

Rosenau, James N. *Turbulence in World Politics: A Theory of Change and Continuity* (Princeton, N.J.: Princeton University Press, 1990).

———. *The Study of Global Interdependence* (New York: Nichols, 1980).

Ruggie, John Gerard. *Constructing the World Polity* (London: Routledge, 1998).

———, ed. *Multilateralism Matters. The Theory and Praxis of an Institutional Form* (New York: Columbia University Press, 1993).

Sassen, Sonia. *Losing Control? Sovereignty in an Age of Globalization* (New York: Columbia University Press, 1996).

Smith, Peter H. *Talons of the Eagle: Dynamics of U.S.–Latin American Relations* (New York: Oxford University Press, 1996).

———, ed. *The Challenge of Integration: Europe and the Americas* (Miami: North-South Center/Transaction, 1993).

Tella, Guido di, et al. *América Latina: de la marginalidad a la inserción internacional* (Santiago: Fundación CIPIE, 1998).

Tulchin, Joseph, ed. *The Consolidation of Democracy in Latin America* (Boulder, Colo.: Lynne Rienner Publishers, 1995).

———, Francisco Rojas Aravena, and Ralph H. Espach, eds. *Strategic Balance and Confidence Building Measures in the Americas* (Washington, D.C.: Woodrow Wilson Center Press/Stanford University Press, 1998).

———, Andrés Serbín, and Rafael Hernández, eds. *Cuba and the Caribbean* (Wilmington, Del.: Scholarly Resources, 1997).

# The Contributors

**Thomaz Guedes da Costa** is a political scientist and an analyst for the Brazilian National Research Council in Brasília.

**Jorge I. Domínguez** is director of the Weatherhead Center for International Affairs at Harvard University, and the Clarence Dillon Professor of International Affairs.

**Ralph H. Espach** is program associate of the Latin American Program at the Woodrow Wilson International Center for Scholars, Washington, D.C.

**Guadalupe González** is professor of political science and international relations at the Centro de Investigación y Docencia Económica (CIDE) and El Colegio de México in Mexico City.

**Robert O. Keohane** is James B. Duke Professor of Political Science and Co-Director of the Program on Democracy, Institutions, and Political Economy at Duke University.

**Ernest R. May** is the Charles Warren Professor of History at the John F. Kennedy School of Government at Harvard University.

**Heraldo Muñoz** is a political scientist and currently the Vice Minister of Foreign Relations in Santiago, Chile. Formerly, he served as the Chilean ambassador to Brazil from 1994 to 1998, and Chilean ambassador to the Organization of American States from 1990 to 1994.

**Peter H. Smith** is the Simón Bolívar Professor of Latin American Studies, as well as the director of the Center for Iberian and Latin American Studies at the University of California, San Diego.

**Joseph S. Tulchin** is director of the Latin American Program at the Woodrow Wilson International Center for Scholars, Washington, D.C.

**Alberto van Klaveren** is senior policy adviser at the Chilean Ministry of Foreign Affairs, and director of the Institute of International Studies of the University of Chile in Santiago.

# Index

# About the Book

Placing Latin America in the context of debates on economic globalization and the dramatically changing nature of the international system, this volume offers the perspectives of scholars and policymakers from across the Americas.

The authors argue that the ongoing diversification of economic and strategic ties presents Latin American nations with new options—and also with dangers. A recurring theme is a caution against excessive optimism regarding the effects of globalization. The book bridges discussions of Latin America and broader world politics, advancing critical insights from within the region together with reflections from a global perspective.

**Joseph S. Tulchin** is director of the Latin American Program at the Woodrow Wilson International Center for Scholars. **Ralph H. Espach** is program associate at the Woodrow Wilson Center.

# Woodrow Wilson International Center for Scholars

## About the Center

The Woodrow Wilson International Center for Scholars is the nation's living memorial to Woodrow Wilson, president of the United States from 1913 to 1921. Created by law in 1968, the Center is Washington's only independent, wide-ranging, and nonpartisan institute for advanced study where vital current issues and their deep historical background are explored throught research and dialogue. The American public is informed by the Center through broadcast, open meetings, print publication, and electronic outreach. The Center is supported by both public and private funds. Views expressed in Center publications are not necessarily those of the Center's staff, fellows, trustees, advisory groups, or any individuals or organizations that provide financial support to the Center.

To receive Center publications regularly or to request change of address, please write to Public Affairs, Woodrow Wilson Center, One Woodrow Wilson Plaza, 1300 Pennsylvania Avenue NW, Washington, D.C. 20004, or send e-mail to obriench@wwic.si.edu. Visit the Center on the World Wide Web at http://www.wilsoncenter.org.